RENEWALS 458-4574
DATE DUE

WITHDRAWN
UTSA LIBRARIES

About Island Press

Island Press is the only nonprofit organization in the United States whose principal purpose is the publication of books on environmental issues and natural resource management. We provide solutions-oriented information to professionals, public officials, business and community leaders, and concerned citizens who are shaping responses to environmental problems.

In 1994, Island Press celebrated its tenth anniversary as the leading provider of timely and practical books that take a multidisciplinary approach to critical environmental concerns. Our growing list of titles reflects our commitment to bringing the best of an expanding body of literature to the environmental community throughout North America and the world.

Support for Island Press is provided by The Geraldine R. Dodge Foundation, The Energy Foundation, The Ford Foundation, The George Gund Foundation, William and Flora Hewlett Foundation, The John D. and Catherine T. MacArthur Foundation, The Andrew W. Mellon Foundation, The Joyce Mertz-Gilmore Foundation, The New-Land Foundation, The Pew Charitable Trusts, The Rockefeller Brothers Fund, The Tides Foundation, Turner Foundation, Inc., The Rockefeller Philanthropic Collaborative, Inc., and individual donors.

About the Surface Transportation Policy Project

The Surface Transportation Policy Project (STPP) is a broad-based public interest coalition founded in 1990. The purpose of STPP is to ensure that transportation policy and investments help conserve energy, protect environmental and aesthetic quality, strengthen the economy, promote social equity, and make communities more liveable. STPP emphasizes the needs of people, rather than vehicles, in assuring access to jobs, services, and recreational opportunities.

For additional information contact the Surface Transportation Policy Project at 1400 Sixteenth Street, N.W., Suite 300, Washington, DC 20036, or call (202) 939-3470.

At Road's End

ISLAND PRESS

Washington, D.C. • Covelo, California

At Road's End

Transportation and Land Use Choices for Communities

Daniel Carlson with Lisa Wormser and Cy Ulberg

Surface Transportation Policy Project

Copyright ©1995 by Island Press

All rights reserved under International and Pan-American Copyright Conventions. No part of this book may be reproduced in any form or by any means without permission in writing from the publisher: Island Press, 1718 Connecticut Avenue, N.W., Suite 300, Washington, DC 20009.

ISLAND PRESS is a trademark of The Center for Resource Economics.

Library of Congress Cataloging-in-Publication Data

Carlson, Daniel, 1946–
    At road's end : transportation and land use choices for communities / Daniel Carlson and the Surface Transportation Policy Project (STPP) with Lisa Wormser and Cy Ulberg.
      p.   cm.
    Includes bibliographical references and index.
    ISBN 1-55963-338-7
    1. Transportation—United States—Planning.   2. Transportation--United States—Planning—Citizen participation.   3. Land use--United States—Planning.   4. Land use—United States—Planning--Citizen participation.   I. Surface Transportation Policy Project.
II. Title.
HE206.2.C37   1995
388′.068—dc20   94-28059
                                                                   CIP

Printed on recycled, acid-free paper ∞

Manufactured in the United States of America
10 9 8 7 6 5 4 3 2 1

Contents

List of Case Studies ix
Preface xi
Acknowledgments xiii

Part I. Building Community through Transportation and Land Use Decisions

1. Introduction 3
2. Developing New Coalitions 21
3. A New Place at the Transportation Planning Table 27
4. Replacing Transportation Blunders with Community-Derived Solutions 41
5. Transportation and Regional Growth Management 61
6. Enhancing the Existing Highway System 71
7. Reflections on Serving Community 79

Part II. Implementing the Intermodal Surface Transportation Efficiency Act

8. First Steps under ISTEA 89
9. Public Involvement in the Transportation Planning Process 117
10. Definitions of Enhancement Activities 127
11. Metropolitan Planning Requirements 135
12. Planning, Project Selection, and Financing 145

Afterword: How ISTEA Will Help Us Serve Communities 153
Suggested Reading 157
Index 159
About the Authors 169

Case Studies

Virginia's James River Crossing   22

Maryland's 301 Task Force   28

Connecticut's Merritt Parkway   32

Atlanta's Freedom Parkway   44

Boston's Central Artery/Tunnel   50

Portland's Western Bypass and LUTRAQ   64

Washington State's Mountains-to-Sound Greenway   76

Preface

I remember a conversation with a really smart upper class student my freshman year in college. I asked her what she was majoring in. She told me it was an independent major in a field I had probably never heard of called ecology. That was in 1964. And she was right, I had never heard of the word or the field of ecology. She was kind enough to explain that it had to do with the study of the interconnectedness of natural systems, their interrelationships and interdependencies. Whole communities of plants and animals were constantly influencing one another, creating, altering, and reestablishing a balance.

Thirty years later, half the products on the supermarket shelf are "ecologically friendly" and states have Departments of Ecology. So the communities in which we live and work must be in better internal balance and greater harmony with the environment than ever before. Well, maybe your community is, but many Americans are distraught about the decline in the quality of life in their communities.

This book began as an examination of the effects of the post-war auto-oriented transportation system on the form and feel of our communities. The concern was that the car culture, in the name of providing greater freedom and mobility, was actually destroying much of what has made American towns and cities liveable; that a kind of monoculture of car-based mobility was upsetting the balance of community.

But this book was never intended to be a downer. Its purpose is to offer models of locally based change which coincide with the major federal policy shifts contained in ISTEA (the Intermodal Surface Transportation Efficiency Act of 1991), namely that federal transportation policy now includes not only more and bigger roads, but planning and funding for getting around on foot, by train, bus, bike, and car. Of course many local citizen groups, government officials, and enlightened transportation professionals have been charting such new directions over the past decade.

At Road's End tells many stories of local efforts to rethink and transform freeway projects which would cut through vital neighborhoods or threatened wetlands. These are cases of new processes for reaching public decisions through broader community involvement and alternative dispute resolution methods. The cases emphasize ways to serve community through the implementation of a more ecological, holistic definition of transportation and its relationship to land, environment, community, economic development, and quality of life.

The initial research for this book looked at community efforts which began prior to ISTEA's passage. The cases which focus on the implementation of ISTEA's programs and provisions have been prepared by Lisa Wormser and the Surface Transportation Policy Project. Cy Ulberg helped place the cases in historic and conceptual context by proposing three transportation paradigms, two for the past and one for the future.

This book has two parts. Part I provides background, description, and analysis of transportation and land use choices for communities around the country and reflects on their meaning. Part II details methods for implementing ISTEA and surveys some examples of this implementation.

We hope *At Road's End* provides a new framework for thinking about serving community through transportation. We also hope it will encourage citizen activists to challenge the system and inspire transportation professionals and elected officials to make innovative use of new tools and funding at the local, regional, and state levels.

Daniel Carlson
Seattle, Washington

Acknowledgments

Many people and organizations have shared their experience, information, and support to make this book a reality. The National Trust for Historic Preservation provided funding for the initial research on transportation and community preservation. Bridget Hartman, manager of the Trust's Critical Issues Fund, provided constant encouragement and guidance. Betty Jane Narver, director of the Institute for Public Policy and Management at the University of Washington, did the same.

Mostly it was the generous participation by citizen activists, transportation engineers, planners, and elected officials—the people invested in their communities who provided the stories, history, data, photos, and time to visit and reflect—which has made these case studies valuable to readers across the country. I really want to thank each of you who took the time to talk with me as I visited your community or called you on the phone. Rather than trying to name each individual and risk offending those I might omit, I will simply acknowledge all of you who helped, from the neighborhood activist in California to the corporate attorney in Boston, from the highway administrator in Maryland to the landscape architect in Seattle.

A special acknowledgement to my contributing authors Cy Ulberg and Lisa Wormser, who made the manuscript complete, and my editors Heather Boyer and Nancy Olsen, who made the manuscript into a book.

The Surface Transportation Policy Project is grateful to the project's Planning Committee (Chair: George Marcou, American Planning Association) and the Enhancements Committee (Chair: Sally Oldham, Scenic America) for contributing to the writing of the material on the Intermodal

Surface Transportation Efficiency Act. The following individuals contributed substantial research and writing toward that material:

Deborah Boldt	Center for Neighborhood Technology
John Bosley	National Association of Regional Councils
Phil Braum	Barton-Aschman Associates
Janet Hathaway	Natural Resources Defense Council
Hal Hiemstra	Rails-to-Trails Conservancy
Annette Liebe	Environmental Defense Fund
George Marcou	American Planning Association
Sally Oldham	Scenic America
Bill Roberts	Environmental Defense Fund
Ian Spatz	National Trust for Historic Preservation
Bob Yunhke	Environmental Defense Fund

The many other individuals who contributed their time and ideas to STPP's portion of this book are too numerous to name, but our heartfelt thanks go to them all.

Lisa Wormser would like to personally thank Hank Dittmar, executive director of STPP, and Laurie Garrett, deputy director, for their feedback and support during this project.

_____ **At Road's End**

Part I

Building Community through Transportation and Land Use Decisions

1
Introduction

The federal highway program, more dramatically than any other single public policy or public works effort, has changed the sense of place in urban, suburban, and rural communities. New roads open land to development, alter the environment, create congestion, and often degrade the quality of life that the roads were meant to improve.

For the past thirty-five years, national policy has aggressively promoted car and truck transportation through construction and expansion of the Interstate Highway System. With the passage of the Intermodal Surface Transportation Efficiency Act of 1991 (ISTEA), however, the federal government established new policies that fund a variety of modes of transportation, including cars, trucks, buses, trains, bicycles, and walking. ISTEA requires state and regional authorities to think and plan comprehensively about appropriate modes of transportation for natural and built environments and relate the selected modes to air quality in metropolitan areas and the quality of life in communities in general.

The subtitle of this book refers to the concept that transportation systems are meant to serve communities of people and their activities. The post-war overemphasis on automobiles and highways has caused serious harm to the environment and altered the complex arrangement of social and economic interaction that we call *community*, which provides our emotional and material well-being and offers a sense of safety.

A New Awareness

ISTEA calls for a holistic approach to transportation planning, taking into account a multitude of factors. Whereas the interstate era was characterized by a single-minded focus on completing a high-speed highway system, the holistic approach considers a range of transportation modes; impacts on the natural environment, including farms, wetlands, and wildlife habitat; impacts on the built environment, such as the effects of future changes in land use on architectural design, historic character, and cultural uses; visual and noise impacts; and the need for a more complete accounting of externalities, i.e., health costs and air pollution and other costs imposed on society such as reduced quality of community life.

ISTEA has changed the rules of the game, making highways one of a variety of transportation modes eligible for funding. What is now required is a more comprehensive view of transportation impacts on land use and the environment. But new legislation, however enlightened, cannot instantly change the corporate culture of highway builders or the attitudes of users. After all, the pre-ISTEA highway projects chronicled in this book were subject to such review for environmental impact and historic preservation required under progressive legislation, but the prospect of review did not deter the projects' proponents.

Had these projects proceeded unchallenged, a multi-lane elevated freeway would have soared above Atlanta's Great Park, three new bridges and sixteen whirling off ramps would have crossed the Charles River to connect Boston and Cambridge, and a new outer beltway would have opened farms and wetlands to development in a giant circle around the nation's capital.

These and other real-life case studies described in the following pages illustrate highway plans developed under the "old culture" but modified by new values expressed by community leaders, environmentalists, developers, and transportation planners. The examples pre-date ISTEA and offer successful and inspirational models for grassroots organizations and agency professionals who are interested in thinking and acting holistically when faced with proposed transportation projects.

Case Studies

Seven case studies, described briefly here, are discussed in depth in coming chapters.

- *The Lower James River Crossing*. In Jamestown, Virginia, a coalition of organizations blocked a proposed bridge in favor of existing ferry service, thereby retaining the area's historic character and viewsheds.

- *The Washington Bypass*. The Maryland Department of Transportation and a task force composed of representatives from environmental and civic organizations, developers, and local governments are working to define transportation and land-use options for the corridor near the nation's capital.

- *The Merritt Parkway*. In Connecticut a historically significant landscape threatened by road widening was saved by a coalition of activists.

- *The Freedom Parkway*. In Atlanta a coalition of community groups engaged in a mediated process to modify a four-lane freeway into a two-lane meandering parkway bordered by parks and housing.

- *The Central Artery/Tunnel*. This Boston project is proceeding as a result of a mediated agreement that creates open space and parkland downtown and fundamentally changes the state's public transportation policy.

- *The Western Bypass.* A Portland group, 1000 Friends of Oregon, is pioneering a new integrated approach to transportation and growth management called the Land Use Transportation and Air Quality study.
- *The I-90 Corridor.* In metropolitan Seattle, a new nonprofit civic organization, the Mountains to Sound Greenway Trust, is attempting to create a public/private alternative to "edge city" sprawl.

Historical Background

Until the middle of the last century, Americans traveled primarily by foot when they needed to get around their communities. In 1825, only one city in the United States had a population of more than 50,000. Towns were small—no greater than two or three miles across—and the residents could walk to most places in less than a half hour. Cities began to mushroom in size and number in the latter half of the nineteenth century, however, because of industrial growth, increasing immigration to the United States, and natural increases in population. A better means to move around cities was required.

The horse filled that need. Offering greater speed, strength, and endurance than people on foot, horses became the preferred mode of travel. But the resulting increase in their numbers created problems. Manure, when wet, was a sticky, smelly nuisance and source of pollution, and, when it dried, the dust carried disease as it blew around the streets. Dead horses created additional environmental problems. In 1880, more than 15,000 were removed from the streets of New York City. Moreover, livery stables took significant portions of municipal land.

Even though horses provided greater mobility, they were limited in range and speed by today's standards. Moreover, the poor could not afford them. As a result, urban form remained fairly dense, and residents were inhibited from making nonessential trips. The advent of horse-drawn trolleys spawned the development of suburbs, but the impact on urban form remained relatively minor.

Then came the electric train and automobile, which helped bring fresh food products from the countryside into urban markets. Ironically, when cars were introduced around the turn of the century, they were touted as a means to improve environmental conditions. Also, their speed and range was comparable to that of horses at first, so that they were not responsible for the initial proliferation of suburbs, which was caused instead by the electric railroad. Railway companies made money by selling land along the rights-of-way.

As automobile technology improved, cars became the preferred mode of travel. Cars were more flexible than railways and offered a new freedom that appealed to city dwellers eager to escape to the country during their leisure hours. By the 1950s, the automobile had replaced walking, horses, and electric trains as the primary means of travel. Without the impact of the Depression and World War II, this transformation would have undoubtedly happened sooner. Traffic problems were already severe in some places as early as the 1920s.

Cars provided mobility and freedom previously unknown in human history. The automobile was viewed as an enhancement to modern living. But times have changed. Today, the car's influences on urban form, community life, and the environment are seen as primarily negative.

The manufacture of automobiles has become the world's largest industry. In the United States, there is more than one car for every man, woman, and child. The nation's 250 million cars travel on 3.9 million miles of roads, and many of these roads, in the form of multi-lane interstate highways, have obliterated the very communities that the car was meant to serve. Metropolitan road systems have opened the countryside to further urban and suburban development, displacing farmlands and rural economies.

More than 60,000 square miles of U.S. land have been paved over for roads. This represents 2 percent of the nation's total surface area and the equivalent of 10 percent of all arable land.[1] In dense urban development, nearly half the land area is devoted to roads and public infrastructure.

Increased Reliance on Cars

Americans use the car, usually as a single occupancy vehicle, with greater frequency than ever before. For instance, vehicle miles traveled in Seattle in the twenty-year period from 1970 to 1990 increased by 123 percent, while the city's population grew by only 34 percent. Most of this mileage does not represent commuter trips. Approximately 75 percent of all travel involves simply getting around town to shop, visit, run errands, and make life work in the auto age.

What led to this increase in usage? The simple availability of the technology (the automobile) enhanced the motivation to escape what is perceived as adverse conditions in cities. Moreover, once urban residential patterns lost their compact form, an automobile was required to carry on the normal activities of life.

Automobile manufacturing, residential construction, and associated activities fuel the economy of the United States, comprising about one-fourth of the gross domestic national product. In *The Geography of Nowhere*, James Howard Kunstler ties the unnaturally rapid increase in automobile production and residential building during the 1920s with the advent of the Great Depression, suggesting the car's pivotal role.

It is small wonder that public policy has supported the use of automobiles. Following World War II, suburban sprawl was promoted by a confluence of policies that funded highways while simultaneously subsidizing home ownership. In particular, the Federal Highway Aid Act of 1956 created the Interstate Highway System with its 90 percent federal funding—sums that were justified on the grounds of national defense. In a matter of three decades, this system of high-speed, multi-lane auto and truck roads helped change the land-use patterns of the nation. By the end of the interstate era in 1991, for the first time, a majority of Americans lived in suburbia.

Businesses began to relocate from expensive, crowded downtown locations to relatively inexpensive and expansive suburban office parks located at freeway exits. In *Edge City*, Joel Garreau describes the phenomenon of suburban real estate and employment. Garreau found that explosive growth of edge city office developments coincided with a rise of women entering the workforce in the 1970s. Rather than commuting to the central city, one or both members of the new two-worker families began to drive to suburban locations reachable only by private automobile.

Increased auto usage has a variety of negative impacts on our communities, including greater environmental pollution, increased congestion on the roadways, auto-oriented development of land at the urban periphery, and loss of natural areas. Automobiles and other motor vehicles account for 50 to 90 percent of urban smog and degraded air quality. Water and noise pollution are also significant results of the heavy reliance on autos.

Traffic congestion is an annoyance faced by urban residents on a daily basis. Almost 70 percent of peak-hour travel on the urban interstate system occurs under near stop-and-go conditions.[2] Congestion is consistently identified by metropolitan area residents as one of the most serious urban problems, even when compared with crime, education, and human services.

The economic impact of congestion is significant. Most people consider time spent stalled in traffic as wasted. How that time would be divided between productive work and leisure activities is hard to determine, but *both* alternatives are valuable. Congestion also inhibits the movement of goods, which raises

The fast food franchises and outlet mall shown in the photo at left are typical of development at an interstate highway interchange, such as this one off I-90 near Seattle. Contrast this auto-oriented shopping environment with the pedestrian-scale "village" in the photo at right. Which creates the kind of community you want? It is particularly interesting that these two examples are contemporaneous, both built after the mid-1980s. The "village" is Mashpee Commons in Massachusetts, the nation's first shopping mall converted into a neo-traditionalist mixed-use development. (Photos courtesy of Tom Phillips.)

prices. The U.S. Government Accounting Office estimates that the annual cost of congestion (excluding environmental impacts) in the United States is $130 billion.[3]

Perhaps most insidiously, the automobile destroys the cohesion of our communities. The construction of roads results in physical divisions, and the reliance on automobiles has been partially responsible for breaking down identification with the community. Urban dwellers have become less likely to know their neighbors and shop at local stores.

The familiar kinds of metropolitan sprawl that the automobile has engendered (strip development, large malls, mini-malls, and drive-in stores and services) consist of buildings surrounded by large parking areas facing main arterials or highway interchanges. People who walk or ride bicycles in these environments are perceived as out-of-place, as well as in danger.

The arrangements of activities are not conducive to civic life. Even in shopping malls, which include elements that mimic community life, activities are limited to those approved by the owner of the mall. One is not likely to see a political rally or a soapbox speaker in a shopping mall.

The loss of natural areas caused by auto-oriented development affects all species, including humans. Transportation infrastructure and associated housing and commercial development in rural areas has taken forests, fields, wetlands, and agricultural lands out of use.

The proliferation of auto use has led to numerous negative consequences and has limited the enjoyment of mobility and freedom that automobiles originally promised. To understand how this has come to be and where we may be headed, it is useful to analyze the underpinnings of transportation policy.

Three Transportation Paradigms

During this century, transportation policy has progressed through two paradigms and is on the brink of a third. These three transportation "world views" can be characterized by their respective focus on increasing (1) *capacity*, (2) *mobility*, and (3) *accessibility*.

As the use of motorized vehicles grew and the impacts of traffic became obvious, the first paradigm of transportation policy focused on building infrastructure, primarily in the form of roads and highways. New roads were constructed, existing roads paved and widened, and traffic control technology was improved. The aim was to *increase capacity* by moving more vehicles.

This paradigm has limitations. The car/road construction equation as practiced during the last thirty-five years eludes equilibrium:

> Wherever an automobile route is heavily used, there exists a reservoir of trips that people do not make because the route cannot accommodate them. If a second route is provided, both routes will draw traffic from this 'reservoir,' and the net loss in traffic by the old route will be considerably less than the gain in traffic by the new route.[4]

Even though ISTEA has changed the transportation planning environment, this paradigm of increasing capacity is still with us. State highway departments are not building many new highways, but they are expanding existing ones and improving their efficiency at moving vehicles. Local jurisdictions build and expand arterials on a regular basis.

Transportation system management (TSM) is a transitional set of policies which took hold during the 1970s. The idea behind TSM policies is to manage existing facilities more efficiently in order to move more vehicles without automatically resorting to widening or new construction. The most widely used TSM strategies today are the careful timing of traffic signals and the establishment of High Occupancy Vehicle (HOV) lanes and programs. TSM strategies continue to focus on providing capacity, but their development did open the door to a consideration of some goals beyond facilities construction.

ISTEA continues the capacity paradigm in its Intelligent Vehicle Highway System (IVHS), now renamed Intelligent Transportation System (ITS). The primary aim of most IVHS efforts is to improve the capacity of highways and move more vehicles. Whether this is done through building new facilities or making better use of current ones, this approach still does not deal with the "demand-rises-to-fill-capacity" dilemma.

The second paradigm, *mobility*, began to take hold in the 1970s. The emphasis shifted from moving vehicles to moving people. Spurred by the energy crises of 1974 and 1979, as well as increasing environmental awareness, planners shifted their focus to moving more people by increasing the number of occupants in vehicles and encouraging a longer spread for peak period travel. The aims of mobility-based policies are to induce more people to use mass transit, encourage the use of carpools and vanpools for those who cannot use transit, and persuade others to travel outside the most congested time periods.

The incentives and disincentives for shifting to HOVs and spreading the peak period are known as transportation demand management (TDM). TDM supercedes TSM in that it attempts to influence traveler behavior. Incentives employed in TDM include transit pass subsidies, parking preference and price breaks for ride sharers, and provision of special HOV lanes for buses, carpools, and vanpools. Parking policy has proven to be one of the most potent TDM strategies. Disincentives for driving alone include charging single occupancy vehicle (SOV) drivers for parking and charging tolls for SOV drivers only. A leading TDM expert, Elizabeth Deakin, notes:

> There have been studies of parking pricing being introduced in the San Fernando Valley, that mecca of suburban sprawl in Southern California. They have found that as many as 30

percent of employees decide that car-pooling does make sense for them, or that riding a bus does make sense for them with a relatively modest $30 a month parking charge imposed by the employer to cover the parking cost.[5]

TDM proponents encourage the use of flextime in the workplace to allow people to travel outside the most congested times.

Also included in this paradigm are incentives for using nonmotorized transportation such as bicycling, a highly efficient way to travel. A bike lane is capable of carrying the same number of people per hour as a highway lane, while taking up a much smaller swath of land, creating less noise and air pollution, and consuming no fossil fuel. Although bicycle travel has recognizable limitations, some of the biggest obstacles such as safe parking places and need for shower facilities can be overcome at modest cost.[6] The City of Palo Alto, for example, now requires developers to provide one shower for every 10,000 square feet of office space and one locker for every 10 car parking stalls.[7]

How have we done in this second paradigm? Some would say that the final results are not in, but the reports so far are not encouraging. In the decade from 1980 to 1990, transit share of work trips decreased by 18 percent. Carpooling share decreased by 32 percent and nonmotorized commuting by 29 percent. Despite the money and energy spent to induce modal shift away from SOVs, the number of Americans traveling alone in cars to reach their jobs increased by 22 million between 1980 and 1990. This represents a 35 percent increase during a period when the number of workers increased by 19 percent. The emphasis on transportation demand management cannot be said to have resulted in obvious success.

The third paradigm, *accessibility*, is not new, but it is receiving substantially increased attention. Awareness is growing that mobility for mobility's sake has inherent flaws. Making it easier to move people around simply encourages more moving around, just as making it easier to move vehicles around means more vehicles will be moving around. It is impossible to provide unlimited mobility, and if it were, it would have indirect consequences that are undesirable.

What is important is that people have access to what they need, and that access is provided in a number of ways. New urban designs can improve the accessibility of employment and services so that people do not have to travel to reach them. Some trips can be replaced by electronic communication. Face-to-face human interaction is important to communication and the development of relationships, but it is not essential for all interchanges.

Strengthening communities and emphasizing local self-reliance can help achieve the goal of this third paradigm. Economic development that enhances local business, employment, and shopping opportunities improves identification with one's own community as well as reducing the need to make trips. More social and leisure time can be spent in the community rather than in places that one must reach by automobile. Providing opportunities to work at home or in a local satellite office, at least part of the time, reduces travel and strengthens community life.

In most places community life has deteriorated for decades and will not be simple to re-establish. Several public policy tools, however, can be employed, including (1) new urban design, (2) growth management, (3) increased economic advantages for local business, (4) enhanced opportunities for telecommuting, (5) integrated transportation and land-use planning, (6) full-cost pricing for transportation, (7) least-cost planning, and (8) ISTEA provisions.

New Urban Design

During the last forty years or so, new urban development has been auto-oriented. The undesirable results of that development have given impetus to new ways of thinking about urban

Auto-oriented development (*top photos*) eats up land and creates a hostile environment for people. Many Americans don't know (until they see them) that alternatives to sprawl exist (*middle and bottom photos*). (Photos courtesy of Tom Phillips.)

design that include an emphasis on pedestrian-friendliness and spaces that promote social exchange.

Even though a substantial number of people still prefer to live in suburbs with detached single family houses and large yards, a significant part of the American population feels differently. Practitioners of the community visioning process, led by Anton Nelleson Associates of Princeton, New Jersey, assist residents who feel this way to define a desirable form for their community, using a slide presentation that pictures a variety of housing and landscaping alternatives, streetscapes, and commercial developments. The community visions are then scored by participants on a numerical scale, and the results can be used to define consensus about the elements of community design. In surveys of visual preferences, these residents routinely score auto-oriented development low on a rating scale.

A growing movement of architects and planners is planning for the post-auto-oriented community.[8] Andres Duany and Elizabeth Plater-Zyberk champion the Traditional Neighborhood Development concept, which has roots in small, dense, pedestrian-scaled towns of the nineteenth century. Orientation of residences to the street and sidewalk, placement of the garage in back of the house, and reinstitution of the grid street pattern are all intended to foster communication among neighbors and a fabric of community life that puts people first and cars second.

Similarly, architect Peter Calthorpe is designing transit-oriented or "pedestrian pocket" development, in which a dense, mixed-use development that includes residential, commercial, and employment use is focused within a five- to ten-minute walk of a transit station. The station serves as the core of the central hub for a 120-acre area.

These ideas are not entirely new. Mention must be made of Clarence Stein and his colleagues who created new towns to fit the automobile age in the first decades of this century. Foremost of these was Radburn, New Jersey, a new suburban town sixteen miles from Manhattan. Stein writes:

In 1928 there were 21,308,159 automobiles registered. The flood of motors had already made the gridiron street pattern . . . as obsolete as a fortified town wall. Pedestrians risked a dangerous motor street crossing 20 times a mile. The roadbed was the children's main play space. Every year there are more Americans killed or injured in automobile accidents than the total of American war casualties in any year.[9]

The plan in Radburn was to build homes on superblocks with the fronts facing a common greensward where children can play. The backs of houses face small roadway *cul de sacs* designed for cars and service vehicles. Pedestrians can walk on paths separated from cars using principles employed by Frederick Law Olmsted when he designed New York's Central Park, where the roads pass over the walkways on bridges.

A movement toward pedestrianization and traffic calming,[10] long underway in Europe, is also making its way into American cities. In addition to the design of new communities, efforts are underway to retrofit existing auto-oriented development. A good example is Mashpee Commons in Massachusetts. This former shopping mall has been converted into a pedestrian-friendly "village" with mixed residential and commercial uses and a grid-style street layout. Other similar retrofits are in the planning stage.

Growth Management

During the interstate years, the interplay of highway construction and adjoining land-use changes was understood as a desirable inevitability. Construction of roads through river bottom land in a metropolitan area would pave the way for new residential and commercial development. Agriculture would move elsewhere, often to desert land that was made productive through water diversion and irrigation.

However, this type of urban sprawl was eventually seen to have costs to the public in terms of traffic congestion, the provision of adequate infrastructure and services, and the inefficiencies of widely dispersed services. Twenty years ago, a growth management movement began when Oregon adopted the first comprehensive statewide land-use plan, including restrictions of development within urban growth boundaries. Other states followed suit in the 1980s and 1990s.

The premise was that development can be intentionally managed. Areas of environmental concern and resource lands that support silviculture or agriculture can be protected. The placement of roads and utilities can be timed to support or not support development in appropriate areas.

As logical and simple as this premise sounds, less than a dozen states have adopted comprehensive growth management legislation. In fact, it is not clear that the relationship between transportation and land use is fully comprehended or acknowledged by planning agencies imbued with the culture of growth. Nevertheless, many of the principal assumptions have been incorporated into the comprehensive planning requirements of ISTEA.[11]

The importance of understanding the relationship between transportation and land use is illustrated by two case studies, which will be discussed in depth in later chapters. First, in 1974 the Puget Sound Council of Governments in Washington State prepared an analysis of the impacts on growth of the completion of a seven-mile, eight- to ten-lane western terminus of Interstate 90. The $1.5 billion project would double, or in some cases triple, capacity of the roadway. The new road would cross Lake Washington on a new floating bridge. The net effect was to make nearby rural land accessible to downtown Seattle by driving less than 15 minutes. The report concluded:

> Regional land use patterns will not be changed substantially by developing I-90, as the proposed facility will be responsive to growth patterns that have already taken place rather than initiating development in patterns of land use.... The growth and concentration patterns resulting from automobile accessibility over Lake Washington will stabilize within a relatively short time span.[12]

Since that report was released, the Central Puget Sound area has grown by 700,000 residents, and the I-90 corridor is one of the growth hotspots. At this writing, the Washington Department of Transportation has proposed a widening of the companion floating bridge across Lake Washington to increase auto capacity. To be charitable, in 1974 when the Puget Sound region was just emerging from the devastating aerospace bust of 1970 when Boeing laid off more than 60,000 workers, planners would have had difficulty conceiving of explosive metropolitan growth—and might have actually longed for it.

Northern Virginia land developers certainly seemed to understand the importance of the relationship between transportation and land use when they pushed for construction of an outer beltway southwest of the nation's capital to connect I-95 (the main north-south interstate on the East Coast) with Dulles airport. The outer beltway was to proceed north through farmland and rural areas, eventually reconnecting with I-95 near Baltimore. For large landowners, a modern highway and crucially located interchanges next to an airport gateway spelled office park, hotel, and development heaven.

In 1986 the developers' trade organization, The Greater Washington Board of Trade, sponsored a conference on interstate bypasses. The conference was followed by a feasibility study of the two-state project. The roadway had enormous implications for growth and sprawl in the region—a fact that was effectively demonstrated by the Chesapeake Bay Foundation. The evolution of this case is covered in more detail on pages 28–32, but the point here is that landowners and developers are aware of the extra value added to adjacent property by highway access.

Growth management policy is a way to prevent or at least moderate the free market's tendency to enhance property values by supporting the construction of highways. By directing growth in appropriate areas and into more compact community forms, sprawl can be inhibited and dependence on autos curtailed.

Increased Economic Advantages for Local Business

Since the purpose of almost half of all auto trips is shopping, the distance between residences and opportunities to shop is a significant factor in reducing auto use. Decreasing that distance reduces vehicle miles when autos are used and increases the probability that shoppers will walk or bike to their destinations.

Unfortunately, the trend is against local businesses. Shopping malls, usually accessible only by car, have been supplanting local shopping districts for decades. In recent years, discount warehouse stores have provided an additional threat to local businesses.

One of the major attractions of malls, discount warehouses, and large grocery stores is lower prices. Community-based firms have a hard time competing with regional stores, which do a greater volume of business and benefit from cheaper delivery costs. However, the regional stores receive a hidden subsidy. The shopper, by traveling farther to the store, pays part of the freight costs. In addition, the public—whether they shop at the stores or not—is paying for the transportation infrastructure that provides access.

Public policy can be used to address these hidden subsidies and give local community-based stores a more level playing field. For instance, local stores could be given a tax break since their location reduces the need to provide infrastructure. Regional stores could be required to cover more of the transportation costs they engender. A combination of such policies could allow community-based shopping districts to flourish and serve as centers for community life.

Enhancing Opportunities for Telecommuting

Working at home or a satellite office and staying in touch through telecommunication technologies has been touted as an important mechanism for reducing auto trips. A recent U.S. Department of Transportation (DOT) report suggests, however, that the potential for trip reduction from telecommuting is marginal. Research has shown that, even though the individual worker's productivity increases substantially when working at home, the overall productivity of organizations is not clearly enhanced. Working away from the office provides a good atmosphere for concentration, but also introduces coordination problems with co-workers that cannot be completely overcome through scheduling and electronic communications. Coupling the reluctance of some organizations to embrace telecommuting with the percentage of jobs that lend themselves to telecommuting and the percentage of total auto use that is associated with work explains the minimal impact predicted by the DOT report.

Nevertheless, telecommuting is a growing phenomenon and has beneficial impacts on reducing auto use, as well as potential community-building aspects. Neighborhood satellite offices that are accessible by foot can overcome some barriers to telecommuting, reduce travel, *and* enhance community life. If people spend more time at home or at a neighborhood work center, they are more likely to shop locally and identify with the local community than if they commute every day to some distant workplace. The State of California is currently experimenting with satellite offices.

Integrating Transportation and Land-Use Modeling

Metropolitan growth and development patterns depend upon a complex set of private market choices and public decisions. Transportation and land-use forecasting through computer modeling is used in most metropolitan areas to predict transportation needs and growth patterns. But problems arise if these models are based on old assumptions about growth and urban form, travel patterns, and mode choices and costs.

During the interstate highway era, planners adopted a unidimensional definition of "transportation improvement," namely more roads. As traffic and population increased and more growth was projected for the future, the conclusion was that demand is present for more highways connecting future population centers.

In 1990, in a trend-setting initiative, 1000 Friends of Oregon established a project called Making the Land Use, Transportation, Air Quality Connection (LUTRAQ). (See case study in Chapter 5.) Using a proposed $200 million bypass around the Portland, Oregon, metropolitan region as a demonstration, LUTRAQ was designed to (1) identify alternative land-use development patterns that reduce travel demand and increase the use of alternative travel modes, and (2) develop reliable transportation modeling procedures that forecast the travel behavior associated with these alternative land-use patterns.

LUTRAQ's survey of transportation modeling in the United States reached the summary conclusion that "forecasting procedures have essentially remained unchanged in the majority of our major metropolitan areas for nearly twenty years." The report found that "only two regional transportation agencies (the San Francisco Bay Area Metropolitan Transportation Commission and the Puget Sound Regional Council) have fully implemented tools to predict the ways in which congestion influences land use, while land use patterns simultaneously influence congestion."[13]

Most transportation models deal only with motorized vehicles and not with walking or bicycling. Nor is transit-oriented development factored into the predictive equation. In addition, multiple trips by different household members to work and nonwork locations are not adequately documented.

When urban planners consider future transportation needs, most assume that the auto-oriented travel and development patterns of the last thirty years will continue to be the norm in the future. But public policy based on these models leads to a self-fulfilling prophecy. What is needed is a new way of modeling the future that allows for a different kind of development.

The LUTRAQ contribution is to model an alternative future that accommodates metropolitan growth in the area's fastest growing county through construction of a new light rail line, improvements to existing arterials, and pedestrian-oriented development patterns and zoning. This alternative future could be achieved without construction of a new freeway or transgression of the area's Urban Growth Boundary as currently proposed. Instead, urban form would be more densely defined, farmland would be protected, and air quality enhanced.

Full-Cost Pricing of Transportation

Essential to creating a new awareness of transportation, land use, and the effect on community is understanding society's support for the automobile and highway and the costs that taxpayers bear as a result. The out-of-pocket costs of owning an automobile are estimated at $4,000 annually for fuel, insurance, and car payments. Most households have more than one worker and usually more than one car. In fact 35 percent of American families own two automobiles, and 20 percent own three or more.[14]

Drivers tend to take only marginal cost into account when they decide to use their car for a specific trip. Research has shown that a jump in auto use is a direct result of increased ownership of cars, not the other way around. Yet we subsidize multiple car ownership with discounts for insurance and free residential parking. This encouragement of multiple car ownership could be addressed through license premiums on the second car, separate rent for the parking spaces at multiple family housing sites, and credit for low car ownership on mortgage applications.

Cars must have roads to drive on. In 1989 federal, state, and local governments spent roughly $33 billion on road construction, $20 billion on maintenance, $6.4 billion on police and safety services, $5.4 billion on administration, and $6.3 billion on interest and debt retirement.[15] All told, a little more than $70 billion is spent annually on building and maintaining the roads in the U.S. Approximately 60 percent of the federal, state, and local funds are raised by highway-user-related taxes and tolls. The other 40 percent or approximately $28 billion annually is raised from local property taxes, general funds, and other indirect sources, paid regardless of the amount the taxpayer uses highways.

When cars arrive at their destinations, they must have a place to park. Most parking spaces are provided "free." Customers at most shopping malls do not pay directly for parking. However, the developer pays for the land used for the construction of parking lots and passes that cost along in the form of higher rents to the stores at the malls. Customers then pay for the parking spaces indirectly through higher prices on goods. To the extent that it is possible for a person to patronize a suburban shopping center without a car, that individual is subsidizing other people's parking each time they make a purchase.

The same kind of subsidy is in effect for most of the workforce. More than 80 percent of Americans commute to work by car and receive free parking. Depending on location, parking spaces can be exceedingly expensive. For example, a parking space at a condominium in Boston's exclusive Beacon Hill neighborhood sells for more than $100,000. If one assumes a $500 per year average national value for a parking space, the close to 85 million Americans who park free at work receive more than $40 billion in annual parking support.[16] The U.S. tax code offers an incentive for employers to provide parking as a fringe benefit to employees. Assuming a daily parking rate of $4, the value of free parking amounts to $1,000 annually, and this fringe benefit is not taxed. If an employee wishes to take public transit to work and receive the additional $1,000 as compensation, that amount *would* be taxed. If an employer wishes to promote public transit by offering transit passes to employees, the value of the passes (if it exceeds $15 per month in value) is taxed. (The allowance has recently been raised to $60 per month.)

In addition to the direct costs incurred in building and maintaining roads and the subsidies offered for parking, there are indirect costs—externalities—that are born by society as a whole. Air pollution, noise, health, and safety are prime examples. Motor vehicles are the major cause of air pollutants such as sulfur dioxide and nitrogen dioxide, which create smog, and cars account for 70 percent of lead and carbon monoxide emissions and 45 percent of nitrous oxide emissions.

More than 112 million people live in metropolitan areas that fail to meet air quality standards. The American Lung Association estimates that the medical costs resulting from inhaling gasoline fumes add up to more than 40 cents for each gallon of fuel burned. Researchers at the University of California at Davis have estimated the cost of damages to crops, human health, lost lives, and reduced productivity as totaling between $10 billion and $200 billion annually. The wide range depends on the values placed on each factor, especially the 47,000 Americans who die in automobile accidents each year.

Another important externality is the contribution of an automobile-oriented way of life to the breakdown of communities. Automobile-based development has reduced opportunities for public life and magnified the polarization of our society by aggravating the geographical and time barriers between people with different incomes, and by making it more difficult for those who don't own cars to participate in life outside their communities. The costs of this degradation in community life are difficult to quantify but are obviously substantial.

One method proposed to make these externalities part of each driver's decision to use a car is called "congestion pricing."

Using electronic means rather than toll booths, drivers would be charged for the actual time and distance they drive, rather than the fuel they burn. Differential charges by location and time of day would respond to the higher costs incurred when driving in congested conditions.

Economists have long recommended that the full cost of transportation be charged to users. ISTEA has responded by funding demonstration projects for congestion pricing. Other public policy tools could be employed in like manner to recover the cost of auto use and discourage unnecessary travel. These methods would be more effective if preventative alternatives such as reducing the need for trips are offered at the same time.

Employing Least-Cost Planning Principles

Recently Southern California Edison gave away one million high-efficiency light bulbs to its customers. Other electric utilities are conducting extensive advertising campaigns urging customers to use less of their product. The reason is that utilities are increasingly pursuing a least-cost, comprehensive approach to provision of service. It is cheaper to conserve electricity and utilize existing infrastructure than to build more power plants and new transmission capacity. In the 1980s electric utilities in many areas of the country redefined their mission to provide lighting, heating, and cooling rather than more electricity and more incentives to use electricity.

Steve Burrington, of the Conservation Law Foundation, suggests that:

> The transportation and electric utility sectors present some strikingly similar challenges. They represent the two largest sources of damage to the environment in the United States. They have capital-intensive infrastructures that often seem to be teetering on the brink of failure, threatening to leave us without lights or bridges. In each sector, adding new capacity is now a difficult, drawn-out task—any proposal for a bigger road or new power plant comes at a time when too many wetlands have already been destroyed, the pollutant burden on the air and water is already too great, and the last piece of land that no one cares about has already disappeared. And in each sector, clean, affordable alternatives seem to be available but not to receive serious consideration from the engineers in charge.[17]

Transportation departments and authorities are also being challenged to re-think their missions or lines of businesses. Providing *mobility* through a variety of modes, rather than highways and cars alone, is the post-interstate era mission. Add to that the provision of *accessibility* by reducing the perceived need for trips, and we begin to see some solutions to transportation problems. David Morris, of the Institute for Local Self-Reliance, asks, "In the future is it not possible to imagine transportation authorities paying developers who build compact communities or communication companies that lay in fiber optic cables?"[18]

A conservation-oriented transportation agency would consider least-cost and full-cost scenarios for providing mobility that factor in the costs of preserving the environment and health of a community. Included would be greater collaboration with other interested public agencies and citizen organizations. We may even see the time, as David Morris suggests, when a state DOT could advertise to promote mobility conservation: "Please use less of our mobility product, live in a pedestrian-oriented community, teleconference instead!"

ISTEA Provisions

ISTEA, which was signed into law in December 1991, ushered in a new set of priorities for transportation planning. The emphasis shifted from a single objective—reducing traffic congestion—to multiple objectives that include protecting the environment and community quality.

Support for highways remains a substantial portion of ISTEA, but most of ISTEA's funding programs may be used for a variety of modes. Other modes of transport are also overtly recognized by the law's provision for a National Intermodal Transportation System. States and regional metropolitan planning organizations (MPOs) are given the flexibility to assign federal funds to a variety of transportation options.

Total authorized funding under ISTEA is $155 billion during the six-year period from 1992 through 1997. Completion of the Interstate system is authorized at $7.2 billion, and the 45,000 mile system will be incorporaed into the designation of a National Highway System (NHS) of up to 155,000 miles. Congress authorized $21 billion for the designation and improvement of the NHS. ISTEA also provides up to $17 billion for maintenance and reconstruction of the Interstate System, although additional capacity cannot be added using these maintenance funds, except for the addition of HOV lanes.

The law also created the Surface Transportation Program (STP), which provides funds for roads, transit, nonmotorized transportation, and even ecosystem improvements. A state may use NHS and STP funds for transportation planning and apply a portion or (with federal approval) all of its NHS funds to its STP. Ten percent of STP funds must be set aside for safety construction projects, and another 10 percent must be earmarked for environmentally related activities called *transportation enhancements*.

The enhancements program holds particular significance for those concerned with holistic transportation and the effects of road projects on surrounding natural and built environments. Over the six years of ISTEA funding, $2.8 billion are to be used for any of the following activities:

- Development of bicycle and pedestrian facilities;
- Acquisition of scenic easements, as well as scenic and historic sites;
- Scenic and historic highway programs;
- Landscaping;
- Rehabilitation and operation of historic transportation buildings, structures, and facilities;
- Preservation of abandoned transportation corridors, e.g., rails-to-trails programs;
- Archeological planning and research;
- Control and removal of outdoor advertising; and
- Mitigation of water pollution caused by highway runoff.

In addition, the Urban Mass Transit Administration, renamed the Federal Transit Administration by ISTEA, is authorized to spend $31.5 billion over six years on trains, buses, and rail modernization.

The law also allows for greater freedom in imposing tolls on roads that receive federal aid than was permitted in the past and allows private entities to own toll facilities. Moreover, ISTEA funds five congestion pricing pilot programs in various locations that could involve tolls. Also funded at $700 million is a prototype magnetic levitation transportation project.

Changing the Role of Regional Agencies

ISTEA calls for two related processes at both the regional and state levels. The first is a long-range planning process, required under Sections 134 and 135 (described in detail in Part II of this book). The second is the transportation improvement program (TIP), a short-term slate of proposed projects and activities derived from the long-range plan.

In the long-range process, the overall vision for a community or state is developed through early involvement of all stakeholders, including the public. Although a state or community's long-range plan is likely to include some project-specific information, the measurement of its success rests in the TIP, which includes specific recommendations for funding the proposed projects and provision for them to receive detailed attention for a minimum of three years.

The roots of regional planning for transportation go back to the Highway Act of 1962. Under ISTEA, MPOs are again in the limelight. For the first time in twenty years, federal funds are directly allocated to the largest MPOs and those in regions suffering from air pollution.

MPOs are given local responsibility for developing long-range transportation plans, which must include land use, intermodal connections, methods to enhance transit services and address congestion, and public transportation facilities and equipment. Each MPO must devise a TIP for its area, and the state is also obligated to produce a statewide TIP. Regions with populations of more than 200,000 are designated as Transportation Management Areas (TMAs) within which an MPO selects projects in consultation with the state.

All MPOs have strengthened roles in selecting projects, along with the state transportation agencies. MPOs must include the public in regional planning and project selection, and MPOs are given much greater leeway in considering alternatives to highway construction.

Under ISTEA, each MPO must also deal with issues of air pollution. The Clean Air Act Amendments of 1990 establish National Ambient Air Quality Standards for metropolitan areas. Those regions not meeting air quality standards for ozone, carbon monoxide, or small particulate matter are classified as nonattainment areas by the U.S. Environmental Protection Agency (EPA). Nonattainment areas are placed on a time schedule to meet air quality standards.

Each MPO for such an area must produce a plan that shows how its region will achieve attainment through transportation control measures involving land-use decisions and/or changes in vehicle miles traveled, transportation mode splits, and commuting patterns. ISTEA establishes the Congestion Mitigation and Air Quality Improvement Program with $6 billion for MPOs and states to fund projects such as HOV facilities that will assist nonattainment areas in reaching required air quality standards.

A more detailed history of ISTEA, description of its components, and analysis and strategies for affecting its implementation at the state and MPO level are contained in Part II.

Notes

1. James J. MacKenzie, Roger C. Dower, and Donald D.T. Chen, *The Going Rate: What It Really Costs to Drive* (Washington, DC: World Resources Institute, 1992).
2. MacKenzie et al., "The Going Rate," article excerpted in the *STPP Bulletin* (December 1992), 5.
3. Ibid.
4. Alistair Sherret, BART's First Five Years: *Transportation and Travel Impacts* (Washington, DC: U.S. Department of Transportation, 1992), 14.
5. Elizabeth Deakin, informal remarks at regional growth conference, "Building a Livable Future," Metropolitan Service District, Portland, OR, 1991.
6. Stuart Goldsmith, *Reasons Why Bicycling and Walking Are and Are Not Being Used More Extensively as Travel Modes,* (Washington, DC: Federal Highway Administration, 1993). Goldsmith concludes that weather, safety, absence of showers and lockers, and lack of bikeways are several of the most significant impediments to commuter bicycling.
7. David Morris, "Getting From Here to There: Building a National Transportation System." (paper presented at the 12th International Pedestrian Conference, Boulder, CO, 1991).
8. For current ideas on the subject, see Andres Duany and Elizabeth Plater-Zyberk, *Towns and Town-Making Principles,* (New York: Rizzoli, 1991); Douglas Kelbaugh, ed., *Pedestrian Pocket Book,* (New York: Princeton University Press, 1991); Peter Calthorpe, *The Next American Metropolis* (New York: Princeton Architec-

tural Press, 1993); and Sim Van der Ryn and Peter Calthorpe, *Sustainable Communities: A New Design Synthesis for Cities, Suburbs, and Towns,* (San Francisco, CA: Sierra Club Books, 1986). For earlier and seminal thoughts on new town design, see Ebenezer Howard, *Garden Cities of Tomorrow,* (Eastbourne: Attic Books, 1985) and Clarence Stein, *Towards New Towns for America* (Cambridge, MA: MIT Press, 1957).

9. Stein, *Towards New Towns for America,* 41.
10. Traffic calming employs several techniques to slow traffic and allow the joint use of roads for cars and pedestrians. For a very accessible guide to traffic calming, see the publication by the Citizens Against Route 20, *Traffic Calming* (Queensland, Australia: CART, 1989). CART changed its name to Citizens Advocating Responsible Transportation, and a sister organization in the United States now offers copies of *Traffic Calming*. See bibliography for additional information.
11. Kevin Kasowski, executive director of the National Growth Management Leadership Project, identifies nine states that play active roles in setting rules, guiding local jurisdictions, providing funding, and monitoring progress. Included are Maine, Rhode Island, New Jersey, Georgia, Florida, Vermont, Washington, Oregon, and Hawaii. As many as forty states have some kind of growth management legislation, but most do not have a comprehensive combination of laws and incentives.
12. Larry E. Pflugheoft, "Summary of Regional Issues: I-90 Final Supplemental Environmental Impact Statement, West Shore Mercer Island to Mercer Slough, Dated 8/30/73," (Seattle, WA: Puget Sound Governmental Conference, March 28, 1974).
13. LUTRAQ, Modeling Practices, Volume 1, October 1991.
14. The Surface Transportation Policy Project, *STPP Bulletin* (Washington, DC: STPP, December 1992).
15. MacKenzie et al., *The Going Rate.* See note 2.
16. MacKenzie et al. *The Going Rate,* 10. The WRI researchers estimated parking value at $1000 per year, doubling the figure given here.
17. Stephen Burrington, "Least-Cost Utility Planning: Lessons for the Transportation Sector," (Boston, MA: The Conservation Law Foundation, 1992).
18. See note 7.

2

Developing New Coalitions

The old stereotypes begin to fall apart in the post-interstate era. The infusion of jobs, construction contracts, and promises of congestion relief are powerful incentives for supporting road projects, but many public officials, citizen groups, and even developers are now saying no to new roads. Environmentalists and labor groups are joining forces; historic preservationists and land developers are forming coalitions. A host of interest groups that could have been divided and conquered to make way for new highways are coalescing around quality-of-life issues, and these partnerships are causing a shift in the way transportation agencies select and present new transport schemes.

In a later chapter, we will look at a case study in Boston in which environmental, labor, business, professional, and community groups are supporting a major project. The broad-based coalition, called Move Massachusetts 2000, includes organizations such as 1000 Friends of Massachusetts, Boston Building and Construction Trades Council, Boston Preservation Alliance, Boston Societies of Architects, Civil Engineers and Landscape Architects, Chinatown Neighborhood Association, and the Greater Boston Real Estate Board. The Boston case is detailed on pages 50–59.

We will also look at a Seattle case study in which a fascinating coalition of hiking clubs, preservationists, timber companies, government agencies, bankers, and lawyers is being pulled together to protect a greenway. The coalition is called the Mountains-to-Sound Greenway Trust, and its governing board reads like a who's who of business leaders, local and state government officials, and civic and environmental groups. Hiking and fishing enthusiasts sit side by side with lumber mill executives, suburban developers, and transportation officials. The Seattle case study is described in detail on pages 72–78.

Freeways have been stopped before or delayed for many years by activist groups. Citizens in South Pasadena, California, for example, successfully blocked completion of the Long Beach Freeway, which would have cut a swath through the community, wiping out hundreds of historic houses and thousands of trees. The city of 23,000 has sued the state and even hired a lobbyist in Sacramento to effectively stall (as of this writing) the I-710 highway proposal.

Affluent and more influential communities have fared better in fending off the intrusions of major freeways, as could be expected. In Los Angeles, for example, it is not difficult to understand that a proposed Beverly Hills Freeway was never built because the wealthy and powerful residents of that community were able to influence decision makers to re-think its route.

What we can expect to see with greater frequency in the future is a broader base of actors involved in the transportation and land-use game. In the ISTEA era various interests, ranging from neighborhood groups to diversified business giants, will have greater occasion to hook up together to influence transportation decisions. The first reason is that quality of life and the importance of community and the environment are recognized more than ever. Secondly, a confluence of interest is developing around the view that addressing these factors is good business and good government.

These conclusions are reached in part from the experiences of Virginia communities in defeating an ill-conceived plan to build a new highway bridge across an unspoiled portion of the James River and into the historically significant Jamestown area. The local county government has been grappling with growth management issues in an effort to protect natural areas and the rural qualities that have distinguished the region from suburban sprawl. The Virginia DOT's plans did not take the county's efforts into account. The proposed bridge could lead to increased development, which is what proponents wanted.

The broader question in light of the new federal emphasis on multi-modalism is whether ferry service might not be the most appropriate mode of transport for the area. In the case of the James River Crossing, the primacy of the auto and highway was challenged by a diverse coalition of preservationists, local officials, environmental groups, and a major developer. Good sense and the ferries won out.

Here is their story.

Virginia's James River Crossing
Historical Setting

The Isle of Wight, Prince George, Surry, Charles City, and James City are the counties that border the Lower James River as it makes its way through the low-lying Tidewater region of Virginia to the Atlantic Ocean. Today the sailor arriving at the confluence of the Atlantic Ocean, Chesapeake Bay, and James River is greeted by the naval fleet at Norfolk and the shipyards of Newport News. But in 1607 English colonists sailed about forty miles upriver to claim their first American settlement on a small island on the north shore of the big river. They named it Jamestown.

For an idea of what this part of the world must have looked like to Europeans or the Powhatan Indians who lived there, one need only go to Jamestown National Historical Park. Protected for future generations, the shore and vistas at the park look as pristine as they must have in the early 1600s.

In 1987, however, the view was threatened by a proposed highway bridge that was to replace a ferry that has plied the river since 1925, taking cars between two sections of State Route 31 that connect the towns of Jamestown and Scotland.

Transportation Modes

In the late 1980s, the Jamestown crossing—the only ferry operated by the Commonwealth of Virginia—was made by two boats that carried 1,800 cars a day on a fifteen- to twenty-minute journey. The schedule provided roughly hourly service from 5:00 a.m. to 12:30 a.m. and required an annual operating subsidy of $2 million from the state. The standard fare was two dollars each way for a car and driver, but commuter tickets lowered the fare to twenty-five cents.

The ferry connects James City County on the north shore with Surry County on the south. James City County is home to the nationally known tourist attractions of Colonial Williamsburg and Jamestown Settlement. The county is a growing residential and commercial area connected by major highways to the state capitol, an interstate, and the Chesapeake Bay highway systems. Surry County, with a population of approximately 6,500, is primarily rural in character without the rapid expansion and growth pressures experienced by Williamsburg. Some of the county's residents commute north across the river for employment.

The proposed bridge was designed to supplant the ferry service with its waits and lack of twenty-four hour service. Cost to construct the bridge was estimated at $100 million, which was to be paid by tolls projected at $1 for cars and $2 for trucks, each way, collected over a fifty-year term. Bridge proponents saw land development and residential and commercial growth on the south side as a benefit of the project. Surry's long-time state senator Elmon Gray was a powerful backer, and the leadership of the Virginia DOT was supportive of new highway and bridge projects.

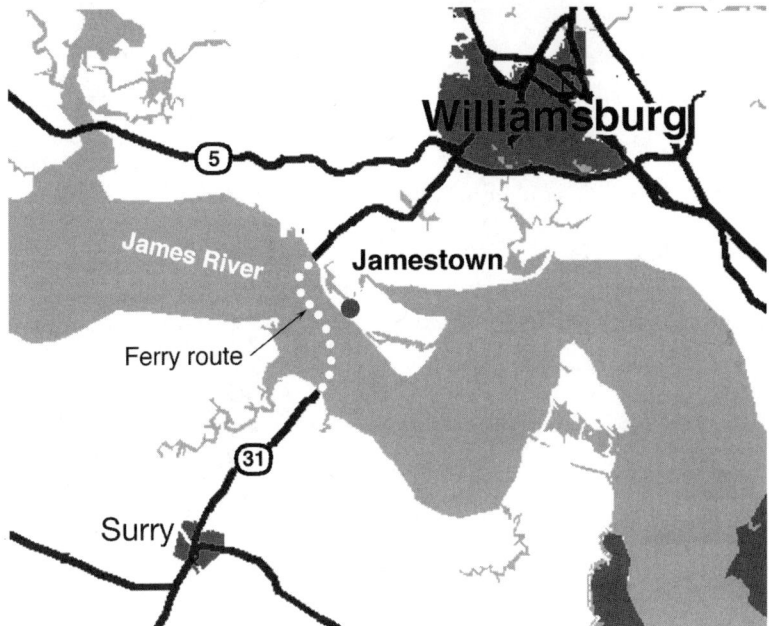

Location of the James River crossing area. (Map courtesy of Steve Durrant of Jones & Jones, Seattle, Washington.)

Growth and Preservation of Place

James City County had previously developed a comprehensive plan in an attempt to control growth in the proposed bridge corridor. Surry County's comprehensive plan made no provision for accommodating the inevitable growth in the bridge corridor, placing its economic development efforts farther south along US 460 and existing rail service.

Prior to 1990, the boards of supervisors of both counties voted against the bridge and in favor of improved ferry service.

The Virginia DOT issued a draft environmental impact statement (EIS) on the project in spring 1989. By then, other public agencies and officials had opposed the bridge, including the City Council of Williamsburg, National Park Service, and state legislators from James City, York, and Southampton

The last ferry in Virginia continues to ply the James River waters now that a proposed bridge has been stopped. (Photo by Nan Brown Maxwell, courtesy of Virginia J. Gabriele.)

counties. At issue were a combination of growth and development factors that would be driven by a new highway connection and would impact the scenic, historic, and environmental quality of the corridor.

For ferry users, tourists, business owners, and officials on both sides of the river, the ferry represents transport, an ambiance, and a way of life: slower paced, quieter, and more connected with the river itself. Vested interests, including tourist attractions in Williamsburg and large land developers, recognized that excessive sprawling development on the Williamsburg side would have negative impacts on the rural, colonial atmosphere that makes their businesses successful.

The Coalition

The proposal under the initial draft EIS corridor alignment placed the bridge immediately adjacent to Jamestown. Even the bridge's supporters soon realized that this alignment would not be acceptable. The next draft EIS corridor alignment put the northern end of the bridge squarely in the middle of Governor's Land, a 1,400-acre, 722-home planned community and golf course, as well as a 200-acre conservation park along the river. This bridge proposal managed to make allies of developers and environmentalists and led to the formation of the James River Crossing Coalition. In addition to the local government and elected officials listed above, the coalition included the following interest groups:

- Colonial Williamsburg Foundation (which owns and operates historic Williamsburg);
- Lower James River Association;
- Chesapeake Bay Foundation;
- Preservation Alliance of Virginia;

- Association for the Preservation of Virginia Antiquities;
- Coalition for Quality Growth, Inc.;
- *Daily Press;* and
- *Virginia Gazette.*

The Lower James River Association initially assumed a lead role in spearheading the coalition, and other members contributed at strategic moments. The formation of such a diverse coalition was itself a significant accomplishment. The fact that the coalition then hired technical consultants to prepare a study to counter the Virginia DOT's assumptions and findings proved critical in the political struggles that followed.[1]

The study, which was issued in March 1990, made the following case against the bridge and for the ferry[2]:

- There is little public support for the bridge;
- Choosing a bridge over a ferry is fiscally irresponsible (the Virginia DOT understated bridge costs and overstated both ferry costs and vehicular demand for a bridge);
- Local land uses will be adversely affected in historic and rural areas;
- The environment will be negatively affected;
- The most significant historic panorama in Virginia (if not the country) will be desecrated; in violation of the Federal-Aid Highway Act of 1968 (Section 4f) and the National Historic Preservation Act (Section 106) because VDOT did not provide for transportation alternatives with a lessened impact on historic and natural resources;
- The bridge will create navigational hazards; and
- The last ferry in Virginia, a valued cultural resource and tourist attraction, will be lost.

Political Power

In January 1990, Governor Douglas Wilder assumed office and appointed John Milliken as the commonwealth's new secretary of transportation. Milliken had previously been a county supervisor and appeared sensitive to the fact that no city or county government had supported the Virginia DOT's James River Crossing proposal. The secretary of transportation chairs the Commonwealth Transportation Board and oversees the department's commissioner.

Governor Wilder appointed four new members to the fifteen-person transportation board, which is responsible for approving bridge proposals. But Milliken still had to contend with a pro-highway, pro-bridge agency and the old-guard members of the transportation board. When the James River bridge came to a vote that year, Milliken crafted a strategy: The bridge would be shelved for now, but a decision on the bridge corridor could be re-examined during the next twenty years if a local government requested the Virginia DOT to do so.

In the fall of 1990 the Surry County Board of Supervisors changed its earlier 4-1 vote against the bridge to a 3-2 vote in its favor. The decision was back in the Commonwealth Transportation Board's lap. During 1991, the coalition carried on intensive lobbying. Three-quarters of the House of Delegates, including the speaker of the house, the majority leader, and the chairmen of the Finance, Roads, and Internal Navigation committees signed a petition opposing the bridge. A critical, and ultimately successful, coalition tactic was to concentrate on persuading the Tidewater area transportation board members to oppose the bridge.

By December 1991 the transportation board was ready to vote. Upon a motion by the Tidewater members, the board decided to scrap the bridge and any effort to preserve a corridor for a future bridge crossing. The board also voted to expand ferry operations to twenty-four hours per day, upgrade existing ferries to carry seventy cars, purchase a new seventy-car ferry, and increase fares so users pay a larger share of the ferry's operating costs.

The Jamestown crossing story is about choices of transportation modes, economic development, growth and sprawl, and the meaning of rural life. It is also about political power and the successful efforts of the James River Crossing Coalition to stop the commonwealth from building another bridge on the lower James.

CONTACT
Patricia Jackson, Executive Director
Lower James River Association
P.O. Box 110
Richmond, VA 23201
(804) 730-2898

Notes

1. The Williamsburg Group, developers of Governor's Land, footed the bill for the transportation consultant. Governor's Land is a development of Dominion Lands. Along with Virginia Power, Dominion Lands is a division of Dominion Resources. The coalition breaks down stereotypes that developers and preservationists must be in opposite camps.
2. David Schoppert, "James River Coalition Study," (Jamestown, VA: Lower James River Coalition, March 1990). This study found that VDOT neglected to account for the costs of operating a toll collection facility, charged the ferry service overhead costs while assuming no overhead for the bridge toll service, and assumed that 2,600 vehicles currently "avoid" taking the ferry without offering evidence of this.

3

A New Place at the Transportation Planning Table

If transportation cannot be disassociated from its land-use and environmental consequences, it is not surprising that the nation's largest estuary protection organization, the Chesapeake Bay Foundation (CBF), selected a highway project to make a public issue of the connection between transportation and environmental quality.

From 1987 to 1990 the Commonwealth of Virginia and State of Maryland studied alternative routes for a new Washington Bypass, an outer beltway around the nation's capital that was supported by developers. In 1990 the Chesapeake Bay Foundation convened a conference to rally political support to stop the bypass. If built, the new outer beltway would become a leading threat to the water quality of the Chesapeake Bay estuary.

In addition to leading to auto-oriented suburban development, highway corridors contribute water and air pollutants. Taken cumulatively, nonpoint sources of pollution in the form of oil dripping from motor vehicles, fertilizer and chemical runoff from suburban lawns, and toxics flushed down home drains constitute the most damaging threat to estuarine water quality.

By weighing in on the Washington Bypass issue, CBF put highway supporters on notice that a powerful and popular

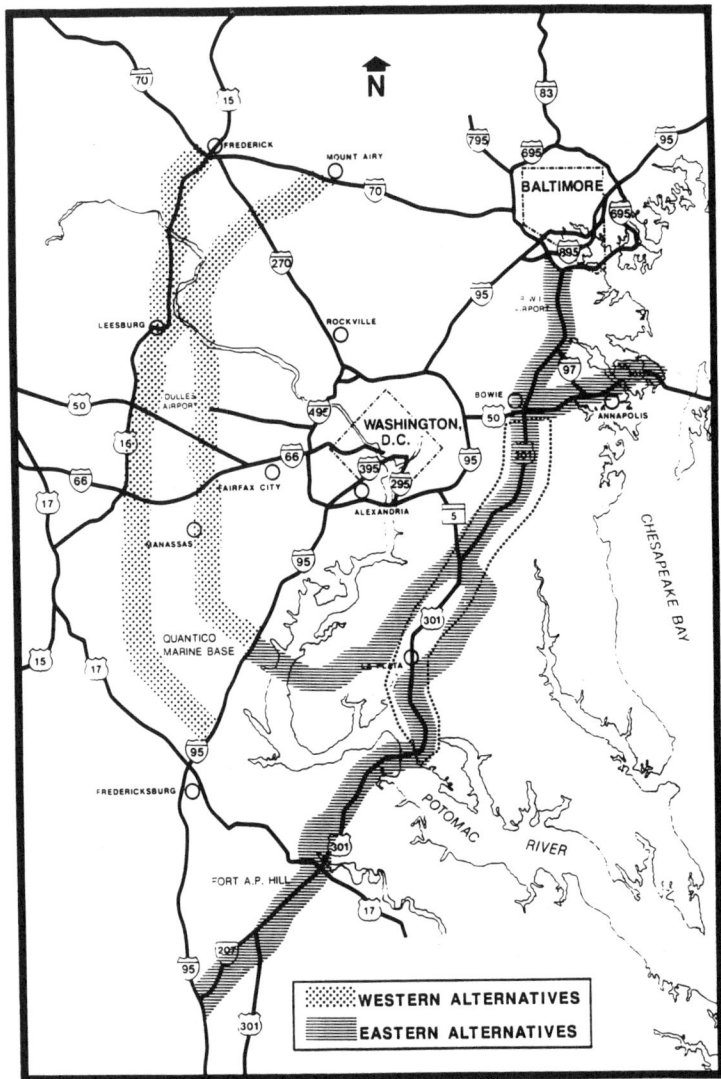

Map of Washington, D.C., and its surrounding area showing alternatives for the outer beltway (bypass) as well as Maryland's U.S. 301 corridor (outlined by dotted line). (Map courtesy of the Maryland State Highway Administration, Planning Department.)

nonprofit environmental group was organizing against the new beltway. The issue of degradation of the natural environment adjacent to the bay was about to be popularized.

The other part of the Washington Bypass story is the response of Maryland's DOT, which came to understand that development of new transportation corridors requires involvement of a broad set of views and participation by many levels of local government.

As the Washington Bypass concept died of its own scale, cost, and popular concern about its impacts, the Maryland DOT, CBF, the Chesapeake Bay Commission, and others began to explore ways to improve Route 301, the existing north-south highway. The 301 corridor is approximately 25 miles east of the nation's capitol and would have comprised about a fifty-mile segment of the bypass.

The Maryland DOT agreed to broaden the scope of discussion on road improvements, impacts on adjacent lands, and transportation mode options for the corridor. Further, the Maryland DOT provided funds to hire a facilitator to assist a task force composed of representatives from environmental and civic organizations, developers, and local governments. The Maryland DOT's actions provide a leadership model for other DOTs as they strive to change the traditional procedures and mindsets that have governed much of their operations under several generations of highway engineers.

Maryland's 301 Task Force

Like many major cities, Washington, D.C., is ringed by a circular interstate beltway. Designed to speed traffic on its interstate journey, beltways have spurred metropolitan growth and sprawl and generated intraregional travel. In the capital area, traffic volume on beltway segments of I-95 and I-495 in Virginia and Maryland has already exceeded designed capacity.

The call for more freeways to relieve the congestion has become insistent.

In 1986 a conference on regional beltways was held in Washington. The conference emphasized the need for a Washington bypass that would create a new interstate-level highway beyond the present beltway, further encroaching upon nearby countryside. In 1987 the Commonwealth of Virginia and State of Maryland authorized a three-year joint bypass study. By May 1990 the study's findings and a first-tier draft environmental impact statement were presented to the public.

Seven alternative routes were examined: three east of Washington, three west of the capital, and one composite route forming a second beltway. Costs were projected to range between $1.4 and $2.9 billion. Forecasts also predicted substantial increases in population, growth in the number of households, economic development, and increased employment along the new routes. Increased highway safety, regional access, truck through routing, and increased crossing capacity over the Potomac River were proposed benefits of the bypass.[1]

In May 1990 the Chesapeake Bay Foundation, a nonprofit organization of more than 82,000 members dedicated to protecting the tri-state estuary, held a conference entitled "The Washington Bypass: Can It Be Done Right?" The foundation was "concerned that construction of a Washington bypass as currently proposed could stimulate extensive, uncontrolled suburban development—one of the most damaging land use patterns affecting the Bay."[2]

According to its organizers, the intention of the conference was as follows:

> to focus public discussion on reconciling the need for a bypass with principles of intelligent growth and environmental protection for the entire region . . . examine the process of highway decision-making . . . present alternatives to a bypass, and initiate a strategy for citizens and community groups to exert unified pressure on the state's highway decision makers.[3]

The CBF conference was successful in drawing attention to the bypass as a major regional issue that transcended transportation alone and would influence growth patterns, lead to loss of farmlands, wetlands, and open space, and denigrate the quality of Chesapeake Bay.

The conference pointed out the limitations of the bypass study, described by one state transportation official as a "classic highway study which didn't consider alternate modes." The study did look at land-use implications, however, such as the loss of 200 to 2,000 acres of farmland. But these figures were based on loss to construction only and did not reflect conversion to residential or commercial use related to development pressure created by the proposed highway. An analysis commissioned by CBF found that 1.1 million acres of land would be at risk of development.[4]

The conference and a subsequent series of public meetings helped create a new political climate. Virginia and Maryland had elected new governors since the inception of the bypass study. In addition, the funding picture for such an ambitious transportation project appeared increasingly uncertain as the U.S. Congress began to revise the Surface Transportation Assistance Act.

The two states had different interests. The proposed western bypass routes directly threatened a Maryland county's pioneering efforts at growth management aimed at concentrating development northwest of Washington and protecting farmland. These western routes were advantageous for landowners and developers in the Dulles Airport area of Virginia where no apparatus for growth management existed. In addition, Maryland's governor was proposing statewide growth management legislation.

Galvanized by the CBF conference, opponents of the

bypass conducted research and developed a position paper during the remainder of 1990. CBF cited as the basis for its opposition:

- Adverse impacts on the Bay and environment;
- Unleashing of sprawling development;
- Conflicts with regional transportation and land-use policy;
- Flawed decision-making process leading to the proposed bypass; and
- Lack of public support.

A New Way of Thinking

CBF proposed a new decision-making process for relieving the "political gridlock" surrounding major transportation proposals such as the bypass. The new planning process would be comprehensive and would integrate land use and transportation planning with environmental protection and economic development. The process would include consideration of a range of alternatives for achieving mobility and would bring together constituencies concerned with regional growth management issues. They would include environmentalists, the business community, and consumers and producers of housing.[5]

CBF developed a strategy to use its political clout to stop the bypass and introduce its comprehensive approach to transportation decision making. CBF and the Chesapeake Bay Commission, a governmental body charged with protecting the Bay watershed, shared a resolve to stop the bypass. Together, the two organizations sponsored legislation in the Maryland assembly that would have required detailed and complicated studies of the eastern bypass US 301 corridor.

The Maryland DOT had concluded that the eastern alignment along existing US 301—a bypass with no connections to Virginia—would be the focus of the state's efforts. Maryland DOT officials were concerned that the proposed legislation would effectively kill their chance to upgrade US 301 and asked the legislature to delay passage of the bill to allow time to work out a new approach to corridor planing with the CBF and Chesapeake Bay Commission.

New Players at the Table

Thus was born an Advisory Task Force for the US 301 Corridor and the beginning of a more comprehensive way of thinking about mobility, environment, and land use. The purpose of the task force is "to focus on transportation and growth management issues associated with US 301. This process will integrate land use planning, open space planning, urban design issues, and enhanced environmental protection into the transportation planning process."[6]

The task force engaged in a two-year study to define and analyze alternatives for the corridor. The group was funded by the Maryland DOT with whom decision-making authority rests. The goal was to provide a basis for sound decisions by developing and evaluating alternative scenarios that attempt to meet the following objectives:

- Enhance mobility in the corridor;
- Foster compact patterns of development;
- Improve safety;
- Reduce automobile dependence (enhance modal choice);
- Protect open space and sensitive areas;
- Comply with the Clean Air Act Amendments of 1990;
- Use financial resources efficiently;
- Incorporate attractive and workable urban design;

- Develop ways to prevent changes to transportation plans and facilities that would compromise their designed purpose; and

- Gain experience with a new study process.

Options to be developed include:

- No action;

- Access-controlled facility with varying number of interchanges;

- Service road options;

- Transit alternatives;

- High-occupancy vehicle lanes;

- Travel demand reduction strategies; and

- Alternative land-use patterns.

Alternatives will be evaluated according to a number of factors, including the following:

- Low-density sprawl effects;

- Air quality impacts, including conformance to the State Implementation Plan and issues associated with the Clean Air Act;

- Water quality impacts;

- Noise impacts;

- Land-use impacts;

- Stream impacts;

- Consistency with local master plans;

- Impact on traffic projections and service;

- Safety impacts;

- Impacts to the Chesapeake Bay;

- Ability of the proposal to meet the project need;

- Economic impacts;

- Farmland impacts;

- Wetland impacts;

- Historic preservation, 4(f) analysis;

- Historic/archeological resources;

- Secondary land-use and environmental impacts; and

- Other environmental issues as identified by the group or dictated by the National Environmental Policy Act.

Participation in the task force includes representatives from the following groups:

- Anne Arundel County Government;

- Audubon Society;

- Chesapeake Bay Commission;

- Chesapeake Bay Foundation;

- City of Bowie;

- Charles County government;

- U.S. Environmental Protection Agency;

- Federal Highway Administration;

- Growth management advocates;

- Legislative representatives;

- Local civic, environmental, and business groups;

- The Maryland DOT—secretary's office;

- Maryland National Capital Park and Planning Commission;

- Mass Transit Administration;

- Minority representation;

- Natural Resources Defense Council;
- Prince George's Civic Federation;
- Prince George's County government;
- Sierra Club;
- State environmental and planning agencies;
- State highway administration;
- Suburban Maryland Builders Association;
- Tri-County Council;
- U.S. Army Corps of Engineers;
- U.S. Fish and Wildlife Service;
- Washington Board of Trade; and
- Washington Council of Governments.

The task force's charge and composition was formulated by staff of the Maryland DOT, Chesapeake Bay Commission, and CBF. The Maryland DOT retained the services of an experienced facilitating firm to staff the task force and will underwrite the technical consulting services, which will be required as the process unfolds.

CONTACTS
Kristin Pauly, Director
Lands Program
Chesapeake Bay Foundation
162 Prince George Street
Annapolis, MD 21401
(301) 261-2350

Heidi Van Luven
Charles Lippy
301 Project Co-Managers
Maryland Department of Transportation
707 North Calvert Street
Baltimore, MD 21203
(410) 333-6431

Connecticut's Merritt Parkway

Another instance of a responsive DOT involving a broader cross-section of stakeholders in a corridor planning process is chronicled in the case of Connecticut's Merritt Parkway, one of America's historic scenic roadways. The Merritt Parkway is a thirty-eight-mile stretch of roadway beginning at the New York State border and extending northeast as far as the Housatonic River, between Bridgeport and New Haven. Its construction began in 1934, and the parkway, billed as "Connecticut's All-Year Gateway to New England," was completed in 1940. The four-lane, limited access highway was designed as a haven for the automobile and its passengers. Commercial traffic and billboards were banned. A wide, landscaped median strip separated the traffic lanes, and rustic wood signs and guard rails blended in with the trees and natural vistas.

"The landscaping was planned to knit the many parts of this complex structure into a greater whole: it was to lead the eye to views beyond and to enhance" its thirty-five bridges—each uniquely designed—"that of all the Merritt's features, have most endeared themselves to its present generation of admirers."[7]

The landscaping is the legacy of the project's landscape architect, Thayer Chase, who catalogued every foot of the parkway prior to construction and after the blasting and construction crews had finished re-created a terrain of new plantings that blended into the surrounding countryside.

The significance of the Merritt Parkway is that it was built with more than the fastest automobile speeds in mind. Schuyler Merritt, whose name the parkway bears and member of the parkway commission, said, "We should see that beauty is kept in view, for the question is not primarily speed, but to enjoy ourselves as we go."[8]

Fifty years after it opened, the Merritt Parkway offers an alternative to interstates. Plans to double its width, which would destroy the historic character of its famous art deco bridges and prized landscaping, led to a well-publicized conference that focused activist and media attention on the issue and put pressure on state officials to justify their plans.

This case study examines the efforts to upgrade the parkway to serve auto users in the twenty-first century, while preserving its unique landscaping and design and protecting the communities along its route.

What Is a Parkway?

The term *parkway* was first used to describe the linear parklike environment that lined the forty-five-mile Long Island Motor Parkway built in 1908. The Long Island road was actually a race course built by William Vanderbilt, Jr. for the Vanderbilt Cup. It offered an alternative design quite at odds with the prevailing view that highways, such as Connecticut's Old Post Highway along the state's shoreline, were designed to serve the abutting properties and businesses.

The nation's first public parkway—the Bronx River Parkway in Westchester County, New York—was built in segments between 1907 and 1924. The New York parkway was part of an effort to beautify the shore of the polluted Bronx River and the slums that lined its ten-mile course. The Bronx road was followed by parkways in Washington, D.C., and several in the New York metropolitan area, culminating in the Robert Moses parkway system on Long Island and Westchester County.

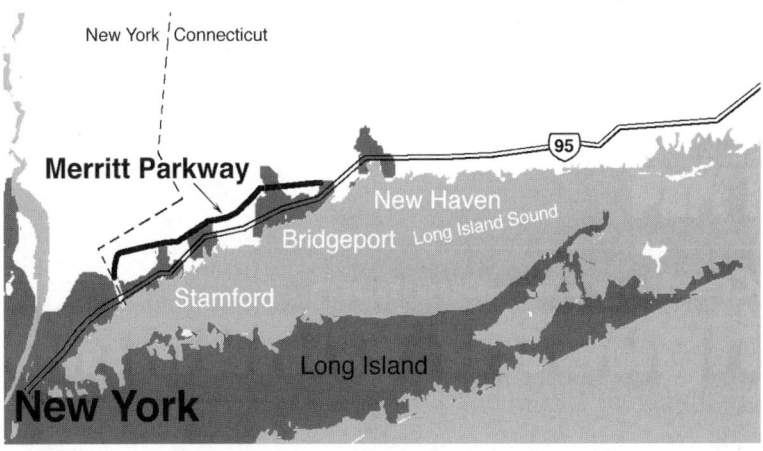

Location of the Merritt Parkway in southwest Connecticut. (Map courtesy of Steve Durrant of Jones & Jones, Seattle, Washington.)

The antecedents to the parkway include the City Beautiful movement with its emphasis on tree-lined boulevards and Frederick Law Olmsted's efforts to create separated rights-of-way designed and landscaped to mimic nature. The activities of the Regional Plan Association (RPA) of New York were another precursor. The RPA was a nonprofit organization comprising the most notable planners, reformers, and thinkers of the time, including Clarence Stein, Lewis Mumford, and Benton MacKaye.

The association foresaw the deleterious effects of urban sprawl and sought alternatives in the form of planned communities designed to safely accommodate the car. The association helped create the first regional plan for the New York metropolitan area and no doubt influenced Connecticut's Fairfield County Planning Association, a group of community leaders who published a pamphlet titled "Fairfield—the First Planned County in New England." The main attraction of the Fairfield comprehensive plan, and the only major element completed, was the Merritt Parkway.

The Merritt Parkway shortly after its opening in 1940. (Photo courtesy of State Archives, Connecticut State Library.)

Pressures on the Merritt

The Merritt's planners anticipated a need for future expansion by acquiring a 300-foot right-of-way and placing the roadway in the northern 150 feet. What the parkway planners probably did not foresee was the pace of growth in southern Connecticut as a suburb of New York City and home for corporate campuses.

The parkway's maximum capacity was 2,800 cars per hour for both directions with a design speed of 40–45 miles per hour (mph). The actual posted speed limit was 40 mph. During 1940, the parkway's first full year of operation, the Merritt exceeded its capacity on more than fifty occasions at the Greenwich Toll Plaza. After World War II, pleasure driving was replaced by commuter traffic, and the speed limit went up to 55 mph.

Interstate 95 opened in 1958, providing a parallel high-speed freeway. The traffic volume on the Merritt dropped by 17 percent. However, by 1976, average daily trips reached 33,000 and, by 1988, had surpassed the 50,000 mark. The higher speeds and volumes amplified the impact of design characteristics that pre-dated interstate highway standards. The absence of acceleration and deceleration lanes at exits impeded the smooth flow of traffic and proved dangerous at the higher speed limits. Trees in the twenty-two-foot medians also proved to be safety hazards and so were removed.

The culture and standards of the state's highway department (later folded into the Department of Transportation) changed over the life of the Merritt. The DOT's primary objectives of providing landscaping and opportunities for pleasure driving gave way to interstate highway standards for road design, maintenance, overpasses, exit and entrance lanes, and signage.

In incremental steps, the design integrity of the parkway was damaged. The road was viewed as anachronistic and unsafe. At seven points along the route, new bridges built according to American Association of State Highway and Transportation Officials (AASHTO) specifications and spanning hundreds of feet conveyed new highways that were bereft of any landscaping over the parkway. Metal guard rails were placed under bridges, aluminum freeway lighting standards were placed at new interchanges, rustic wood signs were replaced with standard metal ones, and the Merritt Parkway was officially renamed Route 15.

In 1973 the state proposed widening the Merritt to eight lanes. One magazine writer described the ensuing uproar:

A "Save the Merritt Committee" was formed and went into action. Newspapers both in and out of the state arose to challenge the planned parkway expansion calling the Merritt a "soothing retreat," a "national landmark among highways," and "Queen of the Parkways." ... The public pressure worked and at length the Governor announced, "The people concerned about this project were right and the designers were wrong."[9]

By 1990 the Connecticut DOT was again proposing to widen the Merritt. In the intervening years, Northwest Greenwich Association and the State Historic Preservation Office had sought to nominate the parkway to the National Register of Historic Places. But then-Governor Ella Grasso would not grant state support to the nomination and appointed a Merritt Parkway Citizens Advisory Committee instead.

It is not difficult to understand the Connecticut DOT's motivation to increase southwestern Connecticut's highway capacity in the Merritt Parkway corridor. The land was already set aside and available without condemnation proceedings. The emphasis on highway expansion in a corridor also served by a major interstate, as well as commuter and intercity rail lines, was an indication that the Connecticut DOT was not thinking along ISTEA lines. Nor did the state have growth management or regional planning systems to manage the relationship between transportation, land use, and sprawl.

Factors That Saved the Merritt

Faced with this new threat, the preservation community again sought to place the Merritt on the National Register. The Connecticut Trust for Historic Preservation began organizing a conference on the Merritt Parkway with the intent of showing the relationship between transportation and land use, congestion, and quality of life.

In the conference announcement, the organizers wrote:

> The Connecticut Trust's interest in the Merritt Parkway stems from our concern about the deterioration of the cultural landscape as our region undergoes a dramatic population shift away from large urban centers toward suburban and small, semi-rural communities. Development pressures caused by this shift all too often result in a homogeneous landscape of sprawl, and this trend is a primary concern of preservationists.[10]

The September 1991 conference was attended by concerned local citizens, land-use activists, preservationists, and the Connecticut DOT's new leadership. The meeting proved to be a political rallying point for efforts to protect the famous road, in large part because the Merritt was finally listed on the National Register that summer—its fiftieth year. The well-publicized conference provided a forum for the Connecticut DOT's new commissioner, Emil Frankel, who came from Fairfield County, to have his deputy announce that the Merritt would not be widened.

A confluence of events served to protect the Merritt Parkway this time around:

- The same kind of public attention that was rallied in the early 1970s was again focused on the issue.

- A new governor assumed office in 1991 and appointed a new transportation commissioner who was not wedded to previous plans.

- The Connecticut DOT began to reassess its highway plans in light of budget constraints resulting from the state's economic and fiscal crises: one city had declared bankruptcy, and cutbacks in personnel and projects were the order of the day. The Connecticut DOT concluded that I-95 was the "obvious choice" for highway improvements in the southwest corridor.

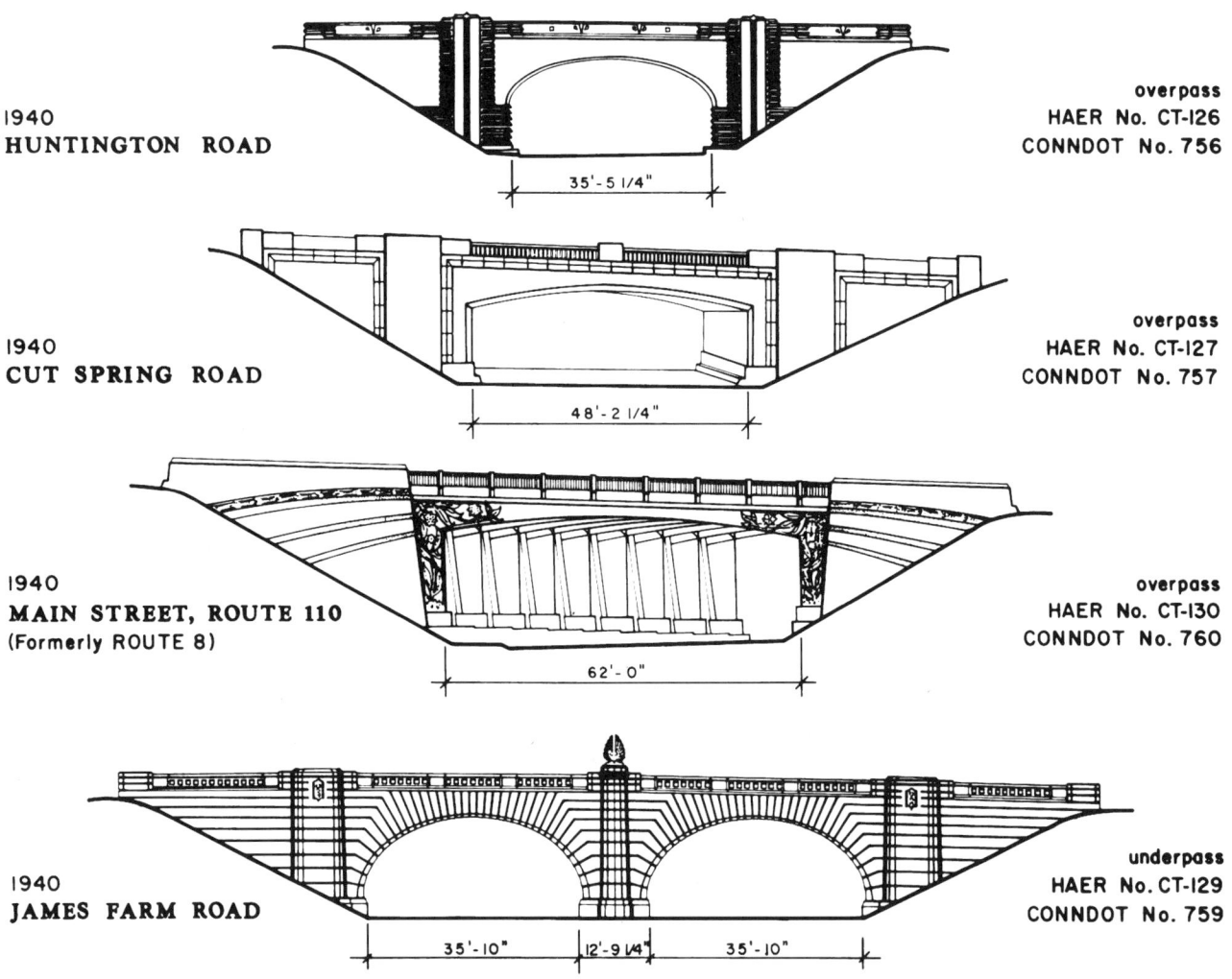

Each of the Merritt Parkway's thirty-five bridges has a unique art deco design (as shown in these examples), adding to the visual and historic value of the parkway experience. (Illustration courtesy of the Connecticut Department of Transportation.)

MERRITT PARKWAY BRIDGE DETAILS
TRUMBULL & STRATFORD, Connecticut

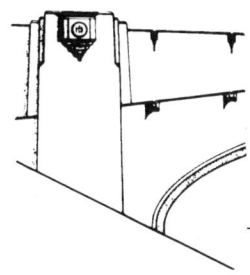

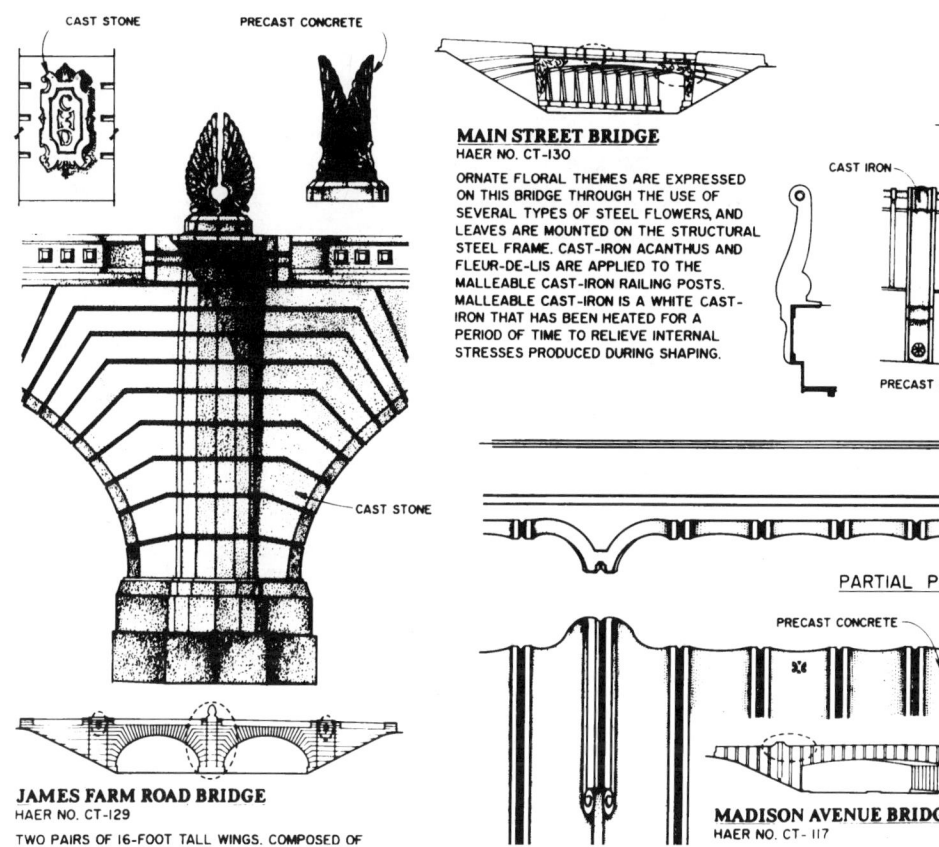

PARK AVENUE BRIDGE
HAER NO. CT-115

THE CAST-IN-PLACE CARTOUCHE ON THE PYLON FEATURES A SEAL OF THE TOWN OF TRUMBULL. THE SEAL DEPICTS A COLONIAL MINUTEMAN FIGURE AND THE YEAR OF THE TOWN'S FOUNDING, 1797.

HUNTINGTON TURNPIKE BRIDGE
HAER NO. CT-124

GRAPEVINE PATTERNS ARE EXECUTED WITH PRECAST CONCRETE, MOLDED-IN-PLACE CONCRETE, AND METAL DETAILS. PRECAST PANELS WITH A FLORIATED BAS-RELIEF OCCUPY NICHES IN THE RAILING. THE TOWN SEAL AND ITS FRAMING VINES WERE CAST WITH REVERSE MOLDS IN THE FORMWORK. THE PYLONS SUPPORT MALLEABLE CAST-IRON GRILLES. A MINIMUM THICKNESS OF 1 1/4" RESULTED IN THREE SECTIONS, EACH WEIGHING 1000 POUNDS, FOR EACH GRILLE OF GRAPEVINES.

CAST MALLEABLE IRON

MAIN STREET BRIDGE
HAER NO. CT-130

ORNATE FLORAL THEMES ARE EXPRESSED ON THIS BRIDGE THROUGH THE USE OF SEVERAL TYPES OF STEEL FLOWERS, AND LEAVES ARE MOUNTED ON THE STRUCTURAL STEEL FRAME. CAST-IRON ACANTHUS AND FLEUR-DE-LIS ARE APPLIED TO THE MALLEABLE CAST-IRON RAILING POSTS. MALLEABLE CAST-IRON IS A WHITE CAST-IRON THAT HAS BEEN HEATED FOR A PERIOD OF TIME TO RELIEVE INTERNAL STRESSES PRODUCED DURING SHAPING.

JAMES FARM ROAD BRIDGE
HAER NO. CT-129
TWO PAIRS OF 16-FOOT TALL WINGS. COMPOSED OF

MADISON AVENUE BRIDGE
HAER NO. CT-117

Compare the attention to detail shown here for the Merritt Parkway bridges with that of today's freeway overpasses. (Illustration courtesy of the Connecticut Department of Transportation.)

- Obtaining approval for new capacity for single occupancy vehicles in a severe nonattainment area like southwestern Connecticut under the Clean Air Act Amendments would be difficult.

The passage of ISTEA in December 1991 provided additional policy incentives and financial rewards for the Connecticut DOT to look at ways to enhance the Merritt. The new state administration is trying to "change the culture" of the department to think in multi-modal terms, increase mobility without new construction, and adopt roadway management techniques that are not based on interstate standards.[11]

One of the September conference's contributions was introduction of the concept of a Merritt Parkway management plan that would provide a guide for preserving the road's integrity and safety. The fact of the matter is that the road crews, maintenance supervisors, and design personnel do not know how to best care for the ornate bridges or the remnants of the original landscaping. The ASSHTO standards book offers no guidance on maintaining and upgrading the safety of a fifty-year-old roadway.

To create a management plan and re-examine the parkway and its restoration and safety upgrading, Commissioner Frankel appointed the Merritt Parkway Working Group. The eleven-person group included three technical advisors from outside the department—a preservationist, architect, and landscape architect. In addition to the commissioner and his executive assistant, other department members were the Deputy Commissioner of Engineering and Highway Operations, District Maintenance Manager (covering the Merritt), Manager of Traffic Engineering, Chief of Design—Engineering, Landscape Designer, and Assistant Planning Director—Policy and Planning.

The group's mission was to help the Connecticut DOT maintain the Merritt Parkway as a safe roadway while enhancing its unique character. The commissioner's personal involvement in the meetings and participation in a van tour of the parkway underscored the working group's significance. Some of the ideas discussed by the group included lighting the bridges at night to highlight their architectural features and designing a Jersey Barrier—the concrete lane divider—with art deco motifs consistent with the Merritt's bridge designs.

To more fully understand the Merritt's history, the National Park Service was contracted to conduct an historic inventory, known as an Historic American Engineering Record Study. This process will provide a baseline record from which to make many design and restoration decisions.

The process set in motion with the Merritt Parkway integrates the positions of highway planners with those of preservationists and designers. It raises important questions about highway design and aesthetic enhancements. One example is whether the original landscape concept with vistas of farmlands through trees is what people have come to love today. What is appropriate to restore or create for the next fifty years? By establishing the working group, a legitimized forum has been created to address these questions and propose solutions from within and outside of the Connecticut DOT.

As in the Maryland case, Connecticut's action is an inclusionary response from the state's highest transportation officials, offering new approaches to bringing concerned activists to the table and educating department of transportation personnel.

CONTACTS
Maribeth Demma
Assistant Director
Office of Intermodal Planning
Connecticut Department of Transportation
2800 Berlin Turnpike
P.O. Box 317546
Newington, CT 06131
(203) 594-2134

Chris Wigren
Connecticut Trust for Historic Preservation
940 Whitney Avenue
Hamden, CT 06517
(203) 562-6312

Final Thoughts

Nationwide, the trend over the past two decades has been to rename state highway agencies and call them "departments of transportation." In some instances, such as Maryland and Connecticut, the state DOT really does plan and operate modes of transportation other than highways, namely commuter rail service. In these cases the current buzzwords of "balanced transportation" and "multi-modal transportation" do have meaning. In many other states, however, the preponderant emphasis remains on funding the construction and maintenance of highways and roads.

Densely populated smaller states may have a more advanced understanding of the meaning of multi-modal transportation, as well as a greater appreciation of the negative consequences of highway-driven urban sprawl and congestion. However, this does not translate into consistent action. Even as the Connecticut DOT was agreeing not to widen the Merritt Parkway, it was proposing construction of a giant new freeway bridge over the Quinnipiac River outside New Haven. The project's draft EIS did not even consider such alternative measures as existing rail or new light rail service. Again, as described in Chapter 9, a coalition of public interest groups intervened to call for consideration of more options.

Another factor involved in both the Maryland and Connecticut cases is the nature of leadership at the departments of transportation. In both states, leadership had been recently assumed by politically astute leaders, attorneys by training, who did not rise through the ranks of highway engineers. The ability to deal with the multidimensional political problems that roads, land use, and environmental and community issues represent will increasingly become an essential asset for transportation leaders.

Notes

1. Maryland and Virginia Departments of Transportation, *Washington Bypass Study Informational Handout* (May 1990).
2. Chesapeake Bay Foundation, conference brochure (1990).
3. Ibid.
4. Resource Management Consultants Inc., *Analysis of Land Use Effects of the Proposed Washington Bypass,* (Washington DC: RMC, 1990).
5. Chesapeake Bay Foundation, "Position Paper on the Proposed Washington Bypass," (Annapolis, MD: CBF, February 7, 1991).
6. Maryland Department of Transportation, "Framework for Advisory Task Force for the U.S. 301 Corridor" (Maryland: MD DOT, no date).
7. Catherine Lynn, "The Golden Anniversary for the Merritt Parkway," *Connecticut Preservation News* (September/October, 1990).
8. George Larned, "Historic Roads: The Road as History, Merritt Parkway," (paper presented at the 70th annual meeting, Transportation Research Board, Washington, DC, January 1991).
9. Charles Monagan, "Queen of the Parkways," *Connecticut Magazine* (1977), 33-37.
10. Conference brochure, "The Merritt Parkway: 50 Years Later," (Hamden, CT: Connecticut Trust for Historic Preservation, 1991).
11. Michael Saunders, Deputy Commissioner for Policy and Planning, the Connecticut DOT, Interview with author, (May 1992).

4

Replacing Transportation Blunders with Community-Derived Solutions

Highway and transportation projects can involve enormous conflict between competing interests over prolonged periods of time. As a state pursues highway projects, it has a variety of advantages over most opponents. For example, it has federal construction and state operating funds—money that most foes and certainly neighborhood groups do not have. The state also has more tools with which to implement its plans, such as eminent domain for obtaining needed property. Moreover, the state has institutional capacity and a structure that persists over time.

In the previous chapter, we examined two instances where a state DOT responded adroitly to community tactics and sentiments by including a variety of community organizations and viewpoints into the process of redefining a transportation corridor. What happens when a DOT is uncompromising in the face of community-based opposition to a new freeway project? At face value the DOT's power is overwhelming compared with that of community groups. In such cases, the tools available to the opponents of new projects are litigation and mediation. From these, constructive outcomes are possible.

Litigation

Challenging a highway project in court is expensive and time consuming, but ultimately may be effective in delaying action until alternative methods of reaching agreement may be employed. In the case studies described in this chapter, we will see two examples of the use of litigation against a state DOT. In the Massachusetts case, the delays inherent in the legal process potentially jeopardized the availability of federal funds for the project, providing an incentive for the state to negotiate an agreement to mitigate project impacts and adopt far-reaching agreements regarding regional transportation decisions.

In Georgia, the state showed greater intransigence when a citizen coalition took it to court to stop a proposed parkway. The Georgia DOT presumed that it would prevail over the grassroots opposition, but community volunteers and dedicated attorneys managed to delay construction until a political climate more favorable to mediation and accommodation prevailed and a creative settlement was reached.

Mediation

Mediation, as a method of conflict resolution, has been applied when major transportation proposals have led to disputes. The affected parties gather in a formalized process with a professional facilitator or mediator to explore disagreements and seek new agreements. Mediation is a multi-step process that involves the following phases:

- Statement of positions;
- Clarifying concerns and interests;
- Agreement on a credible and confidential process;
- Moving away from either/or positions;
- Brainstorming;
- Disaggregating the problems;
- Researching and understanding technical and factual issues;
- Enlarging the pie of options;
- Narrowing the options;
- Creative repackaging of options;
- Displaying impacts and integration;
- Trade-offs and negotiations;
- Deadlines and details;
- Compromise; and
- Resolution—agreement/disagreement: some or all.[1]

The mediation process works when individual participants are unable to proceed with their own agendas. Put another way, they have achieved sufficient equality of power or influence that they must seek compromise because no participant can proceed unilaterally.

Mediation is not always successful as a conflict resolution method. For one thing, parties excluded from the table either by omission or intent do not feel bound by the resulting agreements. Also, if mediation participants get too far out ahead of the groups they represent, the results of the mediation may be repudiated by the larger interest groups. An effective way must be devised for representatives of parties at the table to communicate with and bring along their constituencies. Finally, if the costs that result from not participating in the mediation are insufficient, the process will fail.

Let us briefly consider an example in Kentucky, where Bluegrass Tomorrow, an independent nonprofit public interest group, sponsored a mediation effort to resolve a dispute over widening the Paris Pike near Lexington from two lanes to four. The Lexington-Fayette county urban area was experiencing strong economic growth, but the City of Paris was not enjoying equal prosperity. Paris boosters were convinced that a modernized highway was a key to the city's economic health. Preservationists were equally intent on protecting the two-lane roadway, which was bordered by stone walls passing through a rolling countryside of horse farms.

In 1979 the federal district court ruled in a case brought by the Blue Grass Land and Nature Trust that the proposal to widen the Paris Pike did not comply with section 4(f) of the Transportation Act of 1966. The court issued an injunction stopping construction. Section 4(f) requires transportation plans and projects to protect public lands, parks, and sites of historic significance and consider all feasible alternatives to minimize harm to those areas.

A decade later the road had still not been widened. In 1990 a group known as the Paris Pike Study Committee and consisting of the Kentucky Transportation Cabinet, City of Paris, Lexington-Fayette Urban County Government, and the Bourbon Fiscal Court contributed $90,000 to a conflict resolution effort convened by Bluegrass Tomorrow. The funds purchased the services of a neutral convener and the traffic engineering and planning skills of outside consultants.

The Paris Pike Study Committee developed a range of alternative corridor solutions aimed at increasing traffic flow and safety while protecting the historic and agricultural character of the land and area's economy. After a year of work, the committee failed to reach consensus on how the state should proceed with the Paris Pike. Participants rated the process very highly, and transportation and elected officials believed great progress had been made, but the goal of achieving consensus had proven elusive.

A proposal to widen Paris Pike to four lanes, rebuild the stone walls, and replant the landscaping emerged in 1991. The proposal was signed by state officials but not by the local government, nor by nonprofit land trust and historic preservation organizations. The following year, a new governor proposed an entirely new roadway alignment, which in the end proved unacceptable. Later in 1992, the mayor of

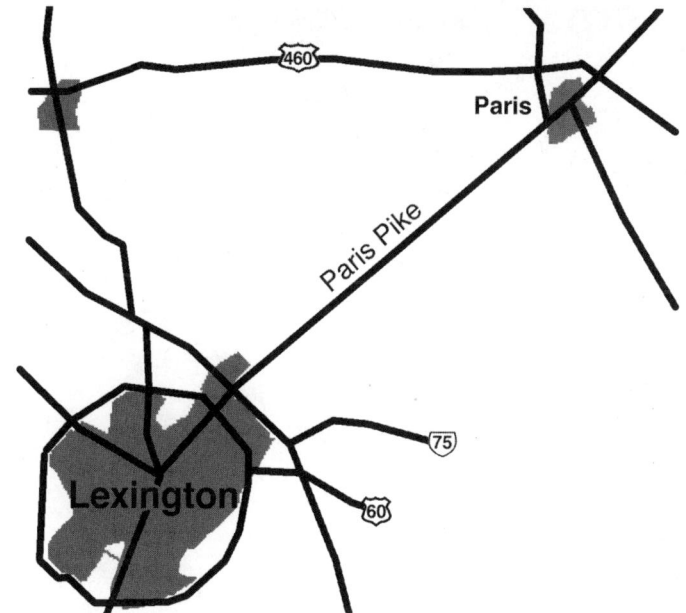

Location of Paris Pike. (Map courtesy of Steve Durrant of Jones & Jones, Seattle, Washington.)

Lexington-Fayette Urban County Government convened another consensus-building group called the Paris Pike Review Committee. This group proposed specific design standards to protect the rural and historic character and prevent urban sprawl. The committee also proposed creation of a corridor commission with authority over key land-use decisions.

In 1993 the federal, state, and local government parties to the Paris Pike dispute reached a memorandum of agreement based on the outcome of the Paris Pike Study Committee process. A second effort at facilitated problem solving provided a framework for compromise and lifting of the Blue Grass Land and Nature Trust's lawsuit. Many factors contribute to the efficacy of mediation, including the chemistry among the key participants, timing, political climate, pending legal action, impending deadlines, and the consequences of inaction.

Widening of Paris Pike means having to destroy or move 18th century stone walls (*top*) as well as encroaching on historic homes (*bottom*). These walls and homes are among the features that give the bluegrass country its sense of place. The Paris Pike agreement may allow for relocation and rebuilding of these walls and protection of historic properties elsewhere in the corridor. (Photos courtesy of Jones & Jones, Seattle, Washington.)

In the two case studies discussed in the remainder of this chapter, a combination of litigation and mediation significantly affected major highway projects.

Atlanta's Freedom Parkway

Ebenezer Baptist Church, made famous by Reverend Martin Luther King, Jr., is just east of downtown Atlanta. Continue east and north toward Emory University for about three miles and you pass through close-in residential neighborhoods and historic districts: Inman Park, Candler Park, Lake Claire, and Druid Hills. Most of this part of Atlanta lies in Fulton County; the rest is in DeKalb County, which also includes affluent suburbs.

In 1961 the Georgia DOT began acquiring land in this area for eventual construction of the Stone Mountain Tollway and Interstate 485 to connect DeKalb County to the airport south of Atlanta. Hundreds of acres of land were purchased as a right-of-way, i.e., a corridor acquired by a government for transportation purposes.

By the early 1970s, neighborhood opposition led then-Governor Jimmy Carter to appoint a blue ribbon Stone Mountain Tollway Study Commission. The commission recommended against construction of the tollway, and Governor Carter killed the project. By 1975 the I-485 project was deleted from state and federal transportation plans, and the land acquired for the interstate project was sold.

The Great Park Alternative

The Georgia DOT retained 219 acres near downtown that it had acquired for the Stone Mountain Tollway. In the 1970s, the close-in neighborhoods around the right-of-way were experiencing a resurgence, with new homeowners rehabilitating the

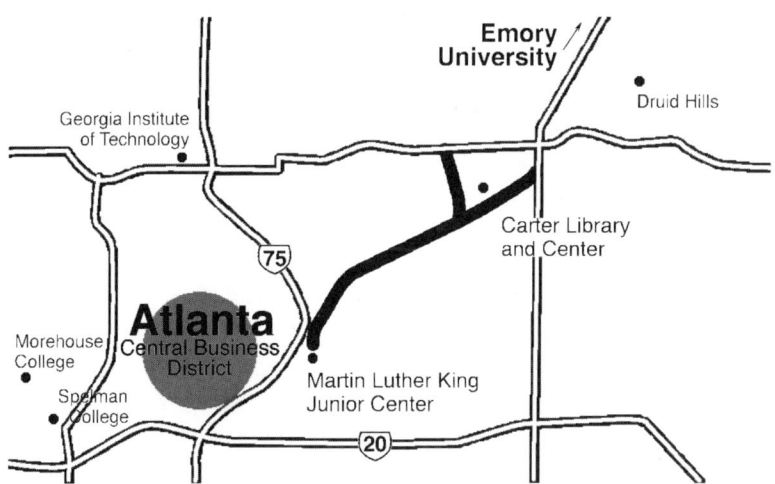

Location of Atlanta's Freedom Parkway. (Map courtesy of Steve Durrant of Jones & Jones, Seattle, Washington).

This abandoned concrete freeway pillar stands covered with kudzu in the middle of the old Stone Mountain right of way in a residential neighborhood: An old monument to the freeway gods?

older homes and tree-lined streets. The established neighborhoods closer to Emory University, laid out by the Olmsted brothers, were continuing to thrive, drawing upon a heritage of five Olmsted-designed parks.

In the late 1970s, a civic commission proposed that the 219 right-of-way acres should become a Great Park. In 1979 the governor appointed Atlanta architect-developer John Portman to head a Great Park Authority to create a master plan for "a unique inner-city Great Park."

Meanwhile the DOT proceeded with a proposal to build a parkway rather than a tollway. The Great Park Authority developed a $160 million concept but included the following warning:

> ... the construction of any major new freeway-type facility in the east-west corridor would be very controversial, would almost certainly be the occasion for further litigation, and would almost inevitably result not only in the demise of any

significant transportation improvement, but also the demise of the Great Park concept.[2]

The Presidential Parkway

Twenty years after the state began acquiring land for the tollway and a decade after scuttling those plans, President Carter returned home to Georgia to site his library and the Carter Presidential Center. In 1981 the former president announced plans to affiliate the library with Emory University and build on state-owned land in the DOT Great Park right-of-way. The Carter Library and Center projected 600,000 visitors annually and desired a limited access freeway. DOT now had a destination and rationale for its road project.

Andrew Young, ambassador to the United Nations in the Carter administration, was running for mayor of Atlanta that year and opposed new multi-lane roads in the city, including roads in the Great Park. But after being elected, the new mayor reversed himself and proposed a four-lane freeway in a new 219-acre Presidential Park that would include open space, the Carter Library and Center, 700 new housing units, and bicycle and jogging paths. The freeway was to be depressed twenty feet below grade in some areas; in others it was to be elevated. The road would have torn through three Olmsted parks, eliminating 9 acres of Candler and Goldsboro Parks and 4.5 acres of Druid Hills Historic District, while cutting across the centermost Shadyside Park.

The Great Park Authority, the City of Atlanta, the Georgia DOT, the *Atlanta Journal-Constitution*, and Jimmy Carter endorsed the plan. With the political forces in alignment, it looked as if a road would finally be built.

CAUTION

Eight neighborhood associations in the path of the proposed freeway banned together to form Citizens Against Unnecessary Thoroughfares in Older Neighborhoods (CAUTION) with a single mission: to stop the Presidential Parkway. This mission unified a neighborhood coalition with various interests and motivations, including an intense desire to preserve their communities from the physical splitting that would occur from a grade-separated, limited access four-lane roadway.

The neighborhood activists were additionally motivated by a sense of betrayal that elected officials and powerful interests had changed their positions, and a sense of moral indignation that middle- and upper-middle-class residents who were reinvesting in the inner city would see the value of their property diminished to satisfy the dreams of DOT planners and a former president.

Many younger residents of the Inman Park and Candler Park neighborhoods and Poncey Highlands cut their political and activist teeth on the freeway issue. This was especially true for many women who participated in the freeway fight when their children were young. A powerful motivator was the fight for a sense of place and community that many of these new urban settlers were intent on creating, coupled with an essential optimism that they could change the system.

The coalition spanned a variety of ages, professions, and income levels. Although some financial support came from the more established communities such as Druid Hills, most of the money was raised from small contributions and fund-raising events like Inman Park's spring festival, home tour, and flea markets.

From CAUTION's perspective, a political deal had been struck between the powerful DOT commissioner, the former governor and president, and the new mayor. In early meetings in 1981 with Carter representatives, community members recount that they were told that they did not hold chips in the political process and their concerns were not subjects for discussion. This reception strengthened their resolve to oppose the project.

CAUTION activists estimate that they raised more than $500,000 during a ten-year effort. All but $50,000 went to pay legal fees from 1982 to 1992. Challenges in the courts at the local, state, and federal levels were key tactics for delaying and defeating the parkway.

In 1984 national assistance and recognition came as the National Trust for Historic Preservation joined with CAUTION and filed suit in U.S. District Court to block the road. Irregularities in putting the road contract out for bid were exposed in court. The DOT's condemnation of public parkland was also challenged and found to be illegal under state law.

Concurrent with the legal process, political opposition was being organized. Three thousand opponents turned out at a DOT public hearing. CAUTION members attended all DOT commission meetings, which were held at various locations around the state. (Decisions on the Presidential Parkway were often made at these out-of-town meetings.) The coalition worked closely with elected officials who opposed the road, notably Congressman John Lewis. Speaking at a rally when he was a member of the City Council, Lewis had declared, "We will use our votes, we will use our money, we will use the courts, we will use non-violent protest to stop this road."

In fact, nonviolent protests began in the winter of 1985 when members of Roadbusters, a protest group willing to engage in civil disobedience, erected a tent city in Frederick Law Olmsted's Shadyside Park. The Roadbusters chained themselves to 100-year-old trees in the freeway's path. Other protesters climbed into trees and refused to leave, remaining in the limbs as the trees were felled by DOT contractors.

The road project was stopped by a court finding that the state could not condemn public parkland. In response, the state created the Commission on the Condemnation of Public Property, which recommended changing state law. During this time CAUTION members were labeled "bored housewives," "frustrated liberals," and the "chablis and brie set" by columnists and editorialists in the city's major newspaper.

Mediation and a New Political Climate

By 1988, toward the conclusion of Mayor Young's second term and two years after the opening of the Carter Library, a DeKalb Superior Court Judge ordered CAUTION and the DOT to engage in mediation to resolve the road dispute out of court. The DOT refused to mediate and appealed the order to the State Supreme Court. DOT's refusal to talk contrasted with CAUTION's public willingness to discuss matters and was probably an important public relations coup for the road's opponents.

Nonetheless, by 1990 when Mayor Maynard Jackson returned to office, a high-ranking member of his administration described the situation as one in which "the community was losing one fight, retreating, losing another, and retreating again." Business interests had focused on another freeway—Georgia 400—and had lost interest in the Presidential Parkway. The new mayoral administration, the same one under which the Great Park plan had been conceived ten years earlier, was opposed to a freeway-type road.

CAUTION's strategies had, at great cost of energy and money to the community groups and the state, proven successful in stopping construction and pushing off a decision to the next decade when the political imperatives and personalities proved to be different. The new factors included the following:

- Mayor Jackson and the Atlanta City Council were opposed to the road.
- A new governor assumed office and was open to changing the DOT commissioners.
- Atlanta was selected as the site for the 1996 Olympics, presenting a new reason and deadline for resolving conflicts.
- The Carter Library had been open for five years and was drawing about one-sixth the number of visitors that had been projected.

In January 1991 Judge Clarence Seeliger, of the DeKalb Superior Court, told the DOT and CAUTION to mediate their dispute again. Two months later, the first session was held under the auspices of the Justice Center of Atlanta, a local mediation center that contributed $25,000 and hired a mediator from outside the state. The City of Atlanta, the DOT, and CAUTION were represented at the table.[3] An important ground rule was that discussions at the mediation table were not to be made public. CAUTION's representatives met with the coalition's full board on a regular basis to discuss issues and reach consensus before returning to the table.

Through the spring of 1991, the group met in seven sessions covering forty-three hours and came close to agreement. The seemingly irreconcilable differences had to do with the size, design, and function of the roadway. The community wanted a small, at-grade road with low speeds and no trucks. The intention would be to better serve local traffic. The DOT wanted to meet larger traffic projections and proximate freeway standards of lane and shoulder size with few if any interruptions or intersections.

Atlanta's Commissioner of Planning and Development, Leon Eplan, suggested a new paradigm for the project. The roadway would connect the Martin Luther King Center to the Jimmy Carter Center and would be called the Freedom Parkway. It would be administered by the National Park Service and designed in the manner of an Olmsted roadway. Working against a September deadline, when the court had scheduled evidentiary hearings, Eplan refined the plan by moving the roadway to the north, bringing it to grade, lowering the speed, and eliminating truck use. He shopped the plan around to build support.

In August negotiations resumed.[4] There was still an impasse. The afternoon session was delayed for several hours while the governor asked his newly appointed DOT commissioner, Wayne Shackelford (replacing long-time commissioner Hal Rives, who had promoted and defended the Presidential Parkway), to become the official state spokesperson and support the Freedom Parkway concept.

The mediation ended with an agreement to build a meandering surface street within a park. The road would be 2.1 miles long, have low speed limits, bicycle lanes, and cost a third of the original price tag. Participants in the mediation and supporters and allies representing all sides celebrated. Former intractable foes were photographed arm in arm with broad smiles on their faces.

After the Celebration

At first, the mediated agreement reached in August 1991 appeared to CAUTION as the victory it had long sought. The agreement marked a political resolution to the Presidential Parkway debate; but it did not design, build, or manage the parkway. The next year was spent intensely involved in translating the agreement into real plans that would yield a parkway that reflected the vision of its proponents.

The Georgia DOT was not in the business of building meandering parkways. It knew of only one type of light standard, for example, for freeways. What would the vertical grade of the roadway be, and what kinds of shoulders and guardrails would be appropriate? CAUTION and the state transportation engineers engaged in a new educational/implementation phase. They found that the professional skills were often unavailable. In one case the Federal Highway Administration "loaned" a transportation engineer who had parkway planning expertise from the National Park Service.

For CAUTION, the post-mediation period was a challenge. The unifying "no road" theme had been modified and no longer applied.[5] The organization had to shift from being an opposition group to being a cooperator on implementation and enforcer of the agreement. Several key board members rolled up their sleeves and participated in the parkway's design process, finding alternative lighting designs, challenging the scale of proposed bike lane bridges, and hammering out the final wording of the Freedom Parkway agreement.

Designing the parkway is one task, managing the parkway is another. Eplan proposed that the National Park Service would manage the Freedom Parkway. CAUTION was wary of any one agency having control and concerned that such an agency could be pressured by powerful interests, like a former president, to change its plans. (Officials at the Carter Library and Center still believe that additional auto and bus capacity will be needed to serve the facility.)

With the Olympics being held in Atlanta in 1996, motivation is high to complete the Freedom Parkway along with other ambitious civic and construction projects. The community coalition that was successful in redefining an expressway into a

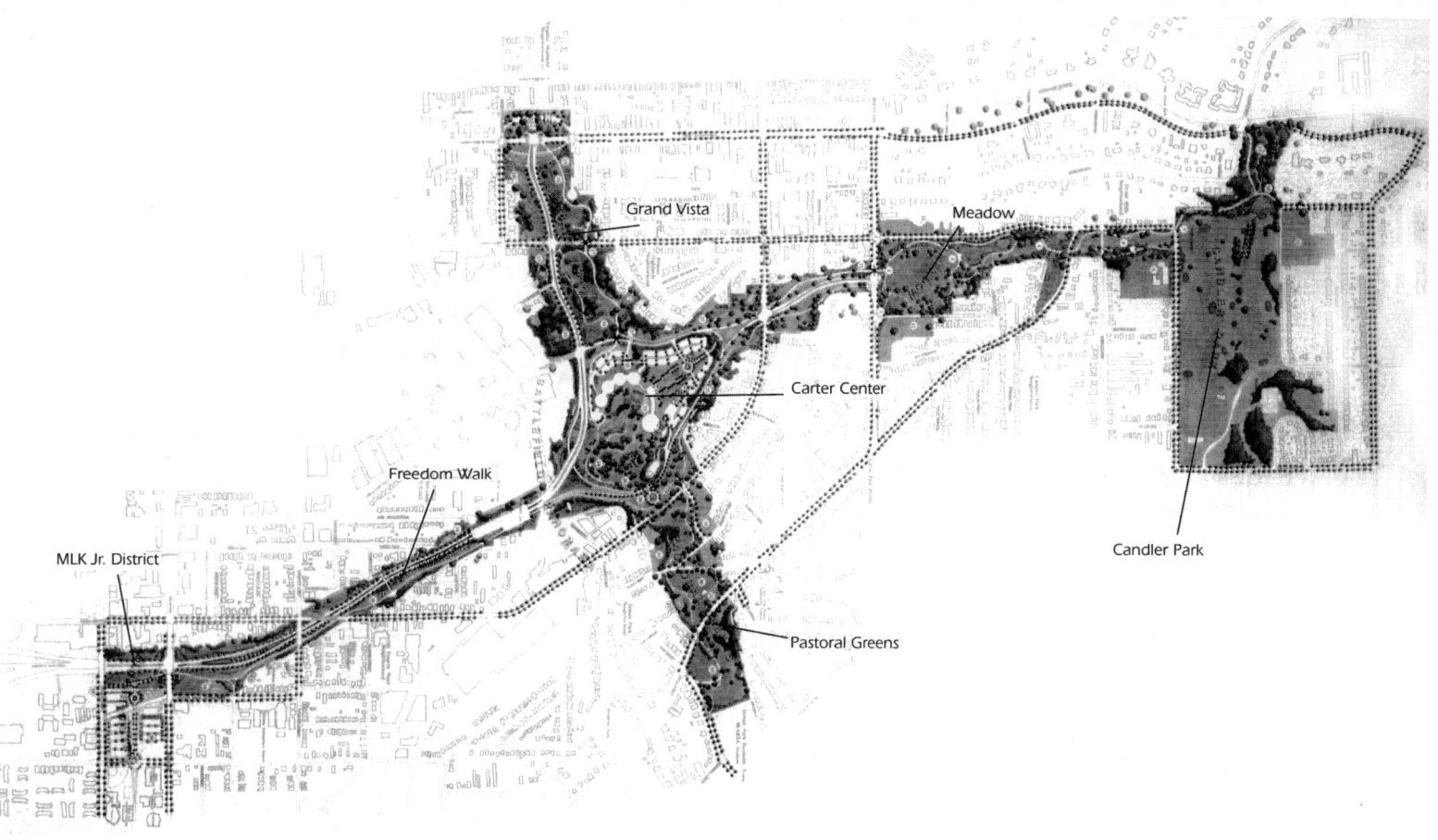

The Freedom Parkway agreement calls for a two-lane, 35 mph, at-grade roadway meandering through a park and serving residential communities. Before citizen action and a mediated settlement it was planned as an elevated four-lane freeway. (Illustration courtesy of Eckbo, Dean, Austin & Williams, Atlanta, Georgia.)

meandering parkway now turns to resolve another element of the parkway agreement, the role and location of new housing in the area.

Lessons from Atlanta

A real or perceived deadline or incentive helps to strengthen a mediation process. In Atlanta, after fifteen years and close to $900,000 spent on litigation, sit-down protests, and political fighting, the neighborhood coalition was able to conclude a mediated agreement with the State of Georgia and the City of Atlanta. The mediated agreement called for a two-lane, at-grade meandering parkway with lowered speed limits. The Freedom Parkway, as it was finally named, would symbolically connect the Martin Luther King Center with the Carter Presidential Library and Center.

By 1991 Atlanta city officials and civic leaders were eager to resolve this unfinished road project. A major incentive was the desire, shared by public officials and private sector leaders, to complete unresolved construction projects in the city prior to hosting the Olympics in 1996.

Another significant factor was the new governor's replacement of the old-guard highway commissioner with an individual willing to compromise on the road's design. Thus, the Atlanta case study also suggests the impact of delaying tactics on successful mediation.

CONTACTS
Cathy Bradshaw
CAUTION
206 Hurt Street, N.E.
Atlanta, GA 30307
(404) 524-4190

Alycen Whiddon
Senior Planner
Atlanta Bureau of Planning
55 Trinity Avenue, S.W.
Suite 1450
Atlanta, GA 30335
(404) 330-6525

Boston's Central Artery/Tunnel

The case study that follows describes a road proposal that ranks among America's largest public works projects. The Central Artery/Tunnel (CAT) project in Boston, conceived in the mid-1970s, is scheduled to cost $7.7 billion over the next decade. As many as 800 engineers and technical experts have been working on the Central Artery since 1986 as part of a joint venture by two giant engineering and construction firms, Bechtel and Parsons Brinckerhoff. For comparison, the City of Boston's entire public works department employs 477 individuals, of which 150 are engineers and technical experts.

The CAT project enjoyed substantial public support because it would replace an ugly downtown elevated highway and relieve traffic and congestion. At present, the Central Artery is a thirty-eight-year-old, double-deck, elevated freeway that cuts through downtown Boston. During the 1980s, the Commonwealth of Massachusetts' Executive Office of Transportation and Construction developed a plan to improve the artery's viaduct, which was believed to be near the end of its structural life as well as being an extremely congested link on the I-90 and I-93 system. The commonwealth's plan involved the following objectives:

- Remove the elevated freeway structure;
- Rebuild it as a depressed (underground) freeway beneath twenty-seven acres of cover;

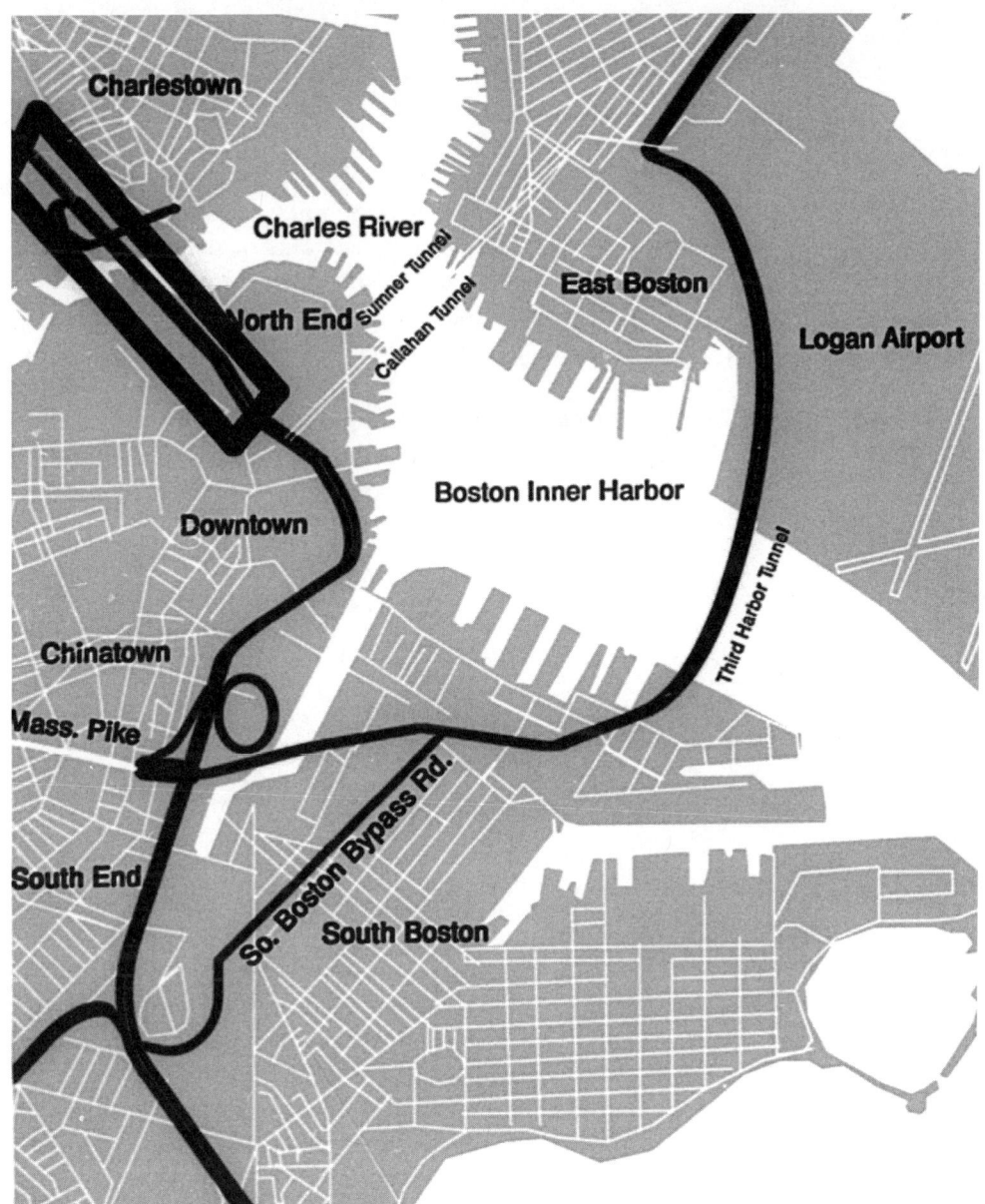

Location of Boston's proposed Central Artery/Tunnel project. (Map courtesy of the Massachusetts Highway Department.)

- Connect the downtown interstate corridor with Logan International Airport by constructing a third tunnel under Boston Harbor; and

- Cross the Charles River to the north via an elaborate new bridge, completing a connection to I-93.

The Central Artery/Tunnel project is of particular interest for a number of reasons. Unlike other highway projects documented in this book, there is widespread agreement—in the transportation, business, and environmental communities—that the existing elevated freeway does represent a problem and a large-scale public works project is needed to solve it. Contention revolved around the project's focus on the private automobile.

The enormity of the proposal has bearing on the local economy; the future design and functioning of downtown businesses and residential communities; air, water, and open space quality; and choices for future transportation modes in greater Boston.

At first glance, the CAT project is an interstate highway built for cars at a time when national policy mandates a multi-modal approach to transportation and a reduction in auto air emissions. The project forces an examination of the relationship of downtown economic development and growth to continued edge city development and the Central Artery's role in metropolitan growth. On the other hand, the CAT project is proposed in the context of a city that already has an extensive light rail, subway, and commuter rail system.

Through years of court challenges and two positive experiences with mediation, many of the players in the political process have found something to like in CAT. The following sections describe the project's highlights.

Political Context

The Central Artery/Tunnel project was proposed early in the 1980s in order to increase auto capacity on the downtown segment of I-93 and capacity to the airport. More than 200,000 vehicles use the Central Artery daily; improvements would increase capacity by another 50,000 to 300,000 vehicles.

The CAT project would affect historic structures and neighborhoods; sensitive environmental areas including shorelines, urban parks, and open lands; and local air and water quality. Opponents decried the absence of any form of mass transit as part of the grand scheme.

While the Massachusetts DOT was addressing these concerns, it was waging a five-year legislative battle to maintain CAT's eligibility for federal interstate funds. A 1985 draft EIS exposed significant concerns about CAT, and the commonwealth worked to redesign and modify the project to address the following problems:

- Dredge disposal in Boston Harbor;

- Loss of public parkland and access to the Boston waterfront and Charles River; and

- Lack of integration of CAT into a broader plan for public transit and HOVs in the corridor.

Enhancements and Mitigation

In connection with each of these major concerns, the Massachusetts DOT strived to gain public support by working with nonprofit groups and public agencies to develop enhancements to the CAT project. One example is a plan to use sediments dredged from the Charles River and Boston Harbor to enlarge Spectacle Island in Boston Harbor. The dredge spoils, which are potentially hazardous, would be capped for containment, artificial reefs would be constructed to attract fish, and the region would have a new park. The suggested approach offers an environmentally acceptable disposal method for waste, while developing recreational opportunities and new wildlife habitat.

Another change to the Big Dig (as the newspapers began to call the project) was a new plan developed in 1989 for the Charles River crossing. The new crossing, which is the point where seven lanes merge into three heading north to Cambridge, would consist of multi-level bridges and spiraling on and off ramps. Named Scheme Z, the new plan became the project's major glitch.

In order to secure federal funding and avoid succumbing to the weight of the opposition, then-Secretary of Transportation Fred Salvucci skillfully built political support for the refined CAT. Timing was critical because the Dukakis administration was scheduled to leave office at the end of 1990. All state approvals needed to be obtained and the final environmental impact statement submitted before a new administration came into office.

By December 1990 the Commonwealth of Massachusetts had signed formal agreements to:

- Link the CAT project with an integrated multi-modal transportation plan for the Boston region;

- Work with the City of Boston and the regional park authority to develop twenty-seven acres in the heart of downtown into parklands that would include tree-lined boulevards, bicycle and pedestrian paths, swimming pools, skating rinks, and even an indoor Winter Garden; and

- Design the CAT to protect the historic character of properties agreed upon by the commonwealth's Historic Preservation Officer, Boston Landmarks Commission, and Advisory Council on Historic Preservation.

CAT incorporated many of the dimensions of ISTEA one year before passage of the landmark federal legislation established that it will be national policy to create multi-modal transportation systems and enhance highway projects. How this came about is a function of the variety of transportation options that exist in the Boston area, the political necessity of making deals to win approval of such a vast and complex project, and the very active role played by a number of sophisticated public interest groups.

Engagement and Opposition

Three public interest organizations played significant roles in linking CAT with changes to commonwealth and regional transportation and environmental policy. The first group, 1000 Friends of Massachusetts, developed a "Massachusetts Transportation Agenda," which was officially adopted by the commonwealth and included as an attachment to the 1990 final EIS. The agenda begins with the following statement:

> Improved mass transportation systems are the backbone of future transportation policy. The Commonwealth must continue its current policy of expanding rail and bus transit routes, improving facilities and developing innovative operating programs. Commonwealth policy will encourage sufficient density of development and quality of transit to make mass transit the preferred transportation for most commuters in urban and suburban regions.[6]

The agenda goes on to declare that the highest priority will be the following improvements to the transit system:

- New equipment;

- Extended rail and rapid transit services;

- Commuter boat service; and

- Constrained transit fares.

The agenda emphasizes the following integrated transportation policies emphasizing traffic demand management and use of HOVs:

- No increase in highway capacity, except High Occupancy Vehicle (HOV) lanes leading into Boston;

- Restrictions on private and public parking in Boston;

- Expansion of suburban parking at public transit stops; and
- Introduction and expansion of HOV lanes.

The second organization playing a major role is the Conservation Law Foundation, a nonprofit dedicated to environmental improvement in New England. The foundation entered into negotiations with the commonwealth and emerged with a memorandum of understanding in December 1990. The foundation, which had previously won a lawsuit forcing the commonwealth to begin cleaning up Boston Harbor, agreed not to oppose the CAT project on the condition that an agreement could be negotiated that would link CAT to an integrated transportation plan. The agreement commits the commonwealth to specific public transit improvements, parking supply reforms, and a construction timetable.

These improvements and reforms (see map on next page) implement the following policies in the transportation agenda that was developed by the 1000 Friends of Massachusetts and adopted by the commonwealth:

- HOV lanes on I-93 north and southbound from the Central Artery at least to Route 128 (the beltway around Boston) and installation of HOV facilities on I-90 if travel time becomes excessive;
- Downtown parking restrictions in Boston and Cambridge to discourage approximately 135,000 commuters from driving from the suburbs, and preferential parking for carpools and vanpools;
- Commuter rail extensions and improvements on six lines by 1995;
- Mass transit (subway, light rail, and bus) extensions, improvements, and stations between 1991 and 2010;
- Public transit fares indexed to the cost of commuting by automobile and inflation so they cannot become more expensive than car travel;
- Commuter parking expanded by 10,000 additional spaces by 1995 and another 10,000 by 1998; and
- A permanent prohibition against additions to the single occupancy vehicle capacity of commuting highway routes into Boston.

The memorandum of understanding stipulates that the Conservation Law Foundation would go to court if the agreed items were not implemented by the state. In fact, the foundation initiated a lawsuit a mere six months after signing the agreement because the Federal Highway Administration failed to include the measures listed above in their record of decision approving the CAT project. The new commonwealth administration settled with the foundation in spring of 1992, affirming that the project "is as much an environmental project as it is a transportation one."

The third pivotal organization, the Boston Greenspace Alliance, saw the CAT project as an opportunity to capture open space and parkland for downtown, the waterfront, and the region. The commonwealth's environmental agency, in its certification of the project, required that 75 percent of the twenty-seven acres of air rights above the sunken downtown freeway would become open space. The expansion of Spectacle Island into a larger park and the agreement between the commonwealth and the regional park district to add bike and pedestrian lanes, waterfront parkland, and other amenities including pools, landscaping, and lighting were benefits derived from advocacy for open space.

Many of the park enhancements were the result of a summer 1990 mediation effort initiated by 1000 Friends of Massachusetts and aimed at offsetting some of Scheme Z's impacts. The commonwealth's secretary of transportation refused to submit Scheme Z itself to mediation, so the talks focused on mitigation measures. Participants in the mediation process, which was facilitated by the quasi-public Massachusetts Mediation Service, included nonprofit and public agencies. In addition to increased communication, the breakthroughs in this effort were the agreements between the commonwealth DOT and the regional Metropolitan Development Commission (which is responsible for parklands) to develop parks and open space.

The Next Twenty Years
A Transportation Blueprint

As a condition for agreeing not to oppose the Central Artery Project, CLF negotiated an agreement to ensure that the project is not just a haphazard highway improvement, but part of an integrated transportation plan. Signed by the Massachusetts secretary of transportation in December 1990, the accord will shape the face of Boston and its suburbs well into the 21st century. The agreement's far-reaching provisions are intended to accomplish one primary goal: to shift Boston- and Logan Airport-bound automobile travelers into efficient, convenient forms of transit.

HOV Lanes
Special "high occupancy vehicle" (HOV) lanes, devoted exclusively to vehicles with multiple passengers, will be installed on Route 93 north of Boston and on the Southeast Expressway. This measure will encourage commuters to drive in carpools or to abandon their cars for more efficient vans and busses. If travel time on Route 93 going north or on the Massachusetts Turnpike becomes excessive, HOV lanes will be installed there as well. To ensure that alternatives to singly-occupied cars remain attractive, the state will take steps to guarantee that HOV lanes do not become jammed.

Parking Freeze
New limits on parking spaces will be imposed in downtown Boston, Cambridge, East Boston, South Boston, and part of Revere. The difficulty of finding parking spots is expected to discourage approximately 135,000 commuters from driving from the suburbs, but preferential treatment in parking lots will be given to carpools and vanpools.

Commuter Rail
Commuter rail service will be reestablished between Ipswich and Newburyport by 1993 and between Framingham and Worcester by 1995. The Old Colony Railroad, connecting Braintree with Middleborough, Plymouth, and Greenbush will be reopened by 1995.

Mass Transit Fares
MBTA fare increases will be indexed to the cost of commuting by automobile—to make transit fares competive with driving expenses.

MBTA Improvements
The state will undertake many new improvements to make mass transit quicker, more comfortable, and more extensive. The Arborway Line will be reopened by 1996. The Green Line will be extended from Lechmere Station to Medford's Ball Square by 2000. Passenger platforms on the Blue Line will be enlarged by 1997, increasing the route's capacity. An underground electric bus line, connecting Boylston Station with South Boston, will be completed by 2010. The state will examine a proposal to construct a circumferential subway line connecting the main peripheral nodes of the existing lines. A study will be conducted on the feasibility of a water shuttle between Boston and the North Shore. A new MBTA bus terminal at South Station will be built.

Commuter Parking
The state will encourage mass transit use by constructing 10,000 additional commuter parking spaces by 1995 and another 10,000 by 1998.

Logan Airport
The state will pursue the installation of separate toll booths at the Sumner Tunnel for Logan Airport traffic. A stiff tariff for Logan-bound cars would discourage unnecessary automobile trips to the airport and could fund express airport shuttle services. Suburban "remote terminals" will be built where air passengers can check their bags on flights and can board express shuttles to Logan Airport. By 2010, an extension of the Blue line from Bowdoin station to Charles Street station will allow passengers to transfer directly from the Red Line to the Blue Line, making the airport more accessible to mass transit passengers. The bus access platform at Airport Station will be lowered to the level of the subway platform, to ease the transfer between the Blue Line and airport shuttle busses. The state will undertake a study to examine a proposal for a tunnel connecting South Station by rail to Logan Airport. This connector could continue north, bridging the existing gap separating passenger rail lines north and south of Boston.

Inter-city Rail
Massachusetts will assist Amtrak in introducing high-speed rail service between Boston and New York; Boston and Portland, Maine; and Boston and Hartford, Connecticut. Anticipated to take just three hours, the New York service will compete with air service to New York, thus reducing pressure to expand metropolitan Boston's airport capacity.

Highway Moratorium
Additions to the capacity of commuting routes into Boston are prohibited forever.

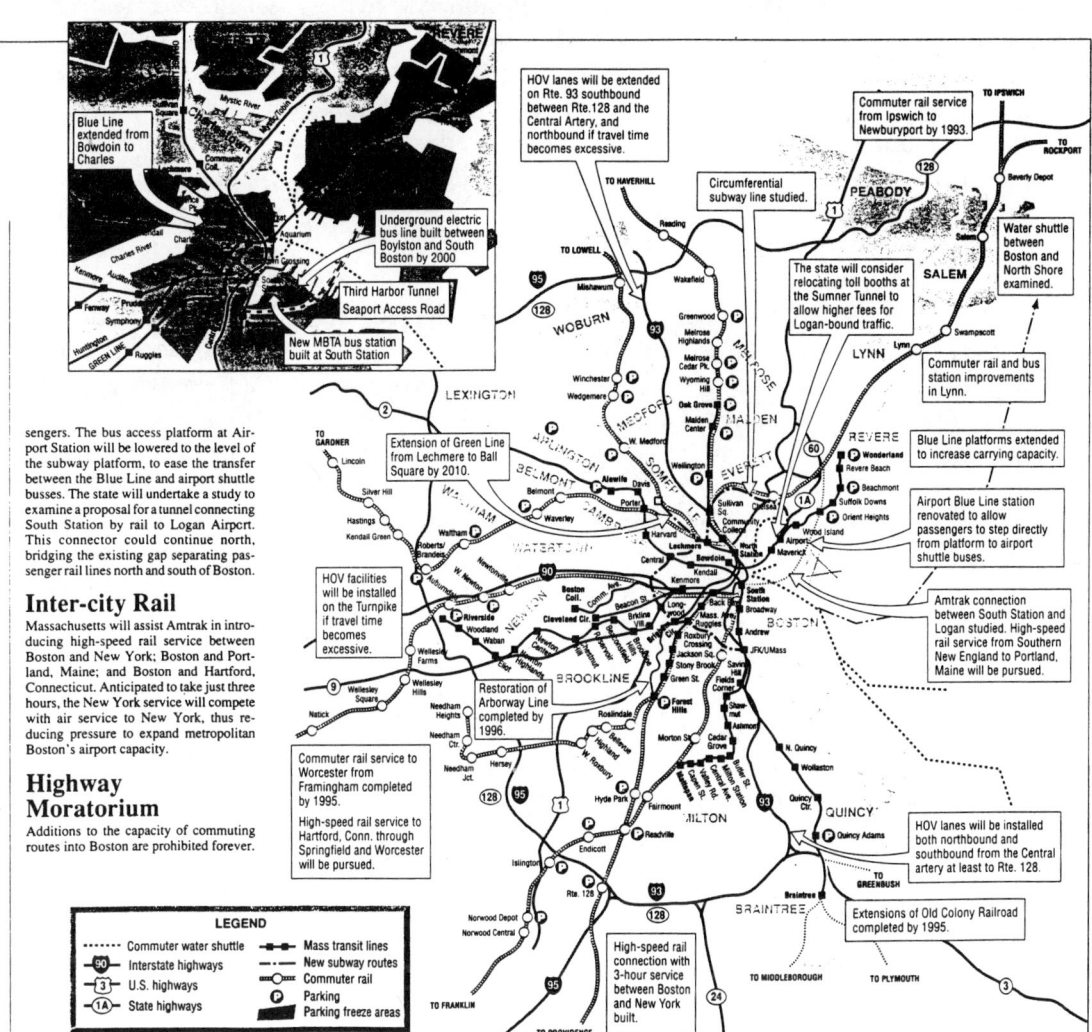

As part of its agreement with the Conservation Law Foundation and other citizen organizations to proceed with the Central Artery/Tunnel project, the Massachusetts Department of Transportation made sweeping commitments for the future development of regional transportation and placements of auto-oriented improvements. The transit, HOV, and parkland commitments are shown here. (Copyright © 1991 the Conservation Law Foundation.)

Not all environmental and public interest groups engaged in the mitigation process. The Sierra Club has opposed any expansion of highway capacity on the grounds that the CAT project will degrade air quality rather than improving it, as the environmental impact statement asserts, and that a rail connection between Boston's two railroad stations should be constructed as an alternative to highway expansion.

Both the foundation and the Boston Greenspace Alliance were courted by then-Secretary of Transportation Salvucci to participate in the mediation process. Both groups engaged in the process because (1) they believed they could reduce auto dependency and increase open space as a result, and (2) they saw a jobs-and-environment connection, confirmed by CAT's strong labor and business support, as well as connections to affordable housing and a desirable climate for continued downtown development. Environmental and growth management advocates participated because they wanted to tie this enormous car-oriented project worth $5.5 billion into a broader statewide transportation and land-use policy emphasizing public transit and HOV lanes.

The Sierra Club and the National Association of Railroad Passengers, by contrast, continued to oppose CAT, believing that increased highway capacity was bad for the environment.

The position of the foundation represents a growth management vision of the city and its relationship to the region. The foundation was influenced by the combined issues of reducing auto dependency and forming regional growth patterns that would be environmentally sustainable. CAT would create a connection between the downtown Central Business District and the waterfront for new development, reinforcing downtown Boston as the region's economic hub. By improving access to the central city and its developability, suburban sprawl and edge city development would be curtailed.

Implementation Methods

CAT, which began as an enormous highway project in 1982, turned into a complex jobs project that redefines commonwealth transportation policy, affects regional growth and development, and creates urban parkland. How will a public agency, especially one that has specialized in highway construction, be made accountable as it implements the project?

Implementation and accountability mechanisms include memoranda of understanding, the power of lawsuits, and establishment of citizen advisory and oversight committees for the enhancement measures. The commonwealth's Executive Office of Transportation and Construction has shown a willingness to try new approaches to make the project work.

One is the establishment—urged by a coalition of environmental organizations—of the Central Artery Environmental Oversight Committee. The committee, which is housed at the Metropolitan Area Planning Council, monitors the progress of hundreds of different commitments and studies spanning years. The oversight committee comprises representatives from nonprofit and public organizations and has an independent staff funded by the commonwealth.

Scheme Z Mediation

Another mechanism is the Charles River Crossing Design Review Committee. In the final year of the Dukakis administration, the Central Artery project almost came unglued. Little noticed by the City of Cambridge or CAT opponents was the manner in which the new freeway would emerge from its Boston depression and cross over the Charles River through the cities of Cambridge and Charlestown. The proposed multi-tiered bridge and overpass structure named Scheme Z would have built as much new elevated highway over the two northern neighbors as would have been eliminated downtown—at a cost of $500 million to boot.

As this became plain, the Cambridge City Council voted to oppose the bridge. Five new lawsuits were filed. The issue remained unresolved while the commonwealth pushed to obtain certification for its 1990 final environmental impact statement. John DeVillars, head of the commonwealth's Environmental

Protection Agency, wrote in his certification letter that he "strongly recommended" establishment of a committee charged with improving the Scheme Z crossing. DeVillars intended that its membership would include specific nonprofit and public agencies and recommended that the committee be convened by February 1, 1991.

The incoming administration of Governor William Weld did in fact appoint such a committee, consisting of forty-two members including representatives of the cities of Boston and Cambridge, commonwealth agencies, and neighborhood and regional private groups representing a broad spectrum of views. The committee included professional, business, environmental, governmental, and community leaders, architects, engineers, planners, lawyers, residents, and labor and business people. Five of the parties suing the commonwealth over Scheme Z and CAT were members.[7]

One ingredient was not part of DeVillars' recommendation: a professional mediator hired by the commonwealth's secretary of transportation to facilitate the process. John Wofford, attorney and former transportation official, had been instrumental in the state's decision twenty years earlier to drop highway plans for the Southwest Corridor and replace them with a new subway line and an urban park corridor.

The committee served an advisory function. Its meetings were open to the public and press, and typical attendance reached seventy-five individuals. The facilitator, protected under the state's mediation statute, served in a confidential relationship with each member of the committee. The process began with a statement of position from each committee member and a site tour, and moved quickly toward mutual understanding of the members' underlying concerns and objectives.

Indeed, the committee moved very quickly. Four months after it commenced work, the committee voted unanimously to abandon Scheme Z and recommended a new configuration combining a tunnel under the Charles River and a single bridge. By October the Bridge Design and Review Committee submitted its report to the Secretary of Transportation. The report included a recommendation that the committee continue to advise on design refinements for the new concept.

The committee continued to simplify and improve the tunnel/bridge recommendation. By March of 1992 the Cambridge City Council, which had sued to stop scheme Z, unanimously voted to authorize the city manager to negotiate on the committee's recommended alternative. By mid-March the Bridge Design and Review Committee unanimously endorsed the tunnel/bridge design. At the same time, the Conservation Law Foundation reached agreement with the commonwealth on environmental and mass transit measures, avoiding a court battle.

The first step for the committee was establishing trust among themselves and toward the facilitator and the assistant secretary of transportation in charge of the Charles River Crossing. Everyone was new to the "job." The next task was examining Scheme Z.

It was an article of faith under Salvucci's administration that a tunnel could not be constructed under the Charles River. Scheme Z was predicated on that contention. As an alternative, the scheme proposed sixteen lanes crossing the river on three separate bridges and six loop ramps on the north side of the river. Scheme Z included all the moves of a typical highway cloverleaf interchange, but stacked on top of each other in a single quadrant instead of four "leaves."

During the brainstorming phase of the committee process, all assumptions about the crossing were challenged. The committee retained five independent experts on bridges, tunnels, traffic, rail, and air quality to develop new approaches and design sketches. The CAT project's consultant team also provided technical analysis and assistance.[8]

The work of the committee was expedited by formation of subcommittees on visual impacts, open space, and traffic and transportation, as well as an executive committee. The committee evaluated new options using a matrix that included many of the concerns listed at the beginning of the process.

Models of Boston's Central Artery/Tunnel project alternatives (all models are views from the north looking south): The state originally proposed crossing the Charles River to Cambridge and points north with three bridges and sixteen whirling off ramps in the Scheme Z plan (*top left*). After citizen opposition and a mediation process, a refined design (Alternative 8.1D Mod 5) featuring a smaller bridge over the river and a tunnel under it was proposed (*top right*). The preferred alternative of the Massachusetts Department of Transportation (known as the Non-River Tunnel Alternative) in its final environmental impact statement eliminates the tunnel under the river and instead places it under Boston's North End (*bottom left*). (Photos are from the Charles River Crossing DSEIS/R, Central Artery/Tunnel project, courtesy of the Massachusetts Highway Department.)

As trust built, so did new alliances and collaborations among players who would not have talked with each other a few months earlier. The process also opened a door for new players with new ideas. For example, a local science teacher with an engineering background encouraged the committee to re-examine the key constraint, the idea that a tunnel could not be built under the Charles River. Obviously a tunnel would reduce the scale of the bridges overhead. Several of the engineers in the project's joint venture design team also came forward in support of a tunnel's feasibility. Freed from the constraint of a previous paradigm, the mediation group could explore new information and create a solution that better served the surrounding communities.

Agreement on the alternative Charles River Crossing was "as significant for this project as tossing the tea in the water was for the American Revolution," claimed K. Dun Gifford, president of the Committee for Regional Transportation and an ardent foe of Scheme Z.

The mediation process in the Boston case was speedy and productive. It was characterized by the strong support of the new secretary of transportation and his deputy. They were willing to examine anew many of the assumptions that were underpinnings of Scheme Z.

The mediation processes employed in the Atlanta and Boston cases were part of a larger context of court challenges to the proposed highways and externally perceived deadlines for the proposed projects.

Contacts

Jack Wofford
Mediator
148 State Street
Suite 806
Boston, MA 12109
(617) 723-7340

Steve Burrington
Conservation Law Foundation
62 Summer Street
Boston, MA 02110
(617) 350-0990

Mike Lewis
Assistant Project Director
Central Artery/Tunnel Project
One South Station
Boston, MA 02110
(617) 951-6034

Notes

1. Adapted from Endispute Inc., *'15 Points' Dispute Resolution Approaches and Stages* (Cambridge, MA: Endispute, 1991).
2. "Atlanta Great Park Authority: Final Report," (Atlanta: 1981), as quoted by Paul Cloverdell in the *Atlanta Journal-Constitution*, 1987).
3. Thirteen individuals participated in the mediation process, including two mediators: Michael Keating, of Providence, Rhode Island, and Edie Primm, of the Atlanta Justice Center. Cathy Bradshaw, Gale Walldorf, and Richard Ossoff represented CAUTION, and Rob Remar served as CAUTION's attorney. The city was represented by John Reid, Atlanta's executive officer, and Commissioner of Planning and Development Leon Eplan, and city attorneys Kendric Smith and Michael Coleman. The state was represented by Massachusetts DOT Commissioner Hal Rives and state legal counsels Charles Richards and George Shingler.
4. By this time the original $25,000 mediation grant had been exhausted, so each of the parties agreed to pay $500 per session.
5. Following the mediation, Richard Ossoff, a CAUTION board member and one of three negotiators, said, "Our position was 'no road,' but we always understood there would be improvements in the right-of-way that would encompass parks and transportation. The only question was what that would be."
6. 1000 Friends of Massachusetts, "Massachusetts Transportation Agenda" (Lincoln Center, MA: 1000 Friends of Massachusetts, 1990).
7. Portions of the description of the mediation process are taken from a summary entitled *Conflict Resolution and the Charles River Crossing* prepared by Endispute Inc., the firm hired to conduct the mediation, April 1992.
8. The Joint Venture of Bechtel and Parsons Brinckerhoff possessed enormous talent. Its expertise, however, was associated with the Scheme Z proposal and the efforts of former Secretary of Transportation Salvucci. Freed from previous political constraints, some of the engineers stepped forward to propose new technical options to the committee.

5

Transportation and Regional Growth Management

The fundamental tenet of growth management is that a region can choose the manner and direction of its growth and development through conscious protection of natural features and resources and provision of infrastructure and services timed for desired growth in nonsensitive areas. In historically mature regions like the Boston metropolitan area, new highways lead to peripheral growth of edge city centers for new technology and commerce, exodus of urban residents and businesses, and intensification of sprawl and congestion. In newer metropolitan areas like Portland, Oregon, that are closer to undeveloped land, uncontrolled urban sprawl eats up farmland and open space and suburbanizes the environment.

In Portland, growth management and environmental groups such as 1000 Friends of Oregon and Sensible Transportation Options for People have pressed for adoption of a variety of strategies to use existing highways more efficiently and rely increasingly on rail, bicycle, and pedestrian modes of transportation in an effort to manage increasing sprawl and enhance the quality of life.

Transportation Demand Management

As soon as one breaks away from the belief that more highways serving more cars is the answer to our transportation future, one can discover some deceptively simple transportation demand management ways of making the existing highway system capacity go further. If three people ride in one vehicle, each highway lane triples its capacity. HOV lanes for transit transportation modes (buses) increase capacity even further. HOV lanes also speed travel time by moving freely while single occupancy vehicles (SOVs) crawl in traffic.

Another simple TDM strategy is to promote flex-time work schedules to spread rush hour traffic over a longer period of time. The effect is to reduce the number of vehicles in each highway lane during peak hours and increase traffic flow.

Drivers' habits are price sensitive. As previously described in Chapter 1, most Americans commute to work in single occupancy vehicles and are given a parking space for their vehicles at no cost. When drivers are required to pay for parking, they are more inclined to carpool or take transit.

Another TDM method, congestion pricing, is in effect on two toll bridges in the San Francisco Bay Area. The Golden Gate Bridge toll of three dollars is waived for cars carrying three or more people. The San Francisco-Oakland Bay Bridge imposes a peak hour toll that has also created some interesting commuting practices in which "commuter pick-up" areas allow SOV drivers to locate prospective passengers to join them in the morning's ride into San Francisco. On toll roads proposed elsewhere in California, variable rates will be charged, depending on the use of the facility at peak or nonpeak hours.

The point is that TDM measures transcend physical transportation facilities and begin to address travel behavior. TDM measures can ultimately affect the form of community itself. If people ride light rail to work and live within a ten-minute walk of the transit station, then the need for new highway capacity could be obviated. The new community form would be the transit-oriented, pedestrian pocket, urban village development planned or in place in new communities such as Laguna West, a light rail suburb of Sacramento, California, and Mission Bay, a new planned development one mile south of downtown San Francisco.

Today public zoning laws usually require auto-oriented development patterns that have precisely the opposite effect of the impacts of holistic transportation. It is not uncommon for a zoning code to require 3,000 square feet of parking space for every 1,000 square feet of new office space. With requirements like that, a compact pedestrian-oriented village around a transit station is an unlikely outcome.

State laws are forcing the introduction of TDM methods that are consistent with ISTEA's policy and funding framework. The State of Washington, for example, passed the Commute Trip Reduction Act of 1991, which requires employers of 100 or more people to enact a carpool and HOV program to reduce SOV miles by 15 percent by 1995, 25 percent by 1997, and 35 percent by 1999. Oregon adopted a transportation planning rule that requires an actual reduction in vehicle miles traveled of 20 percent during the next thirty years. In order to comply with these laws, public agencies and private businesses will need to employ and fund alternatives to the one-person private car.

Transportation System Management

TSM integrates roads, rails, HOV lanes, bus systems, walking, and bicycling into a multi-modal system that increases mobility while achieving related goals of cleaner air and reduced congestion. For example, TSM coordinates a feeder bus system with a transit station and HOV lanes with park-and-ride lots that serve transit stations.

On one level TSM is about rational cost effectiveness.

Building new freeways in urban areas is extremely expensive. Approximately $100 million per mile is a fair estimate, although the price tag can rise even higher; the Century Freeway in Los Angeles is costing nearly $1 billion per mile.

TSM can save money by substituting other ways to stretch the capacity of existing systems or by accommodating people on other modes. Proper signalization of arterial intersections, for example, is far less costly than adding another lane or building fly-overs and has a cost-benefit ratio that runs thirty to one in many typical applications.[1] Lowering speed limits on busy freeways can actually increase their capacity (since safe stopping distance between cars is reduced).[2] Similarly, new bikeways for bicyclists would accommodate commuters who identify concern for their safety on busy roads as a primary reason for not biking to work.

TDM, TSM, and Growth Management

TDM and TSM directly relate to growth management and the nature of community form. The placement of transit lines and stations can reinforce denser, more pedestrian-oriented growth patterns. A modified grid system of arterials can facilitate the flow of traffic through communities, reducing suburban congestion and the clamor for more and bigger roads. These two transportation changes would also allow more people to live comfortably in the same land area and thereby slow the rate of sprawl.

The Boston case study in the previous chapter offers an example of a transportation plan that could dramatically affect the nature of regional growth and development. As we have seen, the Conservation Law Foundation withdrew its lawsuits opposing the Central Artery/Tunnel project when the commonwealth's DOT agreed to an integrated regional transportation plan.

The Massachusetts plan incorporates many TDM strategies and is a truly multi-modal transportation system incorporating light rail, high-speed rail, buses, and subways. (See map in Chapter 4.) The agreement calls for a moratorium on any highway additions that add SOV commute capacity into Boston. Instead, HOV lanes will be installed on Route 93 north of Boston and on the Southeast Expressway. If travel times become excessive on the Massachusetts Turnpike, HOV lanes will be installed there as well.

Parking limits are imposed in downtown Boston, as well as close-in portions of the city and neighboring cities such as Cambridge. The limits are expected to discourage approximately 135,000 commuters from driving into Boston in SOVs. HOVs will receive preferential access to these parking facilities. The commonwealth will construct 10,000 new commuter parking spaces near transit stations by 1995 and add another 10,000 by 1998.

Commuter rail service will be re-established and extended on north and south lines. The Metropolitan Boston Transit Authority will extend its subways and electric bus lines and build new ones, as indicated on the maps in Chapter 4. Fares will be indexed to the cost of commuting by car so that transit fares remain competitive.

The Boston area transportation agreement is comprehensive, transit-oriented, and consistent with growth management principles. It was reached a year before ISTEA was passed into law. However, its brief history symbolizes the resistance that highway-oriented transportation agencies and their supporters will exert in order to circumvent such plans. In May 1991, five months after the terms of the memorandum of understanding were incorporated into the final environmental impact statement for the Central Artery/Tunnel project, the Federal Highway Administration issued a decision allowing the state to proceed with CAT without the comprehensive traffic and transit measures contained in the memorandum.

In August 1991, the Conservation Law Foundation filed suit in U.S. District Court challenging CAT for violating the Clean Air Act and the National Environmental Policy Act because the agreed-upon mitigation measures were omitted from federal approval for the project. It took until March of 1992 for the Commonwealth of Massachusetts and the foundation to settle the suit and again agree on a set of comprehensive transportation measures. The foundation commended ISTEA and its provisions as a "national intermodal transportation system" that facilitated resolution of the lawsuit.

As we will see, the Portland case study described in this chapter heralds the beginning of sophisticated attempts to integrate growth management planning principles with transportation decisions. Planners are provided with technical tools for creating, measuring, and predicting new metropolitan development.

Portland's Western Bypass and LUTRAQ

In 1973 Oregon became the first state to establish a growth management law to shape and control the way new growth occurs and conserve resource and natural lands. Oregon's Land Conservation and Development Commission oversees implementation of the law's nineteen goals through approval of local and regional land-use plans. Oregon, with its twenty years of experience, serves as the nation's model for progressive growth management.

An Urban Growth Boundary—a line separating cities from their surrounding rural/agricultural/forest lands—has proven a key tool in making growth management work in Oregon. The boundary is intended to accommodate all urban growth projected for a twenty-year period. Inside the boundary, urban level infrastructure is acceptable; outside the boundary it is not.

The results can be seen along the I-5 Corridor, which runs through the fertile Willamette Valley on a north-south journey from the Washington border to California. This corridor protects the state's largest industry, agriculture, from suburban sprawl.

At the same time that the state legislature was adopting the nation's first statewide land-use law, plans were moving ahead for the Mount Hood Freeway. The proposed freeway would have cut a swath through southeast Portland destroying an estimated 10 percent of the housing stock and opening rural lands to development.

A citizens coalition called Sensible Transportation Options for People (STOP) formed in 1972 to stop the Mount Hood Freeway. STOP advocated that the state DOT withdraw the project from the federal highway system and in its place substitute a variety of transportation improvements, including removal of the old riverfront freeway and construction of a light rail line to serve the eastside. The result is today's highly touted MAX light rail system operating between downtown Portland and the City of Gresham.

The Western Bypass Freeway

Portland has a population of 415,000 in a metropolitan area of 1.4 million. Washington County, which lies southwest of Portland, is the fastest-growing region. Within the Urban Growth Boundary in Washington County are Nike's world headquarters in Beaverton and a high-technology corridor along Sunset Highway on the way to Hillsboro (see map on next page). Beyond the boundary lies wine country and farmlands.

Rapid growth of multi-family residential housing, retail malls, and commercial centers, coupled with limited arterials and almost total dependence on the automobile, has created predictable and unpleasant suburban congestion.

This gridlock led the Metropolitan Service District (Metro) to undertake a Southwest Corridor Transportation

Study in 1986. The following year, Metro proposed a bypass freeway that would circumvent the congestion by connecting I-5 at Wilsonville with the Sunset Highway high-tech area. Metro then included this western bypass in its regional transportation plan.

A freeway in the southwest corridor would complete three-quarters of a circumferential freeway around Portland. Any future northwest section would breach the Urban Growth Boundary, traverse urban parkland, and entail construction of a third bridge across the Columbia River.

Metro's role in transportation and land-use planning is of particular note. Metro, a regional government model of national significance, is governed by a twelve-member council elected by the region's voters from geographic districts. As the metropolitan planning organization, Metro is the entity empowered to change the Urban Growth Boundary. Moreover, Metro builds and operates regional facilities such as the Oregon Convention Center in Portland. In this one regional organization, elected officials are empowered to plan for transportation and make land-use decisions.

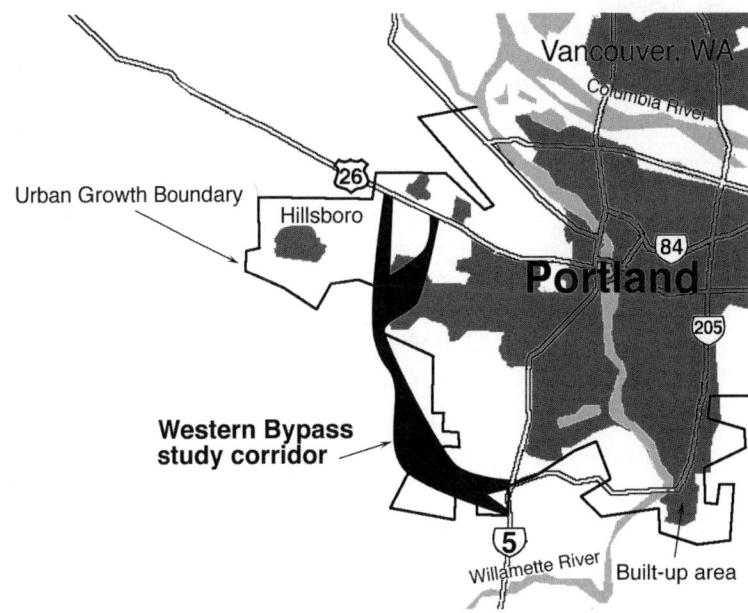

Location of Portland's proposed western bypass. (Map courtesy of Steve Durrant of Jones & Jones, Seattle, Washington).

STOP and 1000 Friends of Oregon

STOP, which re-formed in 1989 under new leadership, has nearly 500 members and a newsletter list of 2,500. This time around, its purpose is to stop the western bypass. STOP views the bypass as an auto-oriented proposal that will not relieve traffic congestion but will increase sprawling urban development into the surrounding countryside. The coalition advocates a variety of alternative approaches, including expanding the MAX light rail line and using the traffic calming techniques employed in Europe and Australia to reduce dependence on cars and lower their impact. Another organization, 1000 Friends of Oregon, was formed in 1972 as a nonprofit advocacy group to watchdog and implement the state's growth management law. Together, the two nonprofits filed suit against Washington County for including the bypass in its land-use plan and against Metro for including it in the regional transportation plan.

The judicial body that decided the lawsuit, the Land Use Board of Appeals, ruled that Washington County had not complied with the state's Land Use Management Act. But the court declared the suit against Metro not ripe for judicial review because inclusion of the western bypass was not a final decision.

These rulings meant that Metro and the Oregon DOT could not proceed with right-of-way purchases and that the project itself was open for further examination since it was not part of Metro's final regional transportation plan.

The STOP strategy has included the following actions:

- Organizing support in the corridor area in Washington County;
- Creating a technical advisory committee to analyze Metro and state DOT information;
- Publishing a newsletter and periodic flyers and studies summarizing technical findings;
- Cultivating the view that transportation issues are inseparable from land-use, growth management, urban form, and related issues; and
- Introducing alternative approaches to improve transportation and the quality of life.

LUTRAQ

In recent years, 1000 Friends of Oregon came to the conclusion that:

> ... the connection between land use, transportation, and air quality is unseverable. To deal responsibly with one issue requires integrated analysis of the others. Failure to do so invariably leads to policies that work at cross-purposes to each other, and inevitably results in increases in traffic congestion, oil consumption, air and water pollution, and suburban sprawl.[3]

In 1991 the organization embarked on a national demonstration project called Making the Land Use, Transportation, Air Quality Connection. The LUTRAQ project is designed to develop methodologies for changing local land-use policies and development designs using the proposed western bypass as a case study. LUTRAQ's purpose is to identify replicable methods for accomplishing the following objectives:

- Using alternative land-use development patterns as a method of reducing travel demand;
- Using land use as a dynamic, interactive variable in transportation modeling procedures; and
- Modifying the more widely used transportation and air pollution computer modeling systems.

LUTRAQ is receiving private and public funding support from national and regional sources, including private foundations, the U.S. Environmental Protection Agency, Federal Highway Administration, and Metro.

Government agencies and private foundations have good reasons for supporting this project. At the federal level, the Clean Air Act does not permit increases of air pollutants generated by additional vehicles in nonattainment metropolitan areas. If LUTRAQ can develop models for predicting air quality impacts and find alternatives to reduce those impacts, then the intent of federal policy will be met and local quality of life will increase.

At the state level, the Oregon Land Conservation and Development Commission with support from the state's DOT adopted the Transportation Planning Rule of 1991, which requires the Portland metropolitan area to reduce total automobile vehicle miles traveled by 20 percent over the next thirty years. The 1991 rule also requires the Portland metropolitan area to evaluate alternative land-use designations, densities, and designs.

> The aims of this rule are lofty: to encourage a multi-modal transportation system designed to reduce reliance on the automobile and assure that planned state, regional and local transportation systems "support a pattern of travel and land use in urban areas which will avoid the air pollution, traffic and livability problems faced by other areas of the country." Towards these ends, the rule adopts stringent standards geared to enhance pedestrian and bicycle travel and, in urban areas over 25,000 population, the use of transit. Simultaneously, the rule takes steps to reduce au-

tomobile usage through reductions in total vehicle miles traveled, parking restrictions, and the like.[4]

At the regional level, LUTRAQ offers Metro a cooperative alternative to the kind of highway planning and air quality battle that was fought and lost by San Francisco Bay Area's metropolitan planning organization, the Metropolitan Transportation Commission, when the Sierra Club took the commission to court for not considering the secondary air quality impacts of approving a new freeway. As a result of LUTRAQ's findings, Metro may be able to enhance its computer simulation models and utilize those refinements in its upcoming regional transportation and land-use planning process, which is known as Region 2040.

At the local level, western bypass opponents will utilize LUTRAQ findings to provide alternatives. The state's DOT is in the process of conducting its Western Bypass Study, which is analyzing alternatives in the southwest corridor. The DOT has agreed to rate a LUTRAQ alternative in the study process.

The LUTRAQ consultant team has completed its first studies on transportation and land-use forecasting on the regional level, including an analysis of Metro's approach, a study of existing land-use conditions in the southwest corridor, and an analysis of the study process that the DOT will use to evaluate the western bypass.

LUTRAQ has prepared a preferred alternative based on transit and pedestrian-oriented land use within the Urban Growth Boundary for inclusion in the DOT study. Next, the study will develop an interactive computer model based on this new form of urban development and the future land uses and travel demand that will be generated. This new approach will be highlighted in a final report and conference presentations regionally around the country. The LUTRAQ study team consists of Cambridge Systematics Inc. for transportation, economics, and computer modeling; The Hague Consulting Group and S.H. Putman Associates, international transportation and land-use modeling; Calthorpe Associates, urban and regional planners and designers; and Blayney Dyett Greenber, growth management and zoning experts.

Outlook for the Western Bypass

How could a new freeway bypass get this far in Oregon of all places—the state that pioneered growth management, withdrawal and substitution of federal highway funds, the modern age of light rail, and reduction of future vehicle miles traveled?

The following factors are contributing to the possibility that a western bypass will be built:

- *Suburban Congestion.* Opponents and proponents alike concur that congestion in the Beaverton-Tualitan-Tigard area is a problem. In a 1986 analysis, Metro planners recognized that traffic diffusion within the Washington County suburban area is restricted by a lack of through-arterials. Studies by the Oregon DOT show that a majority of vehicle trips are within or between urban communities in the corridor. These intrasuburban trips and radial trips to Portland are projected to increase dramatically over the next twenty years.

- *Economic Growth.* Rural land zoned for commercial use in the Hillsboro-Sunset Highway high-tech corridor is becoming very valuable. A new freeway serving this area would increase land values even more. Many Washington County residents and certainly those in the development and real estate communities view increased development with favor.

- *Regional Decision Making.* Metro's transportation advisory committees are composed of elected officials and staff from three counties and a number of cities. Multnomah County has pushed its agenda of making Portland the region's center through construction of a new convention center and expansion of the MAX system's new westside line to Hillsboro. What do Washington and Clackamas County receive in return for supporting Multnomah

County's agenda? Many observers believe Washington County gets Metro support for the western bypass.

- *Difficulty Retrofitting Neighborhoods.* The Southwest Corridor Transportation Study includes upgrades and widenings of several major roads. Widening arterials in residential neighborhoods or pushing arterials through established residential communities, however, elicits a not-in-my-backyard (NIMBY) outcry. Although technically a feasible and perhaps preferable option, creating a modified grid system has high political costs.[5] Going around and outside the problem via a bypass is politically more palatable.

The following factors are contributing to the possibility the western bypass will not be built:

- A popular realization that the western bypass will not reduce suburban congestion. Data from the DOT's Western Bypass Study show that the bypass does not address congestion.[6]

- A recognition that the bypass is not in Portland's interest. Washington County has a population of roughly 300,000. In twenty years projections are that it will have 450,000, the greatest increment of growth expected for any county in the region. Will this growth be at Portland's expense? Candidates in the 1992 Portland mayoral and city council races opposed the western bypass, favoring denser transit-oriented urban villages instead.

- The formidable constraints posed by the combination of the Transportation Planning Rule's reduction of the vehicle miles traveled, the Clean Air Act Amendments' restriction of auto emissions, and the bypass' transgression of the Urban Growth Boundary.

- The presence of capable opponents in STOP and 1000 Friends of Oregon.

- The development of alternative urban and suburban forms through the LUTRAQ process.

Transit-Oriented Developments

The LUTRAQ alternative is based on transit-oriented developments, which are mixed-use neighborhoods of residences, businesses, and civic functions within a ten-minute walk of a transit station. More than half of the transit-oriented developments contained in the LUTRAQ alternative would be concentrated in undeveloped or infill-appropriate land in the existing cities of Beaverton and Tualitan.

Development opportunities for the southwest corridor are confined within the Urban Growth Boundary and are consistent with Oregon's land-use objectives. More than 17,000 acres are identified as suitable for construction of transit-oriented developments by the year 2010. Three categories of land are represented for placement of transit-oriented developments:

- *Redevelopable and Infill Sites.* A total of 6,800 acres are already developed in patterns that under-utilize the land base and could be upgraded to revitalize existing neighborhoods.

- *New Growth Areas.* A total of 10,000 acres are in forty-acre or larger undeveloped parcels of land near planned or potential transit service and represent the easiest option for transit-oriented developments.

- *Dispersed Incremental Infill and Redevelopment.* Approximately 2,000 acres are composed of parcels smaller than fifteen acres surrounded or skipped over by existing development. These sites are too small to support a transit-oriented development by themselves but could be developed to promote transit and pedestrian orientation.

These areas would be served by four light rail lines emanating from Portland and one circumferential line in the Highway 217 corridor. Outlying areas would be served by express buses that would deliver and pick up riders at end-of-line transit stations. Local feeder buses and demand responsive para-transit (dial-a-rides and vans) would serve these stations.

Pedestrians and bicyclists would be served by new paths. Major highways and roads in the southwest corridor would be widened and their intersections improved consistent with the existing regional transportation plan.

A real estate market analysis conducted as part of the LUTRAQ project indicated that 100 percent of projected annual multi-family demand and about 55 percent of single-family demand forecast for Washington County could be absorbed by urban and neighborhood transit-oriented developments. Remaining single-family dwellings would be built outside of the transit-oriented developments. Projections indicate that 6.4 million square feet of new retail gross leasable area will be required in Washington County by 2010. This retail requirement can be accommodated in the proposed transit-oriented developments, as can the county's share of an estimated 2.8 million square feet of Class A office space required by 2010.

Models of the LUTRAQ alternative forecast that the average household in transit-oriented developments would make 22 percent fewer home-based trips per day than the average household in the area under the bypass alternative. More than 20 percent of the workers living in the transit-oriented developments would take transit to work, twice as many as under the bypass alternative. Children living in transit-oriented developments would be more than twice as likely to walk or bike to school.

These forecasts are based on computer models generated by the LUTRAQ study. The models have been installed in Metro's regional transportation computer models to provide greater sensitivity to the effects of urban form on travel decisions, including short trips, walks, and transit trips.[7]

The LUTRAQ study set out to demonstrate that modifications to the existing road system coupled with the introduction of a planned light rail line and a more compact pedestrian-oriented pattern of community development can accommodate projected growth and improve mobility without construction of a proposed new western bypass freeway.

The results of the LUTRAQ analysis show that, compared with the western bypass alternative, LUTRAQ's transit-oriented approach would by the year 2010:

- Increase the share of trips from home to work made by transit by 45 percent;
- Increase the proportion of all trips made either on foot or by bicycle by 22 percent;
- Reduce the number of households owning two or three automobiles by 6 percent;
- Reduce the number of vehicle trips per household by 8 percent; and
- Reduce peak hour vehicle miles traveled by 14 percent.[8]

These findings will be included in the Oregon DOT's review of southwest corridor alternatives, providing an option that promotes mobility and growth management in addition to the traditional "no build" and freeway construction choices.

CONTACTS
Keith Bartholomew
Director
LUTRAQ Project
1000 Friends of Oregon
534 SW Third Avenue, Suite 300
Portland, OR 97204
(503) 223-4396

Molly O'Reilly
President
Sensible Transportation Options for People (STOP)
15405 SW 116th Avenue, #202B
Tigard, OR 97224-2600
(503) 624-6083

Notes

1. Elizabeth Deakin, informal remarks at regional growth conference, "Building a Livable Future," Metropolitan Service District, Portland, OR, 1991.
2. Citizens Advocating Responsible Transportation, *Traffic Calming,* (Queensland, Australia: CART, 1989).
3. 1000 Friends of Oregon, "Making the Land Use, Air Quality, and Transportation Connection: A National Growth Management Research Project" (Portland, OR: 1000 Friends of Oregon, October 25, 1991).
4. Mark J. Greenfield, "Analysis of Transportation Planning Rule," (Portland, OR: Preston Thorgrimson Shidler Gates & Ellis, Attorneys at Law, 1991).
5. A traditional, human-scale city grid system is not possible under Washington County design standards, which require wide (90 feet) roadways and 45 mph design speeds. Neighbors might respond differently if human-scaled streets with sidewalks were proposed instead. See *Traffic Calming* or other guides to pedestrian-friendly design listed in the bibliography.
6. Oregon Department of Transportation, Final Western Bypass Study Evaluation of Strategies—Evaluation Matrix (October 1991).
7. 1000 Friends of Oregon with Cambridge Systematics, Calthorpe Associates, and Parson Brinckerhoff Quade and Douglas, "The LUTRAQ Alternative/Analysis of Alternatives: an Interim Report," (Portland, OR: 1000 Friends of Oregon, October 1992).
8. "The LUTRAQ Alternative/Analysis of Alternatives: an Interim Report." (Portland, OR: 1000 Friends of Oregon, 1992).

6

Enhancing the Existing Highway System

ISTEA breaks new ground in transportation policy in that it funds various modes of motorized and nonmotorized transportation and allows states the flexibility to emphasize or de-emphasize car-oriented projects in certain programs. But ISTEA is also a transitional piece of legislation in that it still segregates highway construction and improvement within other programs, earmarking more than $60 billion over six years to highway, freeway, and bridge projects. Although other ISTEA funds are available for public transportation, the law earmarks only about $20 billion in specific funds for this purpose, most of them in capital programs rather than programs to help fund operations.

Transportation Enhancements

ISTEA's Surface Transportation Program provides $28 billion over six years to states to build roads, rail lines, HOV lanes, and a host of other transportation projects. ISTEA requires that at least 10 percent of those funds be used for transportation enhancements. These are activities that directly link ISTEA to the attainment of social, environmental, and economic goals of communities. Enhancements are cultural, aesthetic, environmental, and historic aspects that define quality of life and, taken together with a new roadway or railbed, create a holistic community fabric.

The ten enhancement activities specified by ISTEA include bike and pedestrian facilities, scenic easements, landscaping, historic preservation, rehabilitation of railroads and canals, control of outdoor advertising, archaeological research, and mitigation of water pollution caused by highway runoff. (See the full list in Chapter 1 on page 17.)

Under the law, enhancement funds do not replace activities required to comply with other laws such as the National Environmental Policy Act. However, enhancements must be or must relate to current projects under construction or planned in the state or metropolitan long-range multi-modal transportation plans.

The Federal Highway Administration suggests three tests for the eligibility of enhancement projects: function, proximity, and impact. A bikeway is an example of a functional relationship, removal of illegal billboards in a scenic highway viewshed is a relationship of proximity, and pedestrian ways that reduce auto use in an area is an impact-related enhancement.[1]

Under ISTEA, it is now possible to construct walkways and bikeways before a road is ever built. It is possible for local communities to use federal transportation funds to protect and restore sites of historic significance, such as revitalizing the historic main street of a small town that may have been bypassed entirely during the interstate era. Enhancement funds can purchase scenic and conservation easements along transportation routes. A potential application of this enhancement would be along portions of Route 301 in Maryland where land-use protection and access control along the corridor are major issues.

Although ISTEA's Surface Transportation Program and enhancements process open transportation planning to greater public participation and flexibility, funds available in the enhancements category are limited—$2.8 billion over six years—and strong vested interests exist within state DOTs to capture those funds for highway-related projects. Metropolitan planning organizations will bear much of the responsibility for determining which kinds of enhancement projects will receive priority attention.

Perhaps the most significant aspect of the enhancements section of ISTEA is the new broader consideration of the relationship of transportation to community quality of life. It is just these quality of life issues—accessible scenery, history, water quality, and outdoor life—that have thrust the Seattle metropolitan area into the national limelight over the past decade.

The Interstate-90 Corridor

A booming economy and a naturally endowed environment that includes snowcapped mountains, lakes, and Puget Sound made the Seattle area a national growth hotspot in the 1980s. Population increased by 700,000 in the Central Puget Sound area, and 600,000 additional residents are projected by the turn of the century. With this rapid regional growth, majestic forests and farmland—symbols of the Pacific Northwest—have been replaced by suburban residential development, shopping malls, and industrial parks.

Nowhere is this incredible transition more evident than in the I-90 corridor. Nationally, I-90 connects Boston on the East Coast (see the Central Artery/Tunnel project, pages 50–59) with Seattle on the West Coast to form the northern tier transcontinental interstate. Locally, the "completion" of the last remaining I-90 link, crossing Lake Washington into Seattle, has accelerated metropolitan growth while pumping $1.5 billion of public works funds into the regional economy.

I-90 provides six lanes of modern interstate roadway from the crest of the Cascade Mountains at Snoqualmie Pass to downtown Seattle, covering a distance of approximately fifty miles. In that span, a motorist traverses several climatic zones and ecosystems. The first twenty miles of this section begin at the Pacific Crest Trail in the Mount Baker-Snoqualmie National Forest, continue past the Snoqualmie Pass ski resorts, descend through Douglas fir forests, and pass snowcapped peaks and waterfalls to the towns of North Bend and Snoqualmie.

These two old mill towns are surrounded by forest and agricultural lands. Twenty years ago, small mills that produced cedar shakes and a large plywood mill dominated the local economy. Today, North Bend is better known for its outlet mall at the freeway interchange, and Snoqualmie has received notoriety as the filming site of Hollywood's *Twin Peaks* television series.

Another ten miles closer to Seattle is the tiny hamlet of Preston. In 1905, a grand total of 105 cars a year passed this spot. In 1990, fifteen million people went by. Five more miles toward Seattle and the motorist leaves the wooded vistas and hits edge city. The freeway widens, traffic congestion increases, and the familiar patterns of American regional sprawl dominate.

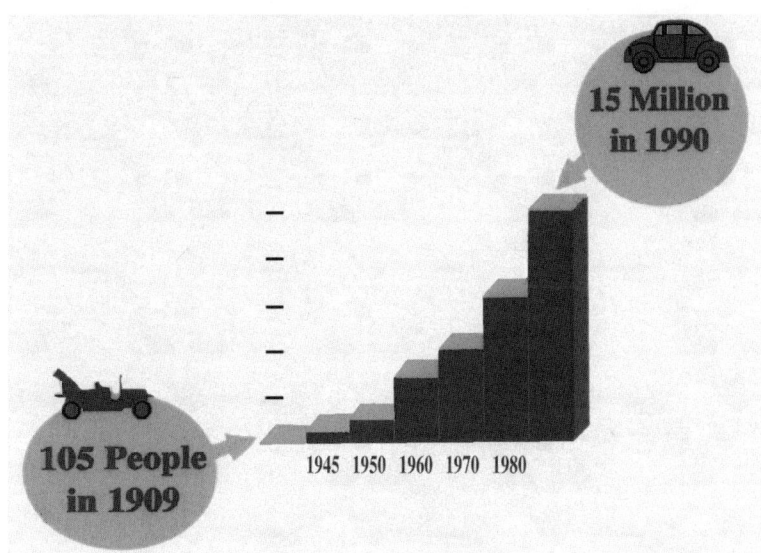

Diagram showing the increasing numbers of people traveling over Snoqualmie Pass between 1909 and 1990. (Figure courtesy of the Mountains-to-Sound Greenway Trust.)

I-90 and Growth

In the 1970s, opponents of the completion of I-90 argued that increasing automobile capacity would degrade the Northwest's famed quality of life and lead to auto-dependent development and sprawl. Transit lanes, they argued, would be more beneficial. Poorer inner-city neighborhoods had powerful allies in the wealthy community of Mercer Island, which would bear the brunt of ten years of construction and increase of traffic, noise, and pollution.

A mediated settlement to a bridge and tunnel segment, reached in 1976, included elaborate mitigation measures to cover the freeway scar on Mercer Island with parklands. Two transit lanes would be added to the freeway bridge crossing Lake Washington. This settlement allowed construction of the bridge and tunnel link to Seattle to proceed by 1980. The widening of I-90 from Snoqualmie Pass to Lake Washington was completed in the 1970s.

As many predicted, the path of growth followed I-90 from Bellevue to Lake Sammammish and then across the lake to the Sammammish Plateau where enormous planned communities of 3,000 and 4,000 units have been built and others are proposed. The Sammammish Plateau represented King County's Maginot Line of protection for the rural areas of the county lying to the east. On the other side of the Sammammish Plateau lies the Snoqualmie Valley, one of the area's most productive and pastoral farming areas. In 1979 residents voted to spend $50 million to buy development rights to this and other King County farmland.

The Snoqualmie Pass highway in 1918. (Photo courtesy of the Seattle Museum of History and Industry.)

Today, I-90 cuts seven lanes through the forested mountains of the Snoqualmie Pass, accommodating over 15 million vehicles annually. (Photo courtesy of the Mountains-to-Sound Greenway Trust.)

Congestion increases to the west as I-90 picks up Seattle's suburban traffic. (Photo courtesy of the Mountains-to-Sound Greenway Trust.)

Interstate-90 traffic is finally deposited into downtown Seattle. (Photo courtesy of the Mountains-to-Sound Greenway Trust.)

The upgraded I-90 began to drive the direction of development locally. It was now possible to commute from North Bend to downtown Seattle quickly. As congestion increased from Issaquah to Seattle, development focus shifted to the interstate segment east of Issaquah, which is utilized at only 30 percent of capacity. Nintendo of America built its distribution facility at the North Bend interchange, and ski resort operators at Snoqualmie Pass began to propose year-round condominium developments for commuters traveling to employment centers along the I-90 route.

Environmentalists were not the only ones who were alarmed by the growth explosion. In 1990 and 1991, the state legislature passed the Growth Management Act which requires cities and counties to protect natural resource and critical areas lands and concentrate future development on lands that already have adequate infrastructure to support development. Popular and institutionalized support emerged for preserving the quality of life that differentiated Puget Sound from the Los Angeles basin.

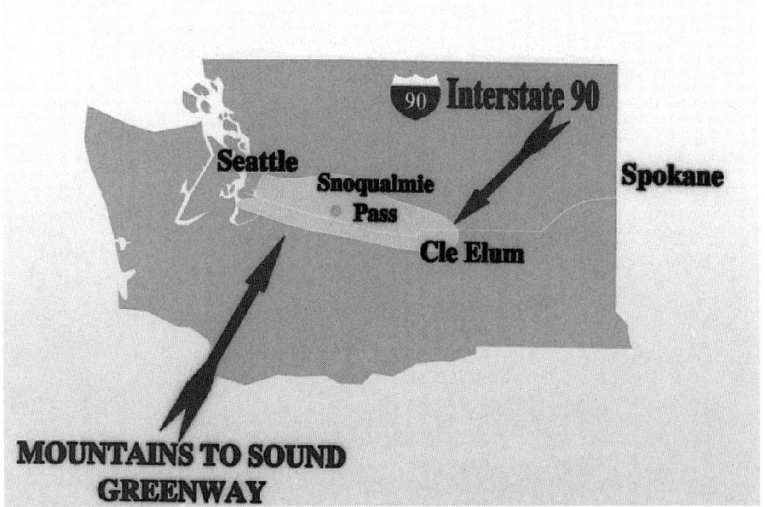

Location of the Mountains-to-Sound Greenway in Washington State. (Map courtesy of the Mountains-to-Sound Greenway Trust.)

Washington State's Mountains-to-Sound Greenway

What if we took an interstate highway and made it the centerpiece of a plan for natural area and heritage preservation? That was the question a group of civic leaders, open space advocates, and business leaders began to ask themselves in 1990. What took form was a holistic concept of linking a natural watershed and drainage basin with a transportation corridor, including Native American trade and hunting trails, railroads and interstates, and the commerce and communities of the past century.

The Mountains-to-Sound Greenway is a proposal to preserve a scenic, historic, and recreational corridor of green space along Interstate-90. The greenway would combine public and private management of commercial forestlands, select acquisitions of parks, and protection of unique features and historic areas.

The goal of the greenway is to keep the I-90 corridor green and scenic, preserve commercial forestry, provide separators between growing urban areas, prevent urban sprawl, maintain wildlife corridors, retain unique natural and historic features and provide recreational opportunities to residents of Puget Sound and the entire state who utilize this major transportation thoroughfare.[2]

To promote this vision, a group of civic, business, and public agency leaders formed a nonprofit organization called the Mountains-to-Sound Greenway Trust. The trust's mission is to accomplish the following objectives:

- Preserve an economic base by retaining working forests and farms;
- Enhance tourist amenities; and
- Interpret and link the history, geography, natural features, and rural landscapes of the region.

The Greenway Trust's board is composed of forty leaders in business, government, and conservation. Its executive committee includes a prominent civic leader, Jim Ellis; officials of the Weyerhaeuser Company, Issaquah Alps Trail Club, Security Pacific Bank, Recreational Equipment Incorporated, and The Trust for Public Land; the Washington State Commissioner of Public Lands; a state transportation commissioner; and the Bellevue City parks director.

The board is supported by a fifty-member technical advisory committee of landowners, government agency officials, conservationists, historic preservationists, and technical experts. The technical advisory committee works through the following subcommittees:

- Transportation and Land Use;
- Economic Development;
- Land Management;

- Recreation;
- Cultural Resources; and
- Natural Resources.

The role of the committee and subcommittees is to bring information that is in the public and private domains to the discussion of the greenway and analyze this data with regard to the corridor's visual, natural, and cultural resources; existing and proposed land uses; and priority sites for protection or acquisition. The results of these efforts will be the starting point of a draft plan for the greenway.

The Greenway Trust is staffed by the Trust for Public Land, which provides expertise to conduct land deals for public purposes. The Greenway Trust is housed in the offices of the Trust for Public Land.

The Greenway Trust's board retained the services of a noted landscape architecture and planning firm to work with the board and its technical advisory committee to prepare a series of documents and maps called the Greenway Concept Plan, which was completed in 1993.

This plan lends the level of definition to the greenway concept needed to rally public and private support. The plan will also provide readily adaptable material for inclusion into the comprehensive plans required of state agencies, King County, and the towns and cities in the I-90 corridor under the state's Growth Management Act.

The Greenway Trust's Approach

The greenway concept transcends the powers of any single public jurisdiction, agency, or private corporation. There is no single corridor management authority. The state's Department of Natural Resources and the Weyerhaeuser Company own large tracts of forestland in the corridor, but not all of it. The Washington DOT maintains the interstate itself, but not the land at the interchanges. King County zones land for rural protection but cannot stop a Weyerhaeuser development subsidiary from annexing 1,400 acres to a town of 2,000 people for a planned community ten times its size.

The Greenway Trust's strategy is precisely not to have a single controlling authority, but rather to utilize the following approaches:

- Bring public jurisdictions and private property owners within the corridor into a regional alliance with shared objectives;
- Establish principles of management to guide the corridor's multiple managers in achieving the overall vision;
- Act as a catalyst, using formal and informal connections and influence, to shepherd the concept along; and
- Build coalitions and strong popular support for the greenway concept.

Jim Ellis has said that the Greenway Trust has to "create a love and history for this place." (This is not hard for a person like Ellis who, as a boy, summered on the Raging River a stone's throw from today's I-90; but at that time he could walk all day amid tall trees and never see another soul.) One of the trust's first tasks was to create a logo that captures the romantic feel of an earlier era. Next was a brochure that introduces the greenway idea through photos and illustrations. Then a glossy photo book and a video documentary were produced.

Equally important, the Greenway Trust's board began to encourage actions to protect and acquire key properties, vistas, and sites along the corridor before the public relations campaign got underway. For example, Rattlesnake Ridge is strikingly visible from I-90. The Trust for Public Land sought and received a $500,000 grant from the Bullitt Foundation to obtain an option on the land from the Weyerhaeuser Company. High-ranking officials of both organizations sit on the Greenway Trust board and smooth the way for this type of action.

Rattlesnake Ridge lies just south of I-90, and just north is Mount Si, a curious peak that rises straight out of a plateau next to North Bend. All of Mount Si recently became publicly protected through a 6,000-acre land exchange between the state's Department of Natural Resources and Weyerhaeuser.

I-90 has a series of such green oases, including some like Cougar Mountain County Park that are smack in the middle of suburbia. At the edge of "edge city" sits Squak Mountain State Park, and a little further out is Tiger Mountain State Forest. Each is a product of enlargement through land swaps and trades. The Trust for Public Land helps facilitate and encourage those swaps.

These green separators are critical to creating an alternative pattern to suburban sprawl. One of the Greenway Trust's ambitious strategies is to use working forests as privately held green separators. Private forests are economically viable if they are more valuable for growing trees than growing suburban tracts. If they can be buffered from the pressures of land development, they will be a key part of the greenway—along with active farms.

The Greenway Trust represents something new in transportation, land use, and community preservation. The greenway is more than mitigation, more than enhancements. It is what Bill Dietrich refers to in his book *The Final Forest* as "ecosystem management across the human landscape."[3] The greenway involves the preservation of working forests as a way of life and as a carbon sink that will provide the metropolitan area with cleaner air. The greenway involves protection of a variety of transportation corridors: interstates for fast-moving cars and trucks, trails for people and bicycles, natural corridors for wildlife, and meandering byways for a leisurely Sunday afternoon drive in the country. The greenway is defined by naturally occurring drainage basins rather than by a highway alone.

I-90 offers an excellent example of a freeway that has opened up the hinterland east of Seattle to suburban development. The efforts of the Mountains-to-Sound Greenway Trust offer an example of the integration of growth management principles with the enhancement objectives of scenic, historic, and cultural protection.

CONTACT
Nancy Keith
Executive Director
Mountains-to-Sound Greenway Trust
506 Second Avenue, Suite 1502
Seattle, WA 98104
(206) 382-5565

Notes

1. This information and detailed interpretations of enhancements can be found in Chapter 10.
2. Mountains-to-Sound Greenway Trust fact sheet, 1992.
3. William Dietrich, *The Final Forest: The Battle for the Last Great Trees of the Pacific Northwest* (Simon and Schuster, New York, 1992).

7

Reflections on Serving Community

Before reflecting on the case studies presented in the first half of this book, let's return for a moment to the transportation paradigms introduced in Chapter 1: capacity (or efficiency at moving vehicles), mobility, and accessibility. Few among us would advocate a less efficient transportation system or less access to information and services. In general terms we value the intent of each paradigm. Our point in the reflections that follow is that although each paradigm has application, efficiency and mobility by themselves cannot achieve their desired goals. Accessibility, on the other hand, broadens the way we think about transportation and community.

In some ways our task is to meld the best of each approach, hence the use of the phrase *holistic transportation*. Perhaps one way is to apply a few simple tests to the transportation approaches and solutions proposed in a given situation: Does it serve the community? Are my neighbors' and my quality of life improved by increased highway efficiency and by multiple modes of getting downtown or visiting with friends? Do we have safer neighborhoods, better access to daycare, more open spaces, more affordable housing?

Are these questions legitimate ones to apply to transportation choices? We think they are. Although a transportation choice alone may not be the sole influencing factor, transportation's powerful influence on land use can either serve or harm communities and their character.

In analyzing the case studies, we come to the conclusion that compact community form and trip substitution strategies can move us toward the third paradigm of accessibility and offer better choices for communities.

Compact Community Form

Seattle's new comprehensive plan calls for funneling residential and employment growth into a series of urban villages of varying size and complexion. These villages will concentrate residences, jobs, and services so that people can access the basic elements of community by foot or public transit. New suburban communities such as Laguna West outside of Sacramento are designed around light rail lines as transit-oriented developments. The Uptown district, an in-city residential and shopping district in San Diego, represents a new wave of dense, pedestrian-oriented development that departs from America's post-World War II suburban themes. In each of these instances new patterns of community development affect reliance on the car. As alternate modes of transportation such as light rail are put into service, they should reinforce this new community form.

Before going any further with this line of thought, it must be acknowledged that for many urban dwellers in cities like New York, Chicago, or San Francisco the concept of an urban neighborhood served by rapid transit is nothing new. Similarly, many suburban communities—in Connecticut, New Jersey, and Pennsylvania, for example—are served by commuter rail lines with stations that are often located in town centers.

So perhaps it is more appropriate to reflect on the meaning of the LUTRAQ and Central Artery cases and the examples just referenced not so much as conceptually new approaches to community design, but as a rediscovery of land-use and transportation relations that have proven over the past century that they work. These success stories simply fell out of our collective short-term memory as automobile and highway development came to dominate our society.

Automobile-oriented patterns have *ipso facto* become synonymous with metropolitan growth in this country. Extensive analysis of regional transportation models and detailed land-use and economic analyses for alternative development, as in Portland's southwest bypass area, are necessary to derail or at least slow the juggernaut of car-based, sprawling development patterns.

The challenge and the import of the LUTRAQ example is that it begins to legitimize, in conjunction with other new policy and development paradigms such as the notion of sustainable communities and urban villages, transit-oriented development patterns.

It is not habit alone that drives continued metropolitan fringe growth. Obviously it is also the substantial economic investment that many landowners have made in the path of anticipated future growth, as well as the ease and lower cost of access to nascent edge city locations. What LUTRAQ suggests is that the ground rules of traditional land speculation and development can be stood on their heads; that land *within* urban growth boundaries can become more valuable for future development; and that investment in public infrastructure can complement private investment and the result will be a higher quality of life in pedestrian- and transit-oriented communities.

Compact community development patterns offer several advantages. The first is the nature of personal interactions and business transactions that can take place in close physical proximity and often in serendipitous ways as one walks from chore to chore or appointment to appointment.

The second is protection of open space and variations in land use. Creating compact communities has the ancillary characteristic of providing abundant open space for recreation, environmental protection, and resource-based economies outside the "town" boundary.

The third advantage is reducing the number of vehicle miles traveled, especially by single occupancy vehicles. The reasons for the reduction in SOV travel are quite straightforward. Trip destinations are grouped together in centers, and public transportation options exist to take people to those centers. The private car does not become obsolete but is used for trips for which it is best suited, such as the freedom of exploring back country roads, visiting grandma in the next county, or a multitude of other trips where spontaneity and flexibility count most.

Trip Substitution

In Chapter 1, we discussed the potential for telecommuting to reduce trips, enhance neighborhood identification, support the development of local businesses, and, generally, build community. The replacement of work trips with working at home or in neighborhood telework centers appears to be a very attractive option in many situations. It is important, however, that potential indirect effects of telecommuting be addressed. Telecommuting can lead to further sprawl if people decide to move even farther from the central city. On the other hand, telecommuting may provide an opportunity to develop rural communities that have suffered from the nation's shift from rural to urban life.

Another way to lessen vehicle miles traveled is to shift more responsibility to delivery service companies such as United Parcel Service or Federal Express. Coupled with the electronic highway's features of electronic shopping and information exchange, delivery service can bring goods directly to one's door. Each delivery replaces another cold start, protecting air quality and removing another vehicle from the roadway.

But doesn't reliance on computer data retrieval, mail order shopping, and similar high-technology options threaten the very sense of community—the face-to-face interaction and interdependence—for which humans as social animals came together in the first place? If each of us lives in an atomized world working at our computer terminals, receiving deliveries at our door, and leaving our cars to rust, are we not missing something?

The thought of isolating people in their homes and having delivery trucks going up and down residential streets all day long does not create an attractive picture. Perhaps there is a way to combine new communication technologies, delivery services, and urban forms that supports the development of community in new ways.

Neighborhoods could have general stores as focal points. The stores could either include telework centers or be located nearby. The stores could have some of the features of a mom-and-pop corner grocery or variety store but would also be the focal point for delivery of goods ordered by telephone, either through voice or computer modem. The idea is to combine the efficiency of delivery service with a meeting place such as a general store and post office. Since the general stores and telework centers would be patronized by residents of the neighborhood on a frequent basis, informal social contacts would increase, and identification with the local community would be enhanced.

If such centers were placed to make them accessible by walking and biking, auto trip-making could be substantially reduced. It is likely that other types of small businesses such as restaurants, cleaners, and the like would become viable in such locations.

The point is that the long-term tendency toward consolidation of work and commerce could easily be reversed with the use of modern technology, and decentralization does not have to mean further increase in travel and erosion of community. Instead, decentralization can be oriented toward increased opportunities for social contact and reduced burden on the transportation system.

It is worth contrasting the notions of compact urban form and trip substitution strategies with an idea that is enjoying great currency and receiving research support: the Intelligent

Vehicle Highway System, recently renamed the Intelligent Transportation System (ITS). The motivating assumption behind ITS is that we can use technology, primarily in the form of better information systems, to improve the efficiency with which we use our current transportation system. As alluded to in Chapter 1, this assumption fails to take into account the fact that, in the absence of any other supporting policies, the latent demand for transportation is so great that any increase in capacity brought on by improvements in efficiency will immediately be swallowed up.

An illustration or two will highlight this problem. One ITS program is aimed at providing better traffic information to motorists. Through the use of traffic monitoring devices and in-vehicle communication systems, drivers can be informed in real time if a certain corridor is experiencing congestion due to an accident or simply too much traffic. The driver then can be given choices of alternate routes to avoid the tie-up. Assuming that the problem of determining which information should be given to whom can be solved, such a system would result in the optimal distribution of traffic throughout the system and minimize average trip times. There are important side issues, such as whether the alternate routes are really appropriate places to put the extra traffic and the potential inequities involved in making the information available only to those who can pay for it. However, the main problem is that such a system, even if it worked perfectly, is actually equivalent to adding additional transportation infrastructure. The extra capacity would be filled by people making more and longer trips.

Another illustration involves the ultimate goal of ITS, the automated highway, which is intended to allow vehicles to travel close together, safely, at high speeds without the driver having to control the vehicle. The automated highway resembles a mass transit system in a way—with people in private compartments.

Technical feasibility aside, this goal has at least two severe complications. One is the perennial latent demand problem. The extra capacity would quickly fill up and eventually require more physical capacity once the technological limits are reached. The second problem is that the automated highway cannot be everywhere. At some point, all these efficiently delivered vehicles will be dumped somewhere and cause traffic problems in the very communities they are meant to serve.

ITS contains elements that can be useful. Some of the technology leading to the automated highway can make for safer driving and better driving conditions. A cautious group of trend-watchers in the public interest community is pointing out the potential benefits of "smart technology" to transit systems and to pricing strategies such as toll collection that differentiates between rush hour and non-rush hour, much as telephone and utility companies are able to distinguish peak and non-peak usage. It is hard to argue against providing better information to motorists, as long as certain limits are respected. However, ITS, as a whole, is a dangerous continuation of the first paradigm of transportation planning. It will not serve community. In fact, it could be as destructive to community as was the Interstate Highway System.

Managing Transportation Corridors

A common theme among at least four of the cases—Atlanta's Freedom Parkway, Maryland's 301 Task Force, Seattle's Mountains-to-Sound Greenway, and Kentucky's Paris Pike—is defining a transportation corridor as including more than a highway and then determining how to manage it. As more citizens and professionals implement the comprehensive planning approaches mandated in ISTEA and the inter-relatedness of environmental land-use features and transportation is examined and understood, the issues confronted in these four examples will become increasingly common.

How do you make major roadway improvements without negatively impacting or destroying the landscape? The 301

Task Force set out to answer this by widening the circle of participants who ask and answer these questions to include environmentalists, local government representatives, designers, and highway engineers. And the task force is looking at implementation tools that include purchase of conservation easements to lands bordering the highway, using ISTEA funds to stabilize the corridor and manage growth patterns.

In the Seattle I-90 case, the widened interstate is already in place and the task is to find ways to stabilize surrounding land uses to protect natural environments and resource-based economies from highway-induced metropolitan sprawl. The question is not only what tools to use to accomplish this, but what organization, agency, or alliance of agencies is equipped to manage a seventy-five mile, multiple-use, and multiple ownership greenway?[1]

At the federal level, the analogous agency could be the National Park Service, which designs, builds, and maintains a series of parkways in the nation's capital, national parks, and new heritage parks. Should state or county park departments be empowered to build and operate roadways where land-use and transportation impacts are inter-related? Or perhaps the model should be the U.S. Forest Service, whose multiple-use mandate has caused the agency to attempt to serve the timber, grazing, mining, and recreational communities simultaneously. Alternatively, perhaps an operating authority such as the Tennessee Valley Authority or the Bonneville Power Administration with broad powers over the land and water in a region is the appropriate model.

In Atlanta and Seattle, citizen activists were determined not to allow one government agency to manage and operate the parkway or greenway. The reason was largely one of lack of trust that any one agency, given existing mandates, could look out for the well-being of the entire corridor, encompassing transportation, conservation, recreation, heritage education, and even housing. The Mountains-to-Sound Greenway Trust concluded that, as a nonprofit organization, it would take the lead in defining a corridor plan, inducing a range of bordering municipalities, businesses, and other interests to buy into the plan. The Trust is coordinating the efforts of various entities to implement their portions of the overall vision.

Perhaps the creation of watershed or ecosystem management authorities could address corridor management issues. These authorities would have power to manage the waters and land-based resources in naturally occurring watersheds or ecosystems. Transportation construction and management would fall under the authority's purview, and the state DOT would abide by the authority's determination regarding impacts on the surrounding local and regional environment. In urban centers and built-up sections of metropolitan areas, the state DOT would need to form alliances with community development, environmental, and recreation agencies to understand and manage impacts on surrounding communities.

In the search for appropriate institutions to implement holistic transportation, it may be helpful to examine the way that society has historically dealt with transportation issues. The earliest roads were often privately constructed toll roads. The streetcar and electric interurban rail systems that flourished in the 1920s were also private ventures. As street railways and subways failed financially, they were often taken over by public agencies. Road building and maintenance became the province of highway departments. In major cities, the bus, subway, and rail systems were sometimes integrated.

At the state level, highway departments flourished after World War II. The notion of a department of transportation was a reform that took place in the 1960s when a federal department was first established. As states followed suit, renaming their highway departments, the reality remained that highways were the main line of business. For all but the most densely populated and urban states like New Jersey, which began to operate failing bus and rail companies, state highway departments had new names but no additional infrastructure to plan or manage.

Oregon developed a unique model that integrated recreation and land-use decisions with highway funding decisions by placing the state parks agency under the highway department. The assumption was that good roads enabled residents and visitors to access the mountains and beaches. The ISTEA era requires state DOTs to expand beyond highways, but can and should the departments engage in integrated corridor management? What new organizational forms will best carry out the integrated land-use and development decisions inherent in transportation corridors?

What if the Central Artery/Tunnel project in Boston had been designed from the outset as a transportation, economic development, park and waterfront enhancement, and regional transportation reform project? Could the same integrated approach to regional transportation and land-use changes have been proposed as was finally worked out during years of legal challenge, community dispute, and mediation?

One driver for such a comprehensive approach would be the availability of additional federal funding for each added public benefit engendered by a transportation project. The park element, for example, might add an additional $150 million, and affordable housing would bring in another $100 million.

Reaching Decisions

It is something of a miracle to watch arch adversaries in a highway dispute emerge from a marathon mediation session with arms around each other and smiles on their faces. In the Boston, Atlanta, and Paris Pike examples described in Chapter 4, the mediation process ended long, seemingly intractable battles with inspiring results.

The importance of these examples is not that mediation is a cure-all. Obviously it does not always work; rather, it offers a decision-making process that could have broader application under an ISTEA/holistic transportation framework than ever before. In both the Central Artery and Freedom Parkway examples, mediation was employed with success when political time was running out and litigation had stalled matters. Boston would have lost its federal funding commitment if it could not proceed with its environmental impact statement, and Atlanta wanted to complete its road project in time for the upcoming Olympics.

The mediation techniques of facilitated discussion and structured problem solving among a wide range of stakeholders can be employed upfront in the planning and decision-making process. The 301 Task Force in Maryland was just such an application; the Maryland DOT, local governments, and nonprofit land-use and environmental groups were gathered to participate in a corridor-wide study.

In the following chapter of post-ISTEA examples, a similar approach is being tried by the Georgia DOT. It remains to be seen whether the potential breakthroughs of a mediation process can occur without the pressure or threat of imminent legal or monetary action.

A further consideration is the ability of mediated settlements to be altered over time as conditions change. Are large unwieldy groups of stakeholders going to be reconvened as new technologies or circumstances alter the previously agreed-upon plan? Will the stakeholder organizations that participated in the first agreement still be available for subsequent discussions, and will their representatives be able to bring their groups along in the change process?

Questions like these are intended to acknowledge the difficulty of reaching and modifying the kinds of complex, large-scale, and long-term decisions entailed in major transportation and land-use issues. No one process will offer a perfect way to make these decisions, but mediation and facilitated conflict resolution do provide a workable approach that ought to be and is being employed with greater enterprise.

Transportation and Education

Transportation professionals have traditionally been trained in civil engineering or planning. Our system of university education is geared toward producing experts in particular fields without adequate attention paid to holistic approaches to issues. Using transportation solutions alone to deal with transportation problems has proven inadequate. It is important that civil engineers are sufficiently grounded in understanding human behavior to make the right connections between transportation facilities and community life. It is equally important that planners move beyond physical design issues and implementation processes to understanding the human needs in communities. A university transportation curriculum that includes social psychology, anthropology, history, economics, and the arts, as well as technical design and planning issues would develop a cadre of transportation professionals who approach problems with a more holistic viewpoint.

In addition, since transportation and community form are intimately connected and not well understood by the general public, these topics should be part of the educational curriculum starting in elementary school. It is important that U.S. citizens gain a more complete understanding of transportation and land use. Elected officials respond to public opinion; and if that opinion is based on shallow understanding or misinformation, it can lead to very bad policy indeed.

Note

1. Although the distance between Seattle and the crest of the Cascades Mountains is 50 miles, the greenway extends an additional 25 miles.

Part II

Implementing the Intermodal Surface Transportation Efficiency Act

8

First Steps under ISTEA

In this chapter we examine the first post-ISTEA attempts to comply with the new law's requirements for integrating citizen participation into the earliest planning stages, devising new methods of evaluating projects and assessing their impacts, and funding a variety of projects in keeping with the environmental, community, and economic needs of specific regions. Several post-ISTEA planning processes are documented, along with their stated goals and objectives, participants, and mechanisms for prioritizing projects.

The descriptions are not inclusive, nor do they provide the kind of analysis that might allow us to learn from some of the mistakes made in these efforts. This is a subject for further research and documentation. Instead, this chapter highlights a variety of local, regional, and state responses to ISTEA, as well as the new planning processes being developed and their early impacts on funding decisions.

Because the focus of this book is on the ways that transportation planning and projects are changing to serve community needs and quality of life, this chapter also looks at how communities are using the ISTEA transportation enhancements program. Overall commitments of enhancements funding were relatively low in the first few years of ISTEA implementation (17 percent nationwide in 1993). However, where enhancements projects have been put in place, they have galvanized local attention to and public support for transportation's potential benefits to communities. The examples of enhancements processes examined here also illustrate how a coalition which begins around a successful project can be extended to take on a life of its own as the guardian of an ongoing process.

Putting Communities First

ISTEA is tangible evidence of the adage, "When the people lead, the leaders will follow." During the first two years of ISTEA, in the absence of regulations, citizens frequently were the first to recognize and follow through on ISTEA's potential for community change. In mostly rural states like Maine, in states such as Virginia with a mix of highly urbanized areas and very small towns, and in complex metropolitan areas such as Washington, D.C., a variety of citizen groups are developing a new vision of community-oriented transportation planning. In Georgia and Maryland, the ISTEA enhancements program has inspired citizens to collaborate with public officials on transportation corridor management and the establishment of an urban greenways program, respectively.

Each of the examples in the first section of this chapter involved a variety of interests in building consensus around community values. In Maine, citizens persuaded the DOT to give public and special interests a direct role in drafting regulations for the state's Sensible Transportation Policy Act. In Virginia, a group that began as an assortment of community, environmental, and design interests with a stake in the transportation enhancements program has grown into a diverse statewide coalition concentrating on state planning and funding requirements. In Washington, D.C., public interest groups and individuals working on different pieces of the transportation planning puzzle came together to share information, coordinate resources, and develop an alternative vision on which to base the regional planning process. In Georgia, a regional agency recognized the seeds of a multi-faceted heritage corridor in three separate historic preservation projects, while in Baltimore, Maryland, public interest groups joined forces with neighborhood groups to breathe new life into a greenways plan that had languished on the shelf for years. In each case, the fact that disparate and sometimes divergent groups joined forces to educate one another and reach consensus has lent their efforts more credibility and clout.

Maine

The Maine Sensible Transportation Act of 1991 (MSTA) preceded the new federal law by several months. The story of the implementation of Maine's law illustrates the shift in community activism from project-specific highway battles or transit debates to long-term, comprehensive planning strategies.

When citizens in Maine were asked to vote on a 1991 referendum to stop plans to widen the Maine Turnpike, they were also asked to vote for a recommendation that the state establish a Sensible Transportation Policy.[1] The new policy would require the analysis of alternatives to widenings or new construction, and would require citizens to be involved in local and state transportation planning.

Subsequent to passage of the new law, citizen groups urged the Maine DOT to develop a public negotiation process to draft regulations implementing the Sensible Transportation Policy. Representatives of more than sixty groups attended the first meeting in April 1992 and established the Transportaton Policy Advisory Committee. The committee included environmentalists, planners, cycling advocates, rail advocates, paving contractors, and developers. Over a six-month period, the committee members negotiated a set of rules that Maine adopted in December 1992.

The rules call for the Maine DOT to meet seven objectives in planning, capital investment, and project development:

- Promote the coordinated and efficient use of all available and future transportation modes;

- Meet the diverse transportation needs of the people of the state, including rural and urban populations, and the unique mobility needs of the elderly and disabled;

- Ensure the repair and necessary improvements of roads and bridges throughout the state to provide a safe, efficient and adequate transportation network;

- Minimize the harmful effects of transportation on public health, air and water quality, land, and other natural resources;

- Reduce the state's reliance on foreign oil and promote reliance on energy-efficient forms of transportation;

- Be consistent with the purposes, goals and policies of the Comprehensive Planning and Land Use Regulation Act; and

- Incorporate a public participation process in which local governments and the public receive timely notice and the opportunity to identify and comment on transportation concerns.

An important innovation in the state law was the creation of eight Regional Transportation Advisory Committees (RTACs) for the state. Each of these advisory committees is comprised of sixteen to twenty-two people who represent "the concerns of planners, environmentalists, business, commerce, different transportation modes, historic preservation, the elderly, the disabled, and other diverse interests."[2] The Maine DOT is required to cooperate with these committees and metropolitan planning organizations in most aspects of the transportation planning process.

Coupled with ISTEA, the Maine process has opened the door for greater consideration of alternatives to road-building. The Portland Area Comprehensive Transportation Committee (PACTC), for example, allocated half of its nearly $8 million in ISTEA funds toward nonhighway projects in 1994, including bicycling routes, sidewalk projects, the purchase of transit vehicles, and other public transportation improvements. Prior to ISTEA, the regional agency had committed all its available funds, aside from those specifically earmarked for transit, to road projects. The region's 20-year plan has also committed 52 percent of its available funding to nonhighway projects.

The PACTC has taken the crucial first step toward investing transportation funds in new alternatives. However, it has not yet taken on the challenge of implementing land-use tools to guide growth toward existing transportation systems. The Natural Resources Council of Maine, a powerful environmental group in the state, is working with the PACTC to test alternative assumptions for traffic, population growth, and air quality, based on the idea of managing growth rather than serving it by road construction. The goal is to forecast the potential impacts of a wide range of alternatives to road building.

In early 1994, the PACTC initiated its first test of the Sensible Transportation Policy's requirement to analyze alternatives in the case of the proposed widening of Riverside Street in Portland. Although preliminary indications are promising, it remains to be seen whether the new state law will stand up to the test. If the law does succeed in focusing early attention on alternatives to road projects, it could help Maine avoid future conflicts such as the dispute over widening the turnpike.

CONTACTS
Bruce Hammond
Natural Resources Council of Maine
271 State Street
Augusta, ME 04330
(207) 622-3101

Jane Lincoln
Deputy Commissioner for Public Affairs
Maine Department of Transportation
State House, Station 16
Augusta, ME 04333

John Duncan, Director
Portland Area Comprehensive Transportation Committee
233 Oxford Street
Portland, ME 04101
(207) 774-9891

Virginia

The recently formed Virginia Surface Transportation Coalition[3] demonstrates the next wave of citizen influence over public decisions in post-ISTEA planning. The coalition was established in January 1993, following a meeting of activists and transportation professionals at a regional conference entitled "Transportation Planning for Livable Communities." Held in Arlington, Virginia, the conference was one of a series of regional meetings sponsored by several nonprofit groups, primarily federal agencies involved in transportation policy, and the national Surface Transportation Policy Project.

The Virginia coalition initially began as an assortment of groups interested in housing, planning, and liveable communities. Their focus was the implementation of ISTEA's transportation enhancements provision. At the 1993 meeting, activists and local officials became concerned over the lack of information from the Virginia DOT about enhancements.

This information gap was common during the first two years of ISTEA's implementation. Initially, only a handful of states focused on transportation enhancements, which, ironically, was the program most frequently singled out for attention by public interest groups. Many state DOTs seemed reluctant to implement enhancements because the provision was unfamiliar or its goals fell outside their traditional set of goals. The $3 billion enhancements program also is relatively small compared with other ISTEA initiatives. For example, the next-smallest is the Congestion Mitigation and Air Quality Improvement Program, which at an authorized $6 billion through 1997, is double the size of enhancements.

Initially, the Commonwealth of Virginia committed none of its enhancements funds, partly because its enhancements program did not formally begin until 1993, but also because of state limitations on matching funds for ISTEA's more flexible categories. The coalition successfully advocated for emergency legislation to release state fuel tax funds for enhancements during 1993. In the course of this effort the coalition learned of ISTEA's broader potential for transportation reform. The coalition, after acclimating itself to the planning requirements and funding flexibility in the federal law, broadened its base of support to include transit representatives, economic development and downtown interests, and bicycling and pedestrian groups. By the end of 1993 the coalition had a steering committee comprised of thirteen individuals representing public health, environmental, housing, and design quality concerns (see List A in the chapter appendix).

In early 1994, the coalition began working with the Virginia DOT on a series of planning roundtables, the first step toward establishing a collaborative planning process between the commonwealth and citizens. The coalition's discussions with the commonwealth's decision-makers has validated its convictions that commonwealth officials need a push to identify the full range of new planning partners and implement adequate techniques to include them.

In contrast to the James River case, in which activists blocked an existing proposal and then regrouped to propose an alternative, the Virginia Surface Transportation Coalition is seeking early positive input into the planning process before project decisions are made. Although the Virginia DOT is still cautious and slow to respond to the coalition's specific suggestions for the planning process, the department has been open to discussing its public involvement policies. In part, the department's willingness is based on the coalition's representation of diverse citizen interests, which entitles it to communicate a wide range of concerns and allows it to broadcast the DOT's intentions and proposals to a broad constituency.

CONTACT
David Brown, Founding Chair
Virginia Surface Transportation Coalition
c/o Preservation Alliance of Virginia
P.O. Box 1407
Staunton, VA 24402

Washington, D.C.

The effectiveness and clout of a diversified citizen coalition, combined with local commitment to growth management and a politically astute DOT leadership, is also demonstrated by the Washington Regional Network for Livable Communities (WRN), encompassing citizen groups from the District of Columbia and eight counties in Maryland and Virginia.[4] The regional network was organized at about the same time that the 301 Task Force was being formed in Maryland. The network included many of the same participants as the 301 Task Force and was also led by the Chesapeake Bay Foundation.

The groups in the network, instead of continuing to put out local fires, pooled their resources to sponsor a brainstorming session in late spring of 1993. The meeting resulted in an alternative vision for the region's land-use planning, transit investment, and neighborhood design.

The network first established a working relationship with the region's metropolitan planning organization, the Transportation Planning Board of the Metropolitan Washington Council of Governments (WASH-COG). The coalition now acts as a two-way conduit of information about the planning board's activities and citizens' views on those activities. The network also helps to educate activists about the complex and interlocking requirements of ISTEA and the Clean Air Act, plus technical issues such as the principles of transportation demand management, land use, and economic policy related to transportation. Finally, the group serves as a consistent, credible presence at the meetings of the Transportation Planning Board.

In part, the timing of the creation of the network has been responsible for its effectiveness in establishing its presence. At the time the group was formed, the Metropolitan Washington Council of Governments was putting the finishing touches to a four-year effort to encourage more diverse participation in regional transportation and land-use decisions. The Partnership for Regional Excellence, as this outreach and consensus building effort is called, is made up of thirty active and more than 200 participating government, business and citizen representatives.

An earlier special task force established by the council issued a report in 1991 with the following conclusions:

- Business as usual will not work [for the Washington, D.C. region]. New ways must be found to cope with growing traffic congestion, a crisis in infrastructure financing, and continued environmental degradation.

- The region has the power to change in any direction it wishes. Regional cooperation can lead to a satisfying future that preserves the resources and assets of communities in the National Capital Area.[5]

The Transportation Planning Board faces daunting challenges in carrying out its responsibilities under ISTEA. In addition to a dramatic expansion of its geographic planning area, it will need to research and collect more data to comply with ISTEA and the Clean Air Act Amendments of 1990. These realities make groups like the Washington Regional Network, which represents a diverse range of interests and expertise across the tri-state area, especially important.

In 1992, the network contacted major public interest groups that had been working on transportation issues in the region: the League of Women Voters, Audubon Naturalist Society, Sierra Club, Washington Area Bicyclists Association, and Maryland Transit Coalition. Approximately twenty people attended each of two design charettes—intensive brain-storming sessions involving participants from a variety of disciplines—to begin developing a long range vision for the region. These were compiled into "A New Approach," a study containing recommendations shaped by three basic goals[6]:

- Invest in the existing transportation system and use in-place road and transit networks more efficiently.
- Make transit, bicycle, and pedestrian investment a much higher priority.
- Organize new residential and business development around urban and town centers.

Linked with each of these goals are the following specific recommendations:

Goal One: Invest in the existing system.

- Enhance connections between transit systems and create better links to transit for cyclists and pedestrians.
- Equalize the relative costs of driving and transit through user fees, congestion pricing, parking fees, and changes in tax policy to attract transit users.
- Manage automobile parking to discourage auto use.
- Encourage employers and employees to create innovative programs to reduce auto trips.
- Develop systems to manage traffic congestion and travel demand.
- Apply new technologies to make transit systems more efficient.

Goal Two: Raise the priority for investment in transit, bicycles, and walking.

- Establish and meet goals for "mode splits," i.e., the relative shares of travel represented by various modes of transportation. At the time that the study was undertaken, drive-alone trips accounted for 63 percent of all regional trips and 86 percent of all suburban trips.
- Create an efficient transit network by coordinating and connecting transit systems, particularly between existing urban centers and fast-growing areas. Improving transit services among and within satellite centers outside the urban core should receive high priority.
- Serve major facilities, including universities, hospitals, research, and government centers.
- Preserve existing rights-of-way, i.e., the corridors of land previously acquired by the government for transportation purposes.
- Construct pedestrian and bicycle ways on highways.
- Promote pedestrian and bicycle use on streets with low traffic volumes.
- Encourage walking in suburban areas by reorienting suburban streets to make them more pleasant and safe for pedestrians, and creating town centers within a five- to ten-minute walk of suburban neighborhoods.
- Build more trails and greenways.

The capital plan proposed by the network would create twenty-three major new transit projects to be undertaken before the year 2010; eleven new trails and four trail upgrades; improvements on five regional bridges to provide access to pedestrians and bicyclists; improved transit access for people on foot and bicycle; and two suburban/rural bike routes. The plan also provides for scenic enhancements to make alternative travel more attractive and help preserve environmental resources.

Goal Three: Organize new development around centers.

- Each jurisdiction in the region should establish guidelines for growth and focus growth in existing centers.

- New housing and commercial growth should be sited near transit stops.

- Jobs and housing should be balanced within each major jurisdiction.

- Intensive transit should be provided for high-growth areas.

- Existing urban and historic centers should be revitalized.

- Rural areas should be preserved.

- Urban design standards should be revised to emphasize aesthetics and create a pleasant, humane street atmosphere.

- Disincentives to transit use, walking, and cycling, such as mandatory low-density development and minimum parking requirements, should be removed from local zoning codes.

- Banks should be encouraged to make loans for transit-oriented development.

The Transportation Planning Board is examining many of the network's recommendations for possible inclusion in the region's long-range plan. Meanwhile, the network continues to work with the planning board to change its public involvement practices. The changes are not occurring overnight, although the board set aside $500,000 to initiate a public outreach program in 1994.

Because the network has been a consistent, credible presence at public meetings, its members have been invited to present their views at several committee meetings of the Transportation Planning Board. The group also continues to tackle the substantive issues of transportation raised by ISTEA, including congestion management and the implementation of the transportation control measures required by the Clean Air Act.

CONTACT
Kristin Pauly
Chesapeake Bay Foundation
162 Prince George Street
Annapolis, MD 21401
(410) 268-8816

Transportation Enhancements in Georgia and Maryland

Two projects in Georgia and Maryland exemplify how the enhancements program can galvanize programs that otherwise might not receive the attention they deserve.

A 56-mile highway in Georgia is the site for a new heritage program that combines transportation, tourism, scenic and historic preservation, and environmental conservation.[7] The Chattahoochee-Flint Heritage Highway passes through nine communities in three counties, tying together more than twenty cultural sites in a rural landscape of working farms and mountains less than an hour west of Atlanta.

When the Chattahoochee-Flint Regional Development Center (RDC) was asked to assist in three historic preservation projects along the route, it settled on a corridor management approach to coordinating the projects. The center then faced the challenge of bringing together citizens and public officials from nine local governments to realize the concept. In January 1993, using the possibility of ISTEA enhancements funding to motivate participation, the center pulled together a steering committee made up of local preservationists, chambers of commerce, and interested citizens (see List B in the chapter appendix).

The steering committee operated informally during the first phase of the project, reaching its decisions by consensus. The committee is now formalizing its structure and bylaws as a nonprofit organization to oversee the development and long-term management of the heritage highway.

The center prepared an ISTEA funding proposal for a first phase of development, choosing five elements along the corridor that were certain to fit into the plan and for which the necessary local match could be secured. The selected activities encompass five categories of eligible ISTEA enhancements projects: improvements for pedestrians and bicycling, scenic or historic highways, acquisition of historic sites, landscaping, and rehabilitation of historic transportation facilities.

In the first category, the plan will provide access to hiking and biking along the Chattahoochee Trace Bike Path, Wolf's Den Loop, and Pine Mountain Trail. In the second category, the corridor plan incorporates the acquisition and rehabilitation of several scenic or historic sites, including the "Little Brown Jug," a vernacular roadside building from the 1950s, the WPA-era Hogansville Amphitheatre, the turn-of-the-century Dunaway Gardens, and the Moreland Old Mill. The corridor also includes a scenic highway program, landscaping, and rehabiliation of the historic Grantsville Depot.

Several conflicts of intention emerged during the early stages of planning. For example, tourism representatives focused on encouraging more visitors to use the highway, preservationists focused on rehabilitation, and transportation planners wanted to concentrate on traffic speed and safety concerns. The steering committee has invested nine months in meetings to discuss the plan elements one by one and secure funding for the project. Through this process, the committee members began to understand the complexities of their undertaking. Although solutions to the conflicts over focus are only beginning to emerge, the planning process does seem to have given the steering committee a sense of ownership in the outcome of the plan.

In terms of funding, the project has already succeeded. It was ranked fourth among a priority list of forty projects selected by the Georgia DOT staff for funding in the nonmetropolitan round. The state granted a full Phase I request of $121,600 for the heritage highway. In less than a year, the center and other agencies secured $224,000 toward the completion of the $5 million project.

In Baltimore, Maryland, the concept for the Gwynns Falls Greenway dates back to Frederick Law Olmsted's early vision for the area.[8] Restoration of that vision has been proposed off and on for decades, most recently in the 1991 *Strategic Plan for Action*, produced by the state's Department of Recreation and Parks with the Yale University Urban Resources Initiative and the Trust for Public Land.

Stretching for approximately six miles from northwest Baltimore to the redeveloped Inner Harbor, the Gwynns Falls Greenway will serve more than 10 percent of the state's population. The greenway will draw both local users and tourists to the B&O Railroad Museum, Oriole Park at Camden Yards, and the highly successful Inner Harbor retail market and park. The greenway also unites several of the city's neighborhoods and, by connecting to the Patapsco River Greenway, lays the cornerstone for a future urban greenway system. In fact, the Gwynns Falls Greenway initiative has sparked the formation of a new coalition, Baltimore Walks, which will spearhead the creation of a citywide system of trails and walkways.

In 1992, members of TPL's local advisory committee and the city's Departments of Parks and Planning formed a steering committee to gauge public interest in the proposed greenway. The steering committee met with community groups, among them The Franklintown Road Improvement Association, Westport Improvement Association, Citizens Planning and Housing Association's Resource Center for Neighborhoods, Baltimore Bicycling Club, and Carroll Park Restoration Foundation.

Many of these groups were already working on their own to improve the quality of life in their neighborhoods in ways related to the greenway. These groups were monitoring water quality, controlling the use of trails by All-Terrain Vehicles, re-opening closed parks, and cracking down on illegal dumping. In addition, the greenway was already serving area teachers as an outdoor classroom on the environment. The B&O Railroad Museum was studying ways to reuse its recently acquired 26-acre switching yard. After meeting with the steering committees, many local groups saw the greenway's potential for uniting their communities.

By the time Mayor Kurt Schmoke convened a task force on the greenway in 1992, regional supporters included neighborhood groups, planning organizations, private and public museums and institutions, schools, local and regional advocacy groups, businesses, and civic leaders (see List C in the chapter appendix). The mission of the mayor's task force was to develop a feasibility plan for the greenway's restoration, incorporate a vision for urban greenways into the transportation plan of the newly formed Baltimore Metropolitan Council, and secure the funds to make it all possible. The task force, while using the Gwynns Falls Greenway to test its approach, was already looking ahead to a regional system of greenways.

The Mayor's Task Force on the Gwynns Falls Greenway was divided into three working groups:

- The *Eureka* group shaped the overall vision for the project and formed alliances with other institutions and programs to better use the greenway;

- The *Greenbacks* group developed a fundraising strategy targeting both private and public funding sources; and

- The *Hardhats* group focused on trail design and management, particularly access, safety, and environmental concerns. Their goal was to identify a cooperative public/private strategy for long-term maintenance and management of the greenway.

The task force brainstormed for several months on immediate and future needs and coordinated events to raise the project's profile. These events included a stream clean-up coordinated by a Baltimore girls' schools organization GUTSE (Girls United to Save the Environment), and a bicycle ride to coincide with the All-Star Game in the summer of 1993.

The supporters of the Gwynns Falls Greenway integrated their efforts into the regional context by working with the Maryland Greenways Commission to develop the Patapsco River Greenway. The strong public and private support for this project helped it gain the endorsement of the Baltimore Metropolitan Council. The council's endorsement was necessary for the State of Maryland to consider the project for transportation funding.

Maryland was one of the first states to recognize the potential for ISTEA enhancements funding. The state has actively solicited applications from local sponsors since the first year of the federal law, and took a strong lead in pursuing projects as diverse as protection of Civil War battlefields, urban greenways, and the restoration of historic rail stations.

All prospective enhancements projects in Maryland are first reviewed by a technical advisory committee according to the following criteria:

- Benefit to the community/environment;
- Cost;
- Ability to leverage additional funding from local governments, other state agencies, private sources, and organizations;
- Level of support for the project;
- Relationship to other plans and programs; and
- Geographic distribution.

The technical advisory committee works with local municipalities on proposed projects to assure that these criteria are addressed before projects are submitted for final approval by the State of Maryland.

The City of Baltimore's application on behalf of the Gwynns Falls Greenway clarified the need to protect it as a resource. The city affirmed its ability to meet 50 percent of the project's cost, as required by the state. Although a local share of 20 percent is the federal minimum required, Maryland adopted the 50 percent approach in order to leverage additional local and private investment toward completion of a greater number of projects across the state.

The final application was approved by the task force's executive committee, which comprises the secretary of the Department of Natural Resources, Transportation Secretary O. James Lighthizer, the state highway administrator, and the director of the Maryland Historical Trust. In late 1992, the Gwynns Falls Greenway project was awarded funding for the first phase of land acquisition.

Both the Georgia and Maryland examples demonstrate how enhancements projects may be used to reinforce ISTEA's focus on corridor management and regional cooperation.

CONTACTS
Georgia: Chattahoochee-Flint Heritage Corridor
Julie Turner
Historic Preservation Planner
Chattahoochee-Flint Regional Development Commission
P.O. Box 1600
Franklin, GA 30217
(706) 675-6721

Maryland: Gwynns Falls
Chris Rogers
Trust for Public Land
666 Pennsylvania Avenue, SE, Suite 401
Washington, DC 20003
(202) 543-7552

Public Involvement

This section examines how regional agencies and citizen groups in northern California, upstate New York, and western Pennsylvania have tackled the intertwined problems of public involvement in planning, innovative project selection, and linking the analysis of land use trends with transportation systems.

San Francisco Bay Area

The Metropolitan Transportation Commission in northern California is expanding its base of partnerships with the public and incorporating new tools for analyzing alternatives to road widening.[9]

The commission serves as the metropolitan planning organization for the San Francisco Bay Area, which comprises nine counties and includes more than 100 towns and cities. Each year, the commission updates its regional transportation plan and develops a three-year transportation improvement program (TIP), recommending and identifying funds for projects. The commission maintains a variety of advisory councils, several of which include citizens and representatives of public interest groups. Scoring especially high on public representation are committees dealing with transit issues: the county-based Paratransit Coordinating Councils, the Minority Citizens Advisory Committee, and the Regional Transit Productivity Committee. An interdisciplinary Transportation Control Measure Task Force includes voluntary participation by regional business leaders, environmental and community groups, and public health and local government agencies.

The commission also has combined a variety of basic public information tools, such as a lively monthly newsletter and an ongoing relationship with key media, to communicate the immediacy of transportation decisions in people's lives.

The commission has been under pressure since a 1988 legal challenge by the Sierra Club and Citizens for a Better Environment, which charged the commission and other agencies with insufficient progress in implementing the 1982 regional Bay Area Clean Air Plan. Since that time, the commission has changed its priorities to be more responsive to environmental and community concerns. ISTEA's planning and funding flexibility provided a chance to demonstrate how the commission's new commitment could be translated into better investment in existing facilities rather than new roads.

Within a month of ISTEA's passage, the commission organized a conference in January 1992 to bring together local, state, and federal policy makers with Bay Area leaders from the disabled, environmental, and business communities. Members of the general public were also invited. The meeting led to the establishment of several task forces and committees that proved to be instrumental in realizing speedy results from ISTEA in the Bay Area, and created permanent working relationships among planners, elected officials, and the public.

To accomplish the high level of intergovernmental coordination that ISTEA requires, the commission established the Bay Area Partnership, a consortium of three dozen local, regional, state, and federal transportation and air quality officials. A citizens' Blue Ribbon Advisory Council was established at the same time, as the partnership's lifeline to business, environmental, and community groups.

The Partnership's first work program under ISTEA was the Joint Urban Mobility Program, nicknamed JUMP Start. The program's aim was to expedite the use of ISTEA funds for projects that take advantage of the existing transportation network to reduce air pollution and fight traffic congestion. The JUMP Start program has been successful with a wide variety of projects, from pragmatic tinkering with the timing of traffic signals to a demonstration program for a unified regional transit pass.

A particularly visible and popular JUMP Start project has been the deployment of a Freeway Service Patrol to help stranded motorists and assist in accident clearance on freeways. More recently, the JUMP Start approach helped MTC secure federal funding for a telecommuting program and has begun work on a computerized "advanced traveler information system" that will dispense information on road conditions, transit schedules, and parking.

Although the partnership has realized short-term improvements in the existing system, it has also set in motion a new process for selecting new projects. The Ad Hoc Multimodal Priority Setting Committee was founded by the partnership in April 1992. Like the partnership, the committee's representation consisted mostly of city and county officials, transportation planners, and air quality representatives, many of whom had previously "at best politely ignored each other, at worst were prone to open warfare," according to Larry Dahms, Executive Director of the MTC.[10]

The committee invited the public to its regular meetings, and local project sponsors were required to involve citizens directly in developing proposals before the projects advanced to the regional stage. Metropolitan Transportation Commission's existing advisory committees were updated regularly about the priority setting committee's work, and the commission's staff made presentations on the proposed process to a variety of planning and public interest groups.

To establish a common framework, the committee used a new and often overlooked requirement of ISTEA, the establishment of a Metropolitan Transportation System. Section 134(g)(2) of ISTEA states,

> A long range plan shall, at a minimum, identify transportation facilities (including but not necessarily limited to major roadways, transit and multimodal and intermodal facilities) that should function as an integrated metropolitan transportation system, giving emphasis to those facilities that serve important national and regional transportation functions.[11]

Beyond a mere collection of facilities, the MTS is meant to be an integrated, interconnected web of transportation systems and services. The focus is on integrating and improving the performance of existing facilities, rather than investing in new construction as a first resort. The purpose of the system is specifically to take a user's point of view in coordinating a variety of options, including walking and biking.

Employing the planning factors listed in Section 134 of ISTEA, the committee devised a basic process for screening projects. To be considered further, a project had to meet all of the following criteria:

- Consistency with the long range plan;
- Demonstration of "reasonable and likely" sources of federal, state, and local funding for the project;
- Project-specific requirements that precisely define the scope, cost, benefits, and eligibility under ISTEA;
- Air quality requirements; and
- Americans with Disabilities Act requirements.

Projects that passed initial screening were ranked according to four broad groups of considerations:

- Up to thirty points could be awarded for maintaining the existing metropolitan transportation system;
- Up to thirty points could be awarded for improving the efficiency and effectiveness of the metropolitan transportation system;
- Up to fifteen points could be awarded to projects that expand the metropolitan transportation system; and
- Up to twenty-five points could be awarded to projects with a potential environmental, social, or land-use benefit.

The net result of the ranking process was that maintenance- and community-oriented projects gained an edge over projects that focused exclusively on expansion or new construction.

Scorers also were asked to keep four basic principles in mind:

- Tie the solution to the problem wherever possible;
- Use measures that cut across transportation modes, where possible;
- Incorporate standards that judge the performance of systems rather than their inherent characteristics (e.g., how long does a 30-mile trip take at rush hour, versus how many cars a given highway carries at a given time); and
- Rely on and strengthen existing land-use and transportation plans.

In only six months, the partnership established criteria, rounded up and ranked projects, and adopted a three-year, $214 million slate of projects that were significantly more diverse than those funded in previous rounds, when Federal Aid Urban System funds had primarily gone toward traffic and road improvements. Because the commission included the public in the process long before individual projects were considered, the unveiling of its proposals met with public support. State and federal agencies approved the transportation improvement program in January 1993.

As an encouraging coda to the conflicts between the commission and environmental groups in the late 1980s, MTC is now working with a local group, the Regional Alliance For Transit (RAFT), to try out alternative scenarios for population growth and land-use changes. The commission is using its transportation modeling program to compare its Regional Transportation Plan projections to RAFT's assumptions about how the region will grow through 2010.

Both growth projections are based on forecasts for population growth, household, and employment trends by the Association of Bay Area Governments (ABAG). RAFT's alternative retains ABAG's bottom line projections for overall regional growth, but rechannels low-density growth in the outlying areas into mixed use development around existing transit centers. RAFT's projections also assume that the scale of design and development will be suited to pedestrians. RAFT did not drop its growth projections below the 1995 limits set by the Association of Bay Area Governments within the thirty-four transit "superdistricts" defined by the Metropolitan Transportation Commission. In addition to public transportation, RAFT asked the commission to assume an increase in walking, bicycling and transit use in these denser pedestrian-oriented centers. This is an important nuance, since less dramatic or smaller-scale transportation improvements are frequently overlooked in regional scenarios.

CONTACT
Ellen Griffin
Associate Public Information Officer
Metropolitan Transportation Commission
Joseph P. Bort MetroCenter
101 Eighth Street
Oakland, CA 91607
(510) 464-7700

Albany, New York

The Capital District Transportation Committee in Albany, New York, used ISTEA funding as an incentive to spur creative local thinking in a relatively short time.[12] Unlike MTC, which is a well-staffed MPO with a high profile in a politically complex region, the Albany-based committee is smaller, and many of its planning and policy decisions have been more technically than politically oriented. The committee was challenged with creating public awareness and interest in its process from the ground up, while broadening the role of local planning officials in addressing public concerns about the environment and community character.

As the metropolitan planning organization for four counties, the committee conducts regional transportation planning for its 78 towns and cities, including Schenectady, Troy, and the state capital of Albany. The committee's 21 voting members represent local elected officials, regional and state transportation authorities, and the New York State Department of Transportation. Serving in an advisory capacity are the regional administrator for the Federal Transit Administration, and the division administrator for the Federal Highway Administration.

The committee's sixteen-member planning committee evaluates project applications submitted by sponsoring counties, municipalities, and agencies for the region's transportation improvement program (TIP). During the first programming cycle in 1992, the projects submitted by local governments did not represent the full range of activities eligible for federal funds. In an effort to push future project submissions and promote awareness among local governments of the broad flexibility contained in ISTEA, as well as to prepare the ground for an upcoming revision of the long-range regional plan, the committee rewrote its project selection criteria to respond to ISTEA's mandate.

The committee's transportation improvement program extends over a five-year period from 1993 through 1998. The long-range plan, revised in 1990, established many of the same goals included in ISTEA: increased emphasis on diversifying and coordinating transportation modes, renewed examination of bicycling as an important transportation option, broadened consideration of transportation's impact on land use and the environment, and consideration of the full social and economic costs and benefits of transportation options. The committee began revising the plan again in 1993 to create a comprehensive 25-year regional plan.

To increase the link between transportation and land-use decisions, the committee required the transportation improvement program to be consistent with local land-use plans. Projects to expand the road system must include commitments to maximize the roads' useful life through demand management and supplemental transit service. The committee's revision was aided by its long-established practice of analyzing the full costs and benefits of transportation proposals and working with municipalities to forecast the impacts of transportation on land use and vice versa.

The committee's approach to its transportation improvement program shares some characteristics with the Metropolitan Transportation Commission process in northern California. The committee used a set of initial screening criteria to assure the consistency of proposed projects with long-range planning, local boundaries, existing facilities, and "community desires as documented in local land use plans or other policy documents, at public meetings, or through other applicable means."[13] Each project also had to address at least one of the fifteen planning considerations outlined in Section 134 of ISTEA. Safety was added as a sixteenth consideration.

Practical considerations were also screened. Reasonable cost estimates, project scope and major facility needs had to be sufficiently described, but preliminary engineering was not required. A financial plan was required to show complete project funding, which could include existing sources and those expected to be in place by project implementation.

An additional requirement was among the most important in establishing a more ambitious atmosphere for future project proposals. In the initial screening phase, projects also had to demonstrate their eligibility for funds from the Surface Transportation Program or Congestion Mitigation and Air Quality Program funds, based on a list of thirteen eligible categories that the committee derived from the list of Transportation Control Measures in the Clean Air Act.

Projects that passed muster in the screening process were evaluated on the basis of their individual merit, judged by each proposal's potential to move people and goods while fulfilling the other goals of ISTEA for connecting transportation modes, enhancing the existing system, and meeting environmental goals. Where possible, the merit evaluation incorporated values that cut across transportation modes. The value of potential projects also was judged over their full life, which strengthened the cost-effectiveness of low-cost strategies and transit projects.

The committee's TIP process included qualitative criteria that favored projects benefiting communities and the environment. The committee also teamed up with project sponsors to ensure that all project benefits were enumerated, including those not readily quantified, such as the potential to remove traffic from local streets. Other qualitative considerations included safety benefits, savings in travel time, energy efficiency, and life cycle cost savings.

A unique feature of the process was the cost/benefit analysis, which added the following project impacts to more straightforward considerations:

- Congestion relief
- Air quality improvement
- Noise reduction
- Residential traffic impact
- Community and ecological disruption
- Access to public transportation
- Modal integration
- Alternative modes within the project
- Transportation system linkage
- Economic development goals
- Project specific benefits

Finally, all projects were evaluated jointly for their contribution to a balanced program addressing maintenance and management of existing transportation facilities, as well as improvements to those facilities where warranted.

The committee formally adopted its new transportation improvement program in March 1993. Compared with the 1991 TIP, which was devoted mostly to road work (over 70 percent of all funds went to bridges alone), the new TIP recommended a broader range of projects to maximize the efficiency of existing systems. Included are a Guaranteed Ride Home Program, an incentive program for employers to provide transportation alternatives to their employees, and a corridor management plan for integrating local land use and transportation along a major regional route.

The committee's new project selection process must be further refined in light of a new regional long-range planning process initiated in 1993. The committee has now turned its attention to strengthening the link between the long-range planning process and the transportaton improvement program, as well as improving two-way communication with the public. The committee will likely meet its first real test in future rounds when the mix of proposed projects is more ambitious and the public is truly involved in the process from the ground up. The initial process was successful in promoting new thinking among decision-makers, however, and it was an important proving ground for the more complex long-range planning process.

CONTACT
Kristina Younger
Senior Planner
Capital District Planning Committee
5 Computer Drive West
Albany, NY 12205
(518) 458-2161

Pittsburgh

In May of 1992 the Pittsburgh Regional Transportation Partnership, a group of sixty government, business, and community leaders, formed to help move the Pittsburgh region toward long-term integration of land-use and transportation decisions. The partnership was convened by the Southwestern Pennsylvania Regional Planning Commission, the metropolitan planning organization for a six-county region that includes the City of Pittsburgh. The partnership represents the most ambitious attempt by the planning commission to bring citizens, elected officials, and technical experts to the same table to discuss regional land-use and transportation needs.

The commission's board of elected and appointed officials represents six counties, the City of Pittsburgh, the Commonwealth of Pennsylvania, and the region's public transit agencies. Like the Metropolitan Transportation Commission in the San Francisco Bay Area, the commission has established traditional links with the communities it serves. It also had to institute basic changes to its structure and operations in order to accommodate the broad-based planning process called for by ISTEA.

One of the first changes instituted by the commission was to grant formal voting status for the Pittsburgh Port Authority, the city transit agency that had worked with the commission in a nonvoting capacity for many years. The Port Authority is now a recognized player and potential ally to the central city in the regional voting process.

The commission is also seeking ways to involve citizens more directly in its activities. Soon after ISTEA passed, the commission initiated a newsletter and began focusing increased attention to media relations and public information. Two newly created advisory committees provide the commission with directions and feedback on public education, as well as providing citizens with better access to the commission's work. The Public Relations Committee works with commission staff to help raise public awareness of the planning process, encourage public input into the plan, and assure the commission's consideration of public comments. A Citizens Advisory Panel was also created in the spring of 1993 to provide input on the full range of issues being examined in the planning process.

The commission is also working with local governments

to gather the views of citizens. For example, the commission and the Pittsburgh Planning Department co-sponsored a forum for the Working Group on Community Development, an established group of thirty public interest organizations with which the Planning Department routinely works. At the forum, the Working Group participated in setting up criteria for project selection, and recommending and ranking local projects for inclusion in the regional transportation improvement program. A subsequent formal presentation of these recommendations was made to the commission.

The commission's partnership is actually an amalgam of the two most important and broad-based advisory committees created by the commission after ISTEA's passage. A forty-member Transportation Plan Policy Committee is made up of senior representatives from the region's public, private, and nonprofit sectors. A twenty-member Transportation Plan Technical Committee includes planning and transportation agency directors throughout the region. The two committees combine to form the partnership, allowing civic and business leaders to work with technical experts on strategies for the region. The technical committee also serves as a link between the partnership and the commission's staff, advising them in a number of areas related to the long-range plan.

To focus its discussions, the Transportation Plan Policy Committee devised four possible land-use scenarios to consider as they set priorities for future spending. The regional plan is unlikely to be based on any one of these scenarios. Instead, they are research tools to allow the committee to group transportation priorities and policies and test their effects on air quality, traffic volume, land-development patterns, and other considerations mandated by ISTEA.

The following is a brief description of the four scenarios:

- *The Targeted Growth* scenario emphasizes minimal land consumption, reinforces Pittsburgh as the region's commercial hub, emphasizes redevelopment, and focuses new development where infrastructure already exists. Public transportation is favored over highways, and environmental preservation and reclamation are emphasized.

- *The Valley and Suburban Renaissance* scenario seeks to rebuild the distressed industrial communities lining the region's rivers and maximize the use of existing infrastructure.

- *The New Growth* scenario emphasizes new highway construction as a means toward economic growth. This scenario encourages industry to settle in sparsely developed areas of the region where inexpensive land is available and where building costs are low. Low-density housing and rural locations for shopping centers and office space are supported by this scenario.

- *The Radial Growth* scenario directs more transportation investment toward management and operations improvements on existing facilities. This option would reinvest in the region's existing system to improve traffic circulation. The assumption is that new economic growth would follow the alignment of existing roads and transit routes.

Although the partners agreed that land and funding are finite resources, there was less agreement on how land use should be approached. The members of the partnership did not reach agreement on land-use controls as a means of guiding growth and transportation decisions in the region. However, the commission succeeded in defining real land-use choices and demonstrated the mutual cause-and-effect relationship between land-use decisions and transportation options. It remains to be seen whether the new alliances now forming among citizens, business interests, and public officials will be successful in forging agreements on regional growth and transportation patterns.

CONTACT
Peter Longini
Communications Consultant

Southwestern Pennsylvania Regional Planning Commission
The Waterfront
200 First Avenue
Pittsburgh, PA 15222
(412) 391-5590

Institutional Changes at the State Level

This section looks at institutional changes, planning, and public participation initiatives in Georgia, Colorado, Connecticut, and Minnesota, where state bureaucracies are attempting to become more customer-oriented, open to change, and genuinely multimodal in orientation.

Georgia

The Georgia DOT is establishing a new public involvement process for both its statewide transportation improvement program and the statewide long-range planning process.[14] The Georgia DOT decided in 1993 to ask its intended audience to help shape the public participation process. The department set out to establish two-way communication for developing and carrying out a new public involvement program.

The agency began by listing the groups and individuals that ISTEA names for inclusion in the public involvement process:

> . . . citizens, affected public agencies, representatives of transportation agency employees, other affected employee representatives, private providers of transportation, and other interested parties with a reasonable opportunity to comment. . .[15]

After identifying groups in the state that satisfied each of these descriptions, the DOT invited representatives of those groups to a two-day retreat. Participants included environmental advocates, transit representatives, labor interests, utilities officials, port representatives, railroad interests, business leaders, planners, bicycle advocates, county officials, and disability and elderly advocates.

The retreat had two goals: to brief participants on the basic structure, ingredients, and development of the state's transportation improvement program, and to establish communication between the DOT and the varied groups in attendance. Once all participants understood the state TIP process, they were to help identify ways to involve the public at various points in its development process.

To put all parties on a more equal footing, the DOT engaged outside facilitators from nearby universities, rather than using staff members. Participants agreed to basic ground rules, such as reminders to participate, listen to and respect other opinions, stay away from personal attacks, and avoid acronyms and jargon. Participants were then asked for their suggestions for putting together the state's new public involvement process.

The participants at the retreat recommended that the state take several basic actions to involve the public. The first step was a series of regional meetings to educate the public and gain access to public opinions. The retreat participants pledged to assist by reaching out to their constituencies to persuade them to participate. The Georgia DOT would use the meetings as a local kick-off to the public participation process and an opportunity to provide the public with information on the TIP process and its relationship to the long-range transportation plan for the state. Each presentation would also offer the opportunity for comments and questions. Additionally, the DOT would provide contact persons within the agency to answer future questions.

Retreat participants also emphasized the importance of clear and understandable information, including visuals such as maps and other graphics, to illustrate the impacts of proposed alternatives on community and environmental resources. The state was also directed by the participants to establish a formal procedure for responding to the public's suggestions, taking action, and demonstrating the impact of public involvement, since proof of results was likely to stimulate further interaction.

An important team player in this process was the newly established Georgia Transportation Alliance (GTA), a coalition that comprises many interests from environmental activists to public utilities. Within Georgia, the alliance has become the key contact for organizations and individuals seeking information and access to the state planning process.

The retreat created an atmosphere of cooperation among private interests, public interests, and practitioners for the exchange of ideas and information. Participants also came to understand their shared goal of putting together a workable program that would serve the broad range of need. The DOT, by giving participants equal ownership very early in the process, also set in motion the dynamic of shared responsibilities, which becomes important when difficult trade-offs must be brokered toward the conclusion of a planning process.

In November 1993, the DOT extended this retreat approach to a two-day workshop with the state's metropolitan planning organizations and the Surface Transportation Policy Project in Columbus, Georgia. The agencies discussed the nature and structure of the state-regional partnership required by ISTEA, with special attention to public involvement. The workshop participants identified four groups of stakeholders in the transportation planning process: private industry, government agencies, advocates/activists, and the public. The participants specified categories and levels of involvement within these four groups, along with detailed recommendations for ways to increase their involvement.

Among the most interesting findings during this exercise was the distinction between "influence" and "involvement." Both industry and activists were identified as having a great deal of influence over transportation decisions through political, financial, or legal means, but low involvement through participation in decision making. If left unchecked, this situation would lead to inconsistencies between the process and its outcomes. Participants in the Georgia process have come to understand that the question of "outside" influence over their decisions is not a question of "if" but "when." The agencies are beginning to craft ways to include citizen and industry representatives early in the planning process.

CONTACT
Warren Williams
Georgia Transportation Alliance
75 Mike's Lane
Sharpsburg, GA 30277

Colorado

The Colorado Department of Transportation passed legislation in 1991 that anticipated many of the requirements of ISTEA. Colorado's state-required planning process is more specific than ISTEA regarding the mechanism for incorporating regional plans into the state plan. The statewide plan must be developed from a maximum of fifteen regional plans, five of which are the responsibility of the state's existing metropolitan planning organizations.

Soon after the law's passage, the Colorado DOT conducted more than two dozen public meetings and additional meetings with local governments to create fifteen Transportation Planning Regions (TPRs) based on perceived common transportation needs, including social and economic unity and the existence (or absence) of active intergovernmental relationships.

The law called on Colorado's five metropolitan planning organizations to develop partnerships with surrounding rural areas. Two of the MPOs agreed to plan for the rest of their counties to form single-county TPRs. In a third case, a large urban area was incorporated into an existing eight-county area, with the established transportation planning organization taking responsibility for all planning in that area. The two remaining MPOs will coordinate their planning processes with those of their surrounding multi-county areas.

The ten Transportation Planning Regions for less populated areas of the state consist of between two and ten counties. Each of these rural TPRs may form a Regional Planning Commission under the state law. The Colorado DOT does not require the regional plans, which are estimated to cost between $40,000 and $80,000, because the state legislature did not allocate funds to support regional planning. The DOT instead allocated a portion of state gas tax revenues and federal State Planning and Research funds for the development of the regional plans. Currently, the Regional Planning Commissions may contract with the state or a third party to carry out all or some of their regional planning.

The Colorado DOT has assigned a team of twenty planners to the regions on a geographic basis, providing the Regional Planning Commissions with consistent contact with the state agency. The DOT also has undertaken an extensive public participation process. Public forums are strategically timed at key junctures of the planning process to allow active citizen participation.

To assure fairness in funding allocations between urban and rural areas, a statewide Transportation Advisory Committee, composed of one member from each Transportation Planning Region, reviews the regional plans.

The state is also looking at ways to expand its existing public participation process. One approach under consideration is the expansion of annual meetings between local government leaders from each county with the State Transportation Commission. While these meetings are currently limited to discussions of highway projects, the idea is to expand the discussion to include all modes of transportation.

It is too early to tell whether Colorado will succeed in promoting cooperation among urban and rural communities. However, the passage of the state transportation planning law six months before ISTEA was enacted put Colorado ahead of other states in implementing ISTEA. The specificity of the state planning requirement allowed the state DOT to structure its planning process early enough so that it can focus on other issues, such as developing better information on which to base decisions and expanding public access to the process.

CONTACT
Bill Stringfellow
Statewide Planning Unit
Colorado Department of Transportation
4201 East Arkansas Avenue
Denver, CO 80222
(303) 757-9226

Connecticut

In 1992, public interest groups contested the findings of an environmental impact study conducted by the Connecticut Department of Transportation (ConnDOT) for the proposed construction of either an expanded or a new 10-lane bridge across New Haven Harbor on Interstate 95.[16] The Quinnipiac Bridge (Q-Bridge) is a six-lane bridge built in 1958, which currently serves traffic volumes far exceeding those for which it was originally designed.

The November 1991 draft environmental impact statement identified essentially only three alternatives, all of which expanded road capacity along the corridor. A transit or transportation system management alternative was also assumed to be included in all of the alternatives.

The following were the three initial alternatives identified in the draft EIS:

- Widen the existing bridge
- Build a new structure south of the existing bridge
- Build a new structure north of the existing bridge[17]

Several environmental groups, among them the Connecticut Fund for the Environment, filed comments opposing the three alternatives. This action compelled ConnDOT to consider a wider range of alternatives and to open up public discussion of the proposed construction. ConnDOT responded by establishing an Intermodal Concept Development Committee to develop public consensus on alternatives.

In December 1992, more than two dozen groups representing environmental, small business, historic preservation, transportation, neighborhood, and construction interests (see List D in the chapter appendix) met with ConnDOT to begin considering alternatives to the bridge proposal. The purpose was to reach agreement on a "structurally reliable and operationally safe transportation system and . . . to address *as prudently and feasibly as can be achieved*, the needed capacity and access to accommodate travelers."[18] (emphasis is the author's) The study was also meant to focus on "mechanisms which will discourage the use of the single occupant auto as the preferred means of traveling to and from work."[19]

By May 1993, the group had assembled 150 ideas for accommodating travelers along the proposed route. A series of open houses was held to air these ideas. The list was narrowed to 11 construction alternatives for further consideration, plus the alternative of rehabilitating the existing bridge without building or reconstructing additional facilities:

- *No-build/rehabilitate the existing bridge* at a cost of $86 million. The land use, social, economic, and cultural resources impacts would be minimal, traffic would be highly congested for approximately 5 hours each day, and transit ridership would be about 2,600 persons each week.

- *Construct new five-lane bridge to the north of the existing bridge* at a cost of between $486 and 497 million. The proposal would have significant land use, social, economic, and cultural resources impacts. Traffic congestion would decrease to about 1 hour each day. Despite transportation system management strategies such as improved marketing and scheduling, transit use would dramatically decrease to 1,747 persons each week.

- *Construct new five-lane bridge to the south of the existing bridge* at a cost of between $462 and 469 million. The impacts of this project are similar to those of the previous alternative.

- *Construct the previous alternative with the capacity to add a second deck in the future*, at a cost of between $484 and 487 million. The impacts of this project are similar to those of the second alternative.

- *Widen existing Q-bridge to eight lanes* at a cost of $268 million. Except for projected transit ridership increases to about 3,200 persons each week, the impacts of this proposal are similar to those of the second, third, and fourth alternatives.

- *Replace existing bridge with new 10-lane bridge* at a cost of between $514 and 536 million. Again, the impacts are similar to those predicted for the second, third, and fourth alternatives (including the dramatic decrease in transit users).

- *Construct new double-deck bridge to the south of the existing bridge* at a cost of between $569 and 582 million. Again, the impacts are similar to those predicted for the second, third, and fourth alternatives (including the dramatic decrease in transit users).

- *Develop a light rail system connecting communities on both sides of the harbor* at a cost of between $339 and 431 million. The rail line would cross the harbor via the nearby Tomlinson Bridge, and the Q-bridge would be rehabilitated to remain at its existing six lanes. In addition, this alternative incorporates a wide range of incentives to coax people into taking transit, and disincentives for them to drive alone, including congestion pricing for bridge traffic of between two and eight dollars, voluntary flextime, preferential parking for High Occupancy Vehicles, an auto insurance rebate of $40 for HOV/transit users, and deeply discounted transit fares. These incentives and disincentives would result in three to six times the transit ridership projected for the "No-build" alternative, and "extensive" but unspecified impacts to residential and commercial land use in the area of the new rail corridor, as well as slight impacts on farmland in the area.

- *Rehabilitate the existing Q-bridge and institute a wide range of incentives to take transit and disincentives to drive alone,* including a possible High Occupancy Vehicle lane at a cost of between $232 and 254 million. This alternative would about double the projected transit ridership for the "No-build" alternative. The land use, social, and natural resources impacts would be limited.

- *Construct a Rapid Bus Transit System (RBTS) along the same route suggested for light rail* at a cost of $288 to $313 million. This alternative included the strongest set of incentives to take transit and disincentives to drive, including mandatory flextime for nearby employers, mandatory preferential parking for High Occupancy Vehicles, an auto insurance rebate of $80 for HOV/transit users, deeply discounted transit fares, and congestion pricing for bridge traffic of between two and eight dollars. These measures would result in transit use increases of between three and five times those projected in the "No-build" alternative.

- *Rehabilitate the existing Q-Bridge, including a High Occupancy Vehicle lane and a wide range of strong incentives and disincentives to encourage transit use* at a cost of $264 million. Transit ridership would more than double over the "No-build" alternative.

- *Construct a new eight-lane bridge south of the existing Q-Bridge, including a High Occupancy Vehicle lane and a wide range of strong incentives and disincentives to encourage transit use* at a cost of between $350 and 353 million. This alternative would not quite double the transit ridership projected for the "No-build" alternative.[20]

At this writing, the committee has begun to develop criteria for screening the alternatives. The screening process is to address traffic and transportation performance, interpreted in terms of the following criteria:

- How well the proposed alternative meets the needs of local traffic as well as through traffic;
- Structural engineering quality from an aesthetic as well as safety perspective;
- Engineering considerations;
- Environmental impacts, interpreted broadly to include social and economic considerations;
- Costs; and
- Feasibility for implementation and enforcement of incentive/control measures.[21]

In addition to this project-specific approach to resolving conflicts with the public, ConnDOT is now working with the Connecticut Fund for the Environment to draft guidelines for the state's public involvement procedures under ISTEA.

CONTACT
Michael Stern or Curtis Johnson
Connecticut Fund for the Environment
1032 Chapel Street, Fourth Floor
New Haven, CT 06106
(203) 524-1639

Minnesota

The Minnesota DOT (MnDOT) undertook two separate but parallel processes to bring citizens and local officials into transportation planning.[22] First, the Strategic Management Process involves reforming management practices to create a more publicly responsive agency. Second, the Process for Transportation Investment Decisions is the agency's effort to broaden the scope of transportation policy to accommodate shared decision making between local and state agencies, public participation, and preservation of existing facilities. Each process has resulted in new approaches that could inform one another, although the processes are administered separately within the DOT and with varied degrees of success.

The Strategic Management Process was designed to be conducted by "outsiders" brought in as MnDOT staff from the private sector. The outside staffers led a series of eight regional dialogues between June and September 1992 to develop goals and recommendations for the agency. Two-thirds of the participants at each of these dialogues were citizens, and each meeting was hosted by a committee that represented a community cross-section of leaders from various disciplines and interests, including teachers, local officials, business owners, farmers, and human services professionals. To compile a balanced invitation list, the regional host committee used a matrix identifying more than thirty transportation-related issue areas. The first cut was then adjusted for gender balance, geographic balance, and public/private balance.

The eight dialogues resulted in a vision for the future of Minnesota in which collaborative efforts on the part of government, business, and citizens effectively utilize resources, technology, labor, communications, and funds in ways that benefit Minnesotans without penalizing others outside the state. Many of the findings of the Strategic Management Process have been incorporated into the agency's ISTEA implementation and its day-to-day workings. For example, the Strategic Management Committee at MnDOT has formulated three focus areas of strategic goals for implementation:

- Increase the focus on the customer;

- Seek new information and allow new thinking about cutting-edge technological advances; and

- Increase funding flexibility for all modes of transportation.

According to interviews with MnDOT's staff and citizen watchdog groups, top management tends to be more committed to the Strategic Management Process than the agency's 150 mid-level managers are. However, the new strategies are gradually being folded into the department through decisions by the Strategic Management Committee, allocation changes in the agency's budget, and internal directives and specific tasks assigned by top managers to mid-level managers.

The agency's second initiative, the Process for Transportation Investment Decisions, seeks to integrate transportation planning with other important state and regional planning efforts, including those for environmental protection and energy use, and addresses all modes of transportation. Public access at the preliminary stage of the process was primarily through state and local elected officials and the findings of the regional dialogues during the Strategic Management Process. In addition, while the investment decision concept was in development, MnDOT presented it to a variety of groups, including chambers of commerce, metropolitan planning organizations, regional development commissions, and public interest groups.

Based on comments from the public, and local and regional agencies, MnDOT created Areawide Transportation Partnerships as a mechanism for promoting regional cooperation in selecting projects and improving relationships between state and local interests. Each partnership is responsible for assembling a regional transportation improvement program listing proposed projects and activities in its region for a two-year period. The regional TIP must reflect the ten decision-making principles developed by MnDOT to carry out the planning process:

- Decisions will result from comprehensive planning and meaningful involvement of local, regional, and state stakeholders;

- All transportation modes should be included in planning;

- Major transportation investments and funding sources will be considered for priority transportation needs within multi-county geographic regions;

- Statewide principles on transportation investments emphasize preservation and management of existing systems over capital improvements;

- As a beginning for development of a transportation investment program, reasonable "target" funding levels can be identified on a geographic regional basis;

- Some minimum funding guarantees for geographic areas or programs will exist: Transportation Management Areas (areas of 200,000 or more population), rural, safety, enhancement, Congestion Mitigation and Air Quality program;

- MnDOT will work with local elected officials to recommend regional transportation investment priorities;

- Balanced investment decisions should first promote effective and efficient transportation with subsequent consideration of equity (transit/highway, state/local, passenger/freight, rural/urban, geographic, and intermodal);

- All eligible stakeholders will have access to the planning and investment decision process; and

- All eligible proposals will be evaluated fairly.

The investment decision process already has succeeded in forging new partnerships among state and regional agencies, including public transit agencies, and elected officials at all levels of government. This interagency cooperation proved helpful when MnDOT was required to carry out specific short-range tasks, such as establishing the state's enhancements program and contributing its proposed designations to the National Highway System. The establishment of interagency relationships helped MnDOT to achieve consensus on such initiatives in a short time.

Whether Minnesota's new process succeeds over the long term will hinge on its commitment to educate and involve citizens. MnDOT's decision to give citizens indirect access to long-range planning through their state and local officials means that the public's views are subjected to the interpretation of city, county, and regional agencies with differing agendas and points of view. Such fragmentation presents less of a problem if MnDOT continues to improve upon its public outreach through meetings and dialogues with civic, public interest, and business groups.

Citizens have more access to the project selection and implementation stage of decisions, but the delay in direct public access may weaken citizens' ability to contribute constructive suggestions, based on the first of the ten principles established by MnDOT, that "decisions will result from comprehensive planning and meaningful involvement of local, regional and state stakeholders."

Contact

Process for Transportation Investment Decisions
Jon A. Bloom
Director, Highway and Area Planning
Minnesota Department of Transportation
395 John Ireland Boulevard, Room 807
St. Paul, MN 55155
(612) 296-1635

Strategic Management Process
Barbara Nelson, Director
Nan Swift, Manager
Office of Strategic Initiatives
Minnesota Department of Transportation
117 University Avenue, Room 222
St. Paul, MN 55155
(612) 297-7860 or
(612) 296-8602

Trends in Planning

After the first thirty months, the most consistent ISTEA successes have been in the reform of processes which consider a wider range of factors than ever before. Transportation agencies have still favored the investment of federal funds in new projects, rather than investment in activities or maintenance to improve existing facilities. Most state DOTs are still failing to take full advantage of their flexibility to invest in alternatives to roads. And for every citizen group that has organized as an effective participant in the transportation planning process, there are many more communities in which ISTEA is an almost unheard-of acronym.

ISTEA is scheduled for reauthorization in 1997. By then we will know with greater certainty whether its impacts have significantly shaped and nurtured American communities. In the meantime, the rest of this book will consider in further detail the ways in which ISTEA can work toward more balanced and sustainable transportation systems.

Appendix

List A. The Virginia Surface Transportation Coalition Steering Committee

The American Lung Association, Virginia Chapter

The Bicycle Federation of Virginia

The Cedar Creek Foundation

The Chesapeake Bay Foundation

The City of Richmond, Department of Transportation Planning

The Clifton Forge Main Street Program

The Conservation Fund/American Greenways

The Council of Virginia Archaeologists

Moving People, a local citizens group in Northern Virginia

The Preservation Alliance of Virginia

The Valentine Museum of the City of Richmond

The Virginia Downtown Development Association

The York County Planning Office

List B. The Chattahoochee-Flint Heritage Highway Steering Committee Convened by the Chattahoochee-Flint Regional Development Center

The Boutique

Bulloch House Restaurant

City of Warm Springs

Cotton Pickin' Fairs

COWETA CARES

Coweta County Planner

Georgia Conservancy

Georgia Department of Industry, Trade and Tourism

Georgia Transportation Alliance

Grantville Historic Preservation Commission

Hogansville Historic Preservation Commission

Hotel Warm Springs

LaGrange-Troupe County Chamber of Commerce

Little White House Historic Site

Mansions and Magnolias, Inc.

Meriwether County Chamber of Commerce

Meriwether County Historical Society

Nana's Porch

New Forum

Newman City Planner

Newman Main Street

Newman Times-Herald

Newman-Coweta Chamber of Commerce

Newman-Coweta Historical Society

Sacks Route 1

Train Cars

Troup County Historic Preservation Commission

Troup County Planning Commission

Trudy's Corner

Victorian Tea Room

Warm Springs Merchant Association

Warm Springs National Fish Hatchery

Warm Springs Village Mall

The Wind Spinner

List C. Supporters of the Gwynns Falls Greenway Initiative

Baltimore Bicycling Club, Inc.

Baltimore Chesapeake Bay Outward Bound

Baltimore City Department of Planning

Baltimore City Department of Recreation and Parks

Baltimore Refuse Energy Systems Co.

Baltimore Orioles

B & O Railroad Museum

Carrie Murray Outdoor Education Center

Carroll Improvement Association

Carroll Park Restoration Foundation, Inc.

Chesapeake Bay Foundation

Citizens Planning and Housing Association Resource Center for Neighborhoods

Communities Organized to Improve Life (COIL)

Concerned Citizens for a Better Brooklyn

Edmondson Village Community Association

Federal Hill Neighborhood Association

Franklintown Road Improvement Association

Franklintown Land Trust

Friends of Gwynns Falls/Leakin Park

Friends of Maryland's Olmsted Parks & Landscapes, Inc.

Girls United to Save the Environment (GUTSE)

Greater Baltimore Environmental Center

Greater Mill Hill St. Benedicts Housing Council

Gwynns Falls Community Association

Harbor Hospital Center

Hollins Market Neighborhood Association

Hunting Ridge Community Assembly

Kernan Hospital

Maryland Citizen Areas Commission

Maryland Conservation Council

Maryland Department of Transportation

Maryland Environmental Trust

Maryland Greenways Commission

Maryland Science Center

Mayor's Gwynns Falls Greenway Task Force

Mayor's Task Force on Tourism

McHenry-Franklintown Improvement Association

Mill Hill Improvement Association, Inc.

Morrell Park Community Association

Mt. Clare in Carroll Park

National Park Service/Rivers, Trails and Conservation Programs

Neighborhood Design Center

Pigtown/Washington Village Improvement Association

The Parks and People Foundation

Rosemont Neighborhood Association

Save Our Streams

Shipley Hill Improvement Association

South Westem Baltimore Police District

South Baltimore Improvement Association

Southern Baltimore Police District

Trust for Public Land

Union Square Community Association

Westport Improvement Association, Inc.

Windsor Hills Neighborhoods

Yale University Urban Resources Initiative

List D. Interstate-95 New Haven Harbor Crossing Intermodal Concept Development Committee

The Alliance for Architecture

Annex Business Association

Central Long Island Sound Council

City of New Haven

City of New Haven, Parks and Recreation Department

City of West Haven

City Point Action Group

Coalition Organizing for Sound Transportation

Connecticut Construction Industries Association

Connecticut Fund for the Environment

Connecticut Motor Club, AAA

Connecticut Trust for Historic Preservation

Connecticut River Estuary Regional Planning Agency

The Honorable Chris DePino, State Representative

Forbes Area Residential and Commercial Association

Greater New Haven Chamber of Commerce

Highway Users Foundation

Hill Neighborhood Development Corporation

Historic Wooster Square Association

Motor Transport Association of Connecticut, Inc.

New Haven Land Trust, Inc.

New Haven Preservation Trust

Quinnipiac River Watershed Association

Rideworks of Greater New Haven

Schooner, Inc.

Sierra Club

South Central Regional Council of Governments

Town of East Haven

Vietnam Veteran Memorial Committee

Notes

1. This and subsequent information on Maine's implementation of its Sensible Transportation Act are drawn from "Maine's New Rules: Open Rulemaking Process Results in Common-Sense Policy," (Washington, DC: *STPP Resource Guide*, July 1993).
2. *Maine Sensible Transportation Act*, 1991.
3. The information in this section was gleaned by the author through personal interviews with David Brown, President of the Preservation Alliance of Virginia and 1993 Chairman of the Virginia Surface Transportation Coalition, February 1994.
4. The information in this section was derived from "The Washington Regional Network: Citizens Plan for the Future," by Lisa Wormser, (Washington, DC: *STPP Resource Guide*, August 1993).
5. Metropolitan Washington Council of Governments, "A Legacy of Excellence for the Washington Region: Task Force Report on Growth and Transportation," (Washington, D.C.: WASH-COG, June 1991).
6. Joseph Foote, "A New Approach" (Washington, DC: Washington Regional Network for Livable Communities, 1993).
7. The information about the Chattahoochee-Flint Heritage Highway in this section is from "A Heritage Highway with a Future," by Julie Turner, (Washington, DC: *STPP Bulletin*, Volume IV, Number 2, March 1994).
8. This information is from "Greenway Gets a Green Light," by Christopher Rogers and Jennifer Greene, Trust for Public Land (Washington, DC: *STPP Resource Guide*, July 1993).
9. Information in this section is derived from "Bay Area Partnership Pays Off," by Jake Pearce and Lisa Wormser (Washington, DC: *STPP Resource Guide*, March 1993).
10. Quote from MTC's *Transactions* newsletter (Oakland: MTC, February 1993).
11. Intermodal Surface Transportation Efficiency Act, Section 134(g)(2).
12. Information about the Capital District Transportation Committee and Pittsburgh Regional Transportation Partnership was derived from "Regions Respond to Change," by Lisa Wormser (Washington, DC: *STPP Resource Guide*, July 1993).
13. Capital District Planning Commission, 1993–1998 Transportation Improvement Program, Albany, New York, adopted March 23, 1993.
14. The source of this information is an unpublished summary of the Georgia public involvement process, written by Christopher Bender, Surface Transportation Policy Project, February 1994.
15. Intermodal Surface Transportation Efficiency Act, Section 135, as codified in 23 CFR Chapter I, Part 450, Section 212 (Washington, DC: *Federal Register*, Volume 58, Number 207, October 28, 1993). Page 58067.
16. The information in this section was provided by the Connecticut Fund for the Environment.
17. Connecticut Department of Transportation, "Draft Environmental Impact Statement on the New Haven Crossing," November 1991.
18. Connecticut Department of Transportation, information update to the Intermodal Concept Development Committee on the New Haven Crossing, January 1994.
19. Ibid.
20. Ibid.
21. Connecticut Department of Transportation, Report of the

Meeting of the Intermodal Concept Development Committee, January 1993.
22. The information in this section was derived from "States Respond to Change" by Jenny Wilson and Lisa Wormser (Washington, DC: *STPP Resource Guide,* August 1993).

9

Public Involvement in the Transportation Planning Process

ISTEA's planning requirements direct federal and state departments of transportation and metropolitan planning organizations to "provide citizens, affected public agencies, representatives of transportation agency employees, private providers of transportation, and other interested parties with a reasonable opportunity to comment"[1] on transportation plans and programs. Federal law imposes a responsibility to make transportation planning more democratic and provides an opportunity to increase the congruence between transportation investments and community travel needs. (See the two lists in the chapter appendix for detailed public involvement requirements.)

The metropolitan planning organizations must involve the public during the initial planning of their twenty-year long-range plans and the development and approval of their three-year transportation improvement programs. States must carry out their long-range plans in cooperation with the MPOs and give citizens "a reasonable opportunity to comment" when the state long-range plan is being developed. In addition, governors are directed to ensure that citizens are involved in developing the state TIP. At both levels, planning must be coordinated with the development of plans for attainment of national air quality standards.

The regulations governing ISTEA planning, which were

released in October 1993 by the Federal Highway Administration and the Federal Transit Administration, substantially expand on ISTEA's public participation requirement with the goal of "informed and involved citizens who have access to public records and the decisionmaking process."[2] Sections 450.212(a) and 450.316(b) of the new regulations address specific requirements for public involvement in ISTEA, stressing the need for agencies to establish processes that are "proactive and provide complete information, timely public notice, full public access to key decisions, and opportunities for early and continuing involvement."[3] The regulations also stress the need to involve the participants in a public process for defining the nature and parameters of citizen participation.

Some states and metropolitan planning organizations have been creatively involved in expansive contact and communication with community groups for years. But others may find the notion of soliciting views from the public on plans and processes new and vaguely ominous. Fortunately, a variety of new approaches are available to better integrate public participation into agency decision making.

Going Beyond Traditional Practices

Public participation requirements have long been established in laws such as the Administrative Procedures Act and the National Environmental Policy Act, as well as regulations and guidance issued by federal and state transportation agencies. However, meeting the minimum standards set in such laws has not resulted in collaboration and partnerships between transportation agencies and citizens.

The phrase *public participation* may conjure up memories of numbing meetings, during which dozens of people line up before microphones to complain to officials about proposed projects or programs. But this is not the only possible scenario. Neither transportation officials nor citizens are pleased when public participation is reduced to a procession of gripes and pleas falling on deaf ears. The main value of a public hearing is as a safety valve at the end of a long and complicated process, which must include many different chances for two-way communication. Public hearings are almost always insufficient to cull good ideas, answer questions, sift through possible alternatives, and explain the reasoning behind projects, plans, or programs.

Working with new partners is something entirely different. "Working" implies an ongoing, interactive, iterative connection. "Partners" are participants with comparable status and equal legitimacy. The old paradigm was that transportation engineers and officials invite "outsiders"—the public—to hear about decisions made by the "experts." The new paradigm establishes transportation decisions as the product of collaborative work by partners. It is the result of debate and choices made jointly by a variety of governmental and nongovernmental parties.

Transportation is so basic that average people, "nonexperts," have strong views on their travel needs, how well those needs are being met, and the impacts of transportation on other aspects of their lives. Any planning process that excludes affected people, limits their input, or fails to provide the necessary information in readily understandable terms will not be effective, no matter how technically defensible are the products.

The broad scope of fundamental issues to be resolved under ISTEA and the Clean Air Act Amendments makes it unlikely that any single or generically determined approach to public participation will meet all ends. However, it is possible to identify the characteristics of successful participation: inclusiveness, early involvement, and clear, accurate information.

Inclusiveness

The "appropriateness" of public participation is to be measured by the inclusiveness of the process, i.e., whether it involves the range of people whose interests are affected. One can begin by rounding up the usual list: state transportation officials, metropolitan planning organizations, local elected officials, and public and private transportation providers. Others affected by transportation decisions are environmental groups, developers, business leaders—especially large employers—transportation users (including the disabled, aged, or young), design professionals, and community organizations. No abstract definition will do to identify everyone who uses or may use a transportation system or be affected by it.

Involving the public means pinpointing and building on the strengths that various individuals and organizations bring to the planning process. This means identifying and addressing their specific interests, skills, values, and degrees of commitment to a the process. For example, some participants will have no background in engineering or design but know of specific community needs that may otherwise be overlooked by planners or transportation professionals. Some people may have innovative suggestions for investments that could serve multiple goals (such as day care centers at transit nodes), but they may benefit from the advice and experience of others to refine and implement the ideas. The more limited the participation in the process, the more impoverished will be the proposals that result, and the less solid will be the popular support for these proposals.

Early Involvement

The earlier there is a concerted outreach, the greater are the prospects for its success. Attempts at public participation that occur late in the game often generate hostility and may result in stalled projects. By requiring that citizens and others with an interest in transportation be involved in developing transportation plans and programs, ISTEA sets the stage for early participation. In this context, a "reasonable opportunity to comment" must be defined in terms of the public's ability to help shape the earliest drafts of the long-range plan and the transportation improvement program, where specific projects are selected. This change in the law marks a departure from the old practice of soliciting public comment just prior to approval of a draft plan or assembled slate of projects.

Accessible Information

To accomplish the goal of inclusiveness, information is vital. Many citizens are discouraged by the lack of basic information about how and why transportation decisions are made in their communities. Citizens whose "participation" has been ignored grow wary of further involvement. Agency professionals are equally fearful that the public will impede their efforts to solve growing transportation problems. Wide availability of clear, accurate, and complete information on transportation procedures can help put both parties on a more equal and cooperative footing.

Effective information should exceed the traditional graphs and charts that accompany studies. Citizens should be helped to visualize the impacts of plans and proposals on neighborhoods, businesses, and the natural environment. This visualization can be accomplished by the use of maps, models, slides, photographs, computer graphics, and other techniques that portray the potential effects of transportation decisions.

The public needs access to reports, statistics, and proposals in sufficient time to review the material carefully and form a response. Time must be allowed for their reactions to be incorporated into the process. This last step is crucial. No one wants to waste their time thoroughly reviewing and addressing a complex issue only to find that their work has no influence on the decisions. If there are delays in the production of useful background information, other deadlines must be relaxed to grant citizens the time to study and respond to the issue.

It is important not to hide the context assumed by transportation officials when they develop transportation plans. Many community values and goals may be controversial. But if transportation is to serve those values and goals, they must be articulated. Attempts to skirt controversy may lead to misunderstanding and resistance.

Many people care about regional development patterns, transportation options, and the consequences these have for employment, economic growth, air quality, liveable communities, and other values. Almost certainly people will disagree about which goals should be dominant and which means will best serve the goals. What is more, no one can be sure of the consequences of even the best-studied plans. Most people will distrust any pretense that transportation investments are value-neutral and promote everyone's interests equally. Honest dialogue and disagreement may be more constructive than efforts to avoid underlying assumptions about how jobs, urban design, environment, and transportation are affected.

Pulling It All Together

There is no cookbook for successful partnerships between public officials and citizens. Community involvement must be tailored to the community and the issues. The greater the diversity of the interested participants, the greater the controversy and hence the more necessary are a range of approaches.

Nevertheless, here are ten of the ingredients, if not the recipe, for success.

Task Forces

Task forces that reflect the diversity of a community can be convened to address a discrete, short-term issue or ongoing, complex transportation planning.

Task forces seem to work best when their scope is relatively narrow and well defined. Two successful task forces convened by the Metropolitan Transportation Commission in the San Francisco Bay Area demonstrate the importance of narrowing the focus. One of the task forces proposed and evaluated transportation control measures for the commission's consideration. The other meets on a regular basis to discuss the transportation needs of communities of color.

Many participants who served on these two task forces found the experience to be a positive one. Genuine education as well as communication took place. However, it was unclear to one participant whether the enhanced understanding shared by task force participants was relayed to decision makers, particularly those with the greatest authority.

Another potential problem was excessive compartmentalization. Interaction between task forces was often limited or nonexistent. For example, people of color probably have useful and unique insights into designing and evaluating Transportation Control Measures (TCMs), but that opportunity for interactive learning will not occur if, for example, a minority task force operates in isolation from one on managing transportation controls and incentives.

Committees

A common tool for public involvement is the establishment of committees. Citizens' advisory committees and technical advisory committees are two basic types. Dividing groups according to expertise or technical skills may initially ease communication, but it may also result in reduced innovation and education. Some transportation committees are therefore a mix of citizens, business representatives, planners, transportation professionals, and advocates for particular transportation modes (bicycles, rail, transit, trucks). The challenge is to braid the skills and experiences of the various participants in a way that results in creative solutions.

Many communities have used the committee approach

to increase public involvement in transportation decisions. Local professionals and citizen observers suggest that such efforts result in greater respect for the process and more cohesive support for the ultimate decisions. Even when the final outcome is controversial, broad participation helps prevent the high level of dissatisfaction that may lead to legal challenge and stalemate.

In Boston, for example, in 1972—long before the Central Artery/Tunnel project described in Chapter 4—the residents of several neighborhoods united to protest the construction of the Southwest Freeway, an interstate segment for which land was already purchased. Through the efforts of city and state representatives, the governor of Massachusetts commissioned a multidisciplinary team to examine alternatives. The team recommended a new subway line that would follow the same route as the existing Amtrak and commuter rail lines and unite three adjacent inner city neighborhoods via a greenway of parks, sidewalks, and bikeways along the subway route. The process was determined and overseen by a citizens' advisory group of residents, business owners, transit officials, and representatives of the City of Boston.

Public Meetings or Forums

Public meetings or forums may be a good way to solicit ideas and discuss transportation alternatives and goals when plans are at an early stage of development. Open forums may include presentations from officials and citizen groups, as well as invitations to discussion and debate.

One of the major difficulties is to encourage ongoing attendance by diverse individuals and groups. Often, open meetings are intimidating to the public and transportation officials. The latter are sometimes fearful that they will be the targets of blame or vituperative remarks. Citizens sometimes worry that their remarks will be ridiculed, or they will be unable to penetrate the jargon of the experts.

Holding useful meetings is a skill. Civility should be expected of all participants, but agreement should not. Fortunately, respectful treatment of people usually generates polite and respectful responses. Officials need to be ready to hear criticism, but they should establish a positive, constructive tone when responding. They should try to avoid defensive reactions.

Successful meetings depend on airing concerns as well as providing solutions. Public officials should try to avoid promoting a particular outcome—which should be easier if meetings are held early in the process of framing alternatives.

Sometimes negotiation training or sessions in alternative dispute resolution are useful prior to embarking on an ambitious series of public meetings. Both transportation officials and interested public participants should take part. The public will benefit from the intended result—an atmosphere in which people are candid and open to new ideas.

It is also important to encourage wide-ranging discussion at meetings or forums that can be folded back into the traditional planning process. If ideas and suggestions are lost or forgotten once the meeting is adjourned, there is a distinct likelihood that the public will perceive such meetings as a sham and waste of time. Follow-up is essential.

Panel Presentations, Symposia, and Interactive Workshops, Including "Charettes"

Public participation in transportation decisions can be increased through workshops, presentations, and debates. These events can cover a wide range of topics, but they are most useful if tied to issues that have special relevance to the city or region where the discussion takes place.

Such gatherings can be highly technical. They are, obviously, more useful to a broad range of the public if panelists refrain from the use of acronyms and jargon (or at least provide translations for such terms when they do crop up). Topics that may merit technical treatment might include the ways that transportation can reduce air emissions, the techniques for using transportation investments to induce or reduce travel, and the factors to make public transit more attractive, reliable, and usable.

Another model for public inclusion is a team effort called a *charette*. The term is derived from an intensive, collaborative exercise of architects, when operating under deadline pressure, to design a project. A charette was formed during discussion of the I-90 Mountains-to-Sound Greenway project for the Puget Sound region in the State of Washington (see Chapter 6). The purpose was to allow diverse interests to discuss development patterns and transportation alternatives in a cooperative spirit. Although a charette requires a substantial commitment of resources from participants, such an approach fosters consultation and trust while eliciting innovative and collaborative solutions.

Facilitators, Mediators, and Alternative Dispute Resolution Techniques

Facilitation and other alternative dispute resolution techniques may help aid in creating a positive atmosphere for cooperation and problem solving, particularly when a region is embroiled in a controversy over transportation. Experienced, neutral facilitators and mediators often can establish basic ground rules; reduce the tendency of participants to interrupt, ridicule, or intimidate other participants; and encourage speakers to explain confusing or seemingly inconsistent statements. As neutral parties, facilitators may be able to guide discussions to include a greater variety of views and help enable all parties to feel that their insights are being heard. Facilitated meetings can often take less time to result in more productive decisions than meetings that are less structured.

Formal dispute resolution techniques, including regulatory negotiations ("Reg-Negs") such as those described in the Maine case example in Chapter 8, have been used at the federal and state levels to distill complex legal and political issues into alternatives that integrate the concerns of the affected parties. Participants in the Reg-Neg process can include environmentalists, developers, transportation officials, and community organizations—many of whom may otherwise polarize debate over the initiative.

Agency-Initiated Outreach

Metropolitan planning organizations and state transportation agencies may wish to invite members of the public or representatives of groups to events and meetings to increase rapport and understanding. Many agencies also develop a mailing list of people interested in the region's transportation issues and regularly send out notices of upcoming events. Newsletters, updates, and bulletins can be targeted to people who have attended previous meetings, called to request information on transportation planning processes, or been involved in community activities that indicate an interest in transportation alternatives.

Public Education Campaigns

Partnerships can be heightened by innovative education campaigns, which may selectively use public service announcements, advertising, the news media, posters, talk shows, and educational television and radio programming. Campaigns can be developed around current transportation problems, transportation solutions, or policy options.

Regions with air pollution problems, for instance, may want to develop an information campaign on the effects of certain transportation practices on air quality. An example of a possible focus could be the importance of trip-chaining to reduce "cold-start" emissions from vehicles. Practical tips on ride sharing or public transportation services can be presented in ads or public service announcements, as cities such as Seattle and Denver are doing. Ongoing efforts to encourage higher rates of vehicle occupancy can provide the basis for a shift in public attitudes about solo driving of the magnitude experienced over the last decade with recycling.

Public Opinion Surveys, Interviews, Focus Groups, Polls

Polling and related techniques are ways to find out what people need and want. Surveys, interviews, focus groups, and polls are ways to gather opinions on transportation services, alternatives, and potential improvements. The benefit of surveys or polls is the opportunity to reach a wide audience at relatively low cost. But designing surveys is an art: A survey or poll will be useless if it asks unintentionally or deliberately loaded questions, fails to provide room for "none of the above" answers and unstructured feedback, or otherwise stifles honest response and unbiased results.

Focus groups are another way to involve various points of view. In Bethel, Maine, a town with a population of 5,000, citizens were catalyzed into a planning process when one of the area's chief employers, National Testing Laboratory, announced its plans to relocate due in part to land-use conflicts. The town convened twenty-seven focus groups representing interests that ranged from loggers to environmentalists, ski resort owners and innkeepers to crafts people and musicians, and old-timers to summer people. A six-week planning process resulted in a workable plan. An unexpected bonus was the laboratory's decision to remain in the area because of the successful resolution of the conflicts that had motivated it to consider relocation.

Competitions

Some cities have held competitions to reward people whose projects or suggestions promise to improve the use of public transportation or reduce single-occupancy travel. Competitions can be held, for example, to select the best proposal for an educational campaign to increase transit ridership through public service announcements. In addition to a monetary prize, the reward could include broadcasting the winning advertisement on radio or television.

Technical Support

Community groups may be granted funding for assistance to enable them to refine a transportation proposal in a technically sophisticated manner. The federal Superfund law provides grants so that community groups can hire an expert who can help analyze and evaluate hazardous waste clean-up proposals. Transportation plans also involve technically complex issues, and decisions may sometimes benefit from the inclusion of independent experts who can help explain and evaluate alternatives. Community groups may be much more informed and engaged if they can rely on technical advice from a respected consultant, whom they see as serving their interests.

Technical support can also be provided by assigning transportation agency staff to assist in the development of ideas generated by the public. For example, in Tallahassee, Florida, a state bicycle and pedestrian office helps refine citizen-generated proposals for expanding opportunities for non-motorized transportation.

Summary

ISTEA's regulations confirm the need for transportation agencies to develop programs for the early and continued involvement of a well-informed and diverse public. The law's regulations call for citizens to participate in shaping and selecting methods for their own involvement in planning. The law also emphasizes the two-way dialogue necessary for agencies to include and address public concerns in the final decisions. Particularly encouraging is the emphasis on proactive efforts to include those "traditionally underserved by existing transportation systems, such as low-income and minority households which may face challenges accessing employment and other amenities."[4]

Many questions remain, however. The regulations specify a forty-five-day comment period in the case of public involvement plans and a thirty-day comment period for metropolitan transportation plans in areas with nonattainment status for National Ambient Air Quality Standards. Apart from these stipulations, the regulations are not specific.

The regulations also call for periodic review of public involvement processes at the regional, state, and federal levels. Although the regulations acknowledge that public involvement is fundamental to state and regional planning processes, specific criteria for assessing public involvement are not included.

Overall, the expanded public involvement process in ISTEA's regulations may be viewed as a strengthened opportunity rather than as a mandate for specific steps to be taken toward more effective involvement of citizens in transportation investment decisions. Ultimately, it is up to the residents and business leaders of a community to determine how best to become involved in and educated on the complex issues surrounding transportation's role in their lives. The challenge will be for agencies to embrace this opportunity with clear, specific methods for addressing public concerns, while remaining flexible and open to new approaches.

Appendix
Public Participation in State Planning

Section 450.212(a) of the regulations issued October 28, 1993 by the FHWA and FTA states, "Public involvement processes shall be proactive and provide complete information, timely public notice, full public access to key decisions, and opportunities for early and continuing involvement." The processes shall provide for:

(1) Early and continuing public involvement opportunities throughout the transportation planning and programming process;

(2) Timely information about transportation issues and processes to citizens, affected public agencies, representatives of transportation agency employees, private providers of transportation, other interested parties and segments of the community affected by transportation plans, programs, and projects;

(3) Reasonable public access to technical and policy information used in the development of the plan and state transportation improvement program;

(4) Adequate public notice of public involvement activities and time for public review and comment at key decision points, including but not limited to action on the plan and STIP;

(5) A process for demonstrating explicit consideration and response to public input during the planning and program development process;

(6) A process for seeking out and considering the needs of those traditionally underserved by existing transportation systems, such as low-income and minority households that may face challenges accessing employment and other amenities;

(7) Periodic review of the effectiveness of the public involvement process to ensure that the process provides full and open access to all and revision of the process as necessary.

Within metropolitan areas, if the state department of transportation and the metropolitan planning agency agree, metropolitan public involvement activities may satisfy the state planning requirements for that area.

Public Participation in Metropolitan Planning

Section 450.316(b) of the regulations issued October 28, 1993 by the FHWA and FTA states, "The metropolitan transportation planning process shall . . . include a proactive public involvement process that provides complete information, timely public notice, full public access to key decisions, and supports early and continuing involvement of the public in developing plans and TIPs and meets the requirements and criteria specified as follows:

(1) Require a minimum public comment period of 45 days before the public involvement process is initially adopted or revised;

(2) Provide timely information about transportation issues and processes to citizens, affected public agencies, representatives of transportation agency employees, private providers of transportation, other interested parties and segments of the community affected by transportation plans, programs and projects (including but not limited to central city and other local jurisdictional concerns);

(3) Provide reasonable public access to technical and policy information used in the development of plans and TIPs and open public meetings where matters related to the Federal-aid highway and transit programs are being considered;

(4) Require adequate public notice of public involvement activities and time for public review and comment at key decision points, including but not limited to approval of plans and TIPs (in nonattainment areas classified as serious and above, the comment period shall be at least 30 days for the plan, TIP and major amendments);

(5) Demonstrate explicit consideration and response to public input received during the planning and program development processes;

(6) Seek out and consider the needs of those traditionally underserved by existing transportation systems, such as low-income and minority households which may face challenges accessing employment and other amenities;

(7) When significant written and oral comments are received on the draft transportation plan or TIP (including the financial plan) as a result of the public involvement process or the interagency consultation process required under U.S. EPA's conformity regulations, a summary, analysis and report on the disposition of comments shall be made part of the final plan and TIP;

(8) If the final transportation plan or TIP differs significantly from the one which was made available for public comment by the MPO and raises new material issues which interested parties could not reasonably have foreseen from the public involvement efforts, an additional opportunity for public comment on the revised plan or TIP shall be made available;

(9) Public involvement processes shall be periodically reviewed by the MPO in terms of their effectiveness in assuring that the process provides full and open access to all;

(10) These procedures will be reviewed by the FHWA and the FTA during certification reviews for Transportation Management Areas (urbanized areas with population over 200,000), and as otherwise necessary for all MPOs, to assure that full and open access is provided to MPO decisionmaking processes;

(11) Metropolitan public involvement processes shall be coordinated with statewide public involvement processes wherever possible to enhance public consideration of the issues, plans and programs and reduce redundancies and costs."

Notes

1. 23 Code of Federal Regulations, Chapter I, Part 450, Section 212 (Washington, DC: *Federal Register*, Volume 58, Number 207, October 28, 1993). Page 58067.
2. 23 CFR, Chapter I, 450.212(a) and 450.316(b). Pages 58067 and 58072.
3. Ibid.
4. 23 CFR, Chapter I, 450.212(a) and 450.316(b). Pages 58067 and 58072.

10

Definitions of Enhancement Activities

Several provisions in ISTEA recognize the link between transportation decisions and the preservation and enhancement of significant natural and cultural resources. One of the most important of these new provisions is contained in the Surface Transportation Program, where ten types of activities are defined as "transportation enhancements." (See Chapter 1, page 17.) Ten percent of STP funds must be set aside for these enhancements to ensure a dedicated minimum source of revenue for important but often overlooked activities that fall outside the category of routinely undertaken scenic, historic, and environmental programs.

ISTEA includes a detailed list of enhancements, a list that is definitive, not illustrative. In correspondence issued April 24, 1992, the Federal Highway Administration (FHWA) states, "The Congress included language on transportation enhancements as a means of stimulating *additional* efforts in the activities listed." (The emphasis is the agency's.) The correspondence also states, "Several field offices have asked whether the list of activities . . . is exclusive or illustrative. It is exclusive."[1]

Transportation enhancements must be considered in metropolitan and state plans and programs. This requirement links enhancements directly to the attainment of the social, environmental, and economic goals that must be set and met by the planning process. At the metropolitan level, enhancement activities must be reflected in a city's twenty-year long-range plan and three-year transportation improvement program. At the state level, the TIP must reflect priorities for programming and spending enhancement funds. Because states must incorporate metropolitan plans and programs into their long-range plans, decisions and funding priorities for enhancements must also be reflected in state long-range plans.

As indicated in Chapter 1, transportation enhancements are defined by ISTEA as follows:

> ...with respect to any project or the area to be served by the project, provision of facilities for pedestrians and bicycles, acquisition of scenic easements and scenic or historic sites, scenic or historic highway programs, landscaping and other scenic beautification, historic preservation, rehabilitation and operation of historic transportation buildings, structures or facilities (including historic railroad facilities, and canals), preservation of abandoned railway corridors (including conversion and use thereof for pedestrian and bicycle trails), control and removal of outdoor advertising, archaeological planning and research, and mitigation of water pollution due to highway runoff.[2]

According to the FHWA, funds for enhancements are derived from several sources, the primary one being the Surface Transportation Program. Ten percent of Surface Transportation Program funds are available only for transportation enhancement activities. Additional funds from funding categories that are part of apportionment adjustment to the states are also available only for enhancements. However, the amount of funds from sources other than STP are not very significant.

ISTEA excludes from eligibility for enhancements any routine or customary elements of transportation projects, or activities to mitigate project impacts in compliance with existing environmental, historic preservation, and public health and safety regulations. However, determining what constitutes "routine" versus what constitutes "additional" or "special" activity is not always easy. Many states are already struggling with this question, and not every state will arrive at precisely the same answer. The FHWA provides some guidance when it states that "many projects are a mix of elements, some on the list and some not. The project elements which are on the list may be counted as transportation enhancement activities."[3]

As a general rule, it may be understood that activities already required under ISTEA or another federal law such as the Environmental Policy Act may not be interpreted to be enhancement activities, but the enhancement portion of a larger project involving routine activity is eligible for enhancement funds.

In determining eligibility for enhancements funding, the phrase "with respect to any project, or any area served by the project" has prompted debate on how to define the "area served." The FHWA interprets the phrase to mean that a proposed enhancement activity must have "a direct relationship to the intermodal transportation system, but not necessarily to a currently planned highway project." As previously mentioned, FHWA suggests three tests for eligibility: function, proximity, and impact. If a proposed project has a functional relationship to an existing or planned transportation facility, it is actually part of that facility. A bikeway is an example of a functional relationship. A proposed enhancement may also be related through proximity. Removal of illegal billboards in the viewshed of a scenic highway is a proximity relationship. Finally, if the proposed enhancement has an impact on an existing or planned transportation facility, it is eligible for funding. If constructing a system of pedestrian ways reduces auto use in an area, that is an impact-related enhancement.

To be considered eligible as an enhancement, a proposed activity need pass only one of these tests. Once the relationship of the proposed enhancement activity to a transportation facility is established, it makes no difference whether additional work is proposed on the facility itself. The FHWA states:

> The proposed enhancement activity must have a direct relationship to the intermodal transportation system, but not necessarily to a currently planned highway project.... Once a relationship to the intermodal transportation system is established, transportation enhancement activities can be ... developed as parts of larger transportation projects, as parts of larger joint development projects, or as stand-alone projects.[4]

Eligible activities may include land acquisition and construction as well as preliminary architectural and engineering services, related design functions, or preliminary archaeological and historical research.

The Americans with Disabilities Act of 1990 directs that the needs of elderly and disabled persons be integrated into all projects involving public access, not only those involving federal funds. All transportation enhancements projects, particularly those involving pedestrian access, should be responsive to this federal requirement.

The Role of Enhancements in Transportation Planning

The FHWA states in its guidance,

> The metropolitan and statewide planning processes should occupy a central role in the identification, planning, and funding of transportation enhancement activities.... To be funded, transportation enhancement activities must be included in the appropriate metropolitan and statewide transportation improvement programs.[5]

In preparing the long-range plans called for by ISTEA, metropolitan planning organizations must, at a minimum, propose appropriate enhancement activities.[6] Because states must include enhancements as part of their three-year transportation improvement programs, they should also consider enhancements during their long-range planning. They must address several factors, such as tourism and land use, that are directly linked to enhancement decisions. States and metropolitan planning organizations must develop separate long-range plans for bicycle and pedestrian facilities, and such plans are to be incorporated into the overall long-range plans, as called for in Section 135(e). Metropolitan planning organizations must include other types of enhancements as well.

The FHWA also recommends that, "given the widespread public interest in transportation enhancement activities, they should be highlighted in public involvement activities implemented under new metropolitan and statewide planning requirements."[7] States must actively invite public participation in the early stages of the transportation planning process in addition to the current practice of soliciting public comment during the approval stage of projects. The FHWA and the Federal Transit Administration directed states to establish or modify public involvement processes by October 1, 1992 to allow this greater involvement.[8]

In the area of project development, the FHWA has directed state DOTs, MPOs, and FHWA field offices to be aggressive in pursuing enhancement opportunities as part of overall projects. Future environmental approvals should take into account the potential to implement enhancement activities. Other state agencies, local agencies, and private entities may be brought into the development of proposed activities, but the responsibility for the project remains with the state DOT.

An important factor in the success of any planning process is the ability to track and account for the expenditure of funds and the result of public investment. The FHWA has alerted state DOTs that they will be required to track and report on expenditures of their transportation funds, including those spent on enhancements. This kind of accountability can also be an effective mechanism for the public to monitor their local and state agencies' performance on specific areas of transportation decision making, including new programs such as enhancements.

Guidelines for Determining Eligibility for Enhancements Funding

The Surface Transportation Policy Project recommends the following guidelines for determining a project's eligibility under one or more of the ten categories of enhancements.

Bicycle and Pedestrian Facilities

The category, "provision of facilities for bicycles and pedestrians," includes providing facilities in conjunction with a new or proposed transportation project or improving existing transportation beyond what is necessary for safe accommodation of bicyclists and pedestrians.

Safe accommodation should be given full consideration during the design, development, and construction of all federally aided transportation projects. Such facilities are eligible for National Highway System and Surface Transportation Program funds. For new construction and reconstruction projects, routine provisions for bicyclists and pedestrians, such as sidewalks, curb ramps, wide curb lanes, and shoulders on rural roads, are not considered to be enhancements.

Improved bicycle and pedestrian access to existing facilities is important to the development of effective intermodal transportation and is encouraged. When improvements for bicycle and pedestrian access are independent of new construction or rehabilitation projects, activities such as widening curb lanes, striping bike lanes, adding road shoulders, installing sidewalks and crosswalks, and enhancing access to public transportation are considered enhancements.

In addition, expenditures for mitigation required by ISTEA and other federal laws are not eligible for funding under this category under any circumstances.

Scenic and Historic Sites

"Acquisition of scenic easements and scenic or historic sites" includes the use of funds for purchase, donation, transfer, or trade of land that possesses significant aesthetic, natural, visual, or open space values, including acquisition of any property listed in or eligible for listing in the National Register of Historic Places.

Funds may be used for planning and construction costs such as appraisals, surveys, legal costs, or purchase costs. In order to remain eligible for these funds, state DOTs should agree to enforce appropriate mechanisms to preserve significant scenic and historic values.

"Scenic or historic highway programs" include funds for the protection and enhancement of state or federally designated scenic or historic highways. Funds may be used only for projects that will protect and enhance the scenic, historic, cultural, natural, and archaeological integrity and visitor appreciation of an existing highway and adjacent area. Funds may also be used for the planning, design, and development of new state scenic byway programs. Projects designed to protect and enhance the integrity of existing designated highways and adjacent areas should be reviewed by professionals qualified to evaluate scenic, historic, cultural, natural, and archaeological values.

Funds provided under this category are supplementary to those provided under the Scenic Byways Program in Section 1047 of ISTEA.

Eligible projects should not include the construction of safety rest areas, although if a rest area project includes an activity eligible for enhancements funds, that activity is eligible. The FHWA's guidance states:

...a rest area might include a historic site purchased and developed as an interpretive site illustrating local history. The historic site purchase and development would qualify as a transportation enhancement activity.[9]

Adding lanes for any purpose or constructing new scenic or historic highways should also be considered as ineligible, in keeping with ISTEA's significant disincentives to adding lanes or building roads where not warranted by demand and the law's inclusion of language allowing the waiver of federal design standards for scenic and historic roads and byways.

Landscaping and Scenic Beautification

"Landscaping and other scenic beautification" includes landscape planning, design, and construction projects that enhance the aesthetic or ecological resources along highways, other transportation corridors, points of access, and lands in proximity to other transportation enhancement projects. Funds should not be used for routine, incidental, or maintenance activities such as grass cutting, tree pruning and removal, soil stabilization, construction of noise barriers, drainage improvements, and post-construction finish work, such as replanting and reseeding. Seeding and planting vegetation for erosion control or screening purposes should not be considered as an eligible landscaping enhancement project.

Projects that enhance the attractiveness of a transportation facility include planning, design, and construction of scenic vistas and overlooks, restoration of historic landscapes, and construction of landscapes that are compatible with their surroundings. Projects that enhance the ecological balance along a transportation corridor include planning, testing, and planting for restoration or reintroduction of native plant communities and appropriate adaptive species. Activities associated with interpreting sites and providing information about the programs for preserving resources are also eligible for funds.

Funds should be used only for projects consistent with the state's overall landscape policies and programs. Funds may also be used to hire professionals qualified to evaluate the design concept of a proposed activity. No funds should be used to remove trees unless an approved site plan calls for such removal on the grounds of scenic or ecological enhancement or unless a tree is diseased or dead as certified by a qualified professional.

Historic Preservation

"Historic preservation" includes identification, evaluation, documentation, curation, acquisition, protection, management, rehabilitation, interpretation, restoration, stabilization, and maintenance of any historic district, site, structure, object, or landscape included in or eligible for inclusion on the National Register of Historic Places. The objective of activities in this category should be to improve the ability of the public to appreciate the historic significance of the project itself or the area to be served by the project.

Expenditures are not eligible under this category if required by Section 4(f) of the Department of Transportation Act of 1966 (49 USC 303) or Section 138 of Title 23 or if they may be conducted in order to avoid or mitigate the effect of a project on any historic place pursuant to 16 USC 470(f) or its implementing regulations.

Historic Transportation Buildings, Facilities, and Structures

"Historic transportation buildings" are buildings or related structures that are associated with the operation, use, construction, or maintenance of any mode of transportation and that are listed in the National Register of Historic Places or are eligible for listing.

"Structures and facilities" include tunnels, bridges, trestles, embankments, rails or other guideways, nonoperational vehicles, canal viaducts, towpaths and locks, stations, and other built transportation features related to the operation, use, construction, or maintenance of any mode of transportation. Both freight and passenger facilities are eligible.

Another term mentioned in this category, "rehabilitation," refers to the process of returning the property to a state that makes a contemporary use possible while preserving the significant historic features of that property. "Operation" refers to the provision of access to the public and service in a manner related to the continuation of a contemporary transportation or nontransportation use consistent with the historic character of the property.

"Rail corridors" are transportation corridors of varying width in which rail tracks exist or have existed in the past. "Abandoned railway corridors" are rail corridors that have been authorized for abandonment by the Interstate Commerce Commission, rail corridors for which abandonment proceedings are pending before the Interstate Commerce Commission, or rail corridors that have been set aside for future transportation use (i.e., "rail banked') under any applicable federal or state authority. Such corridors include all fee (full title owned) and less-than-fee (partially owned) corridor holdings. Passenger and freight facilities are both eligible.

The preservation of abandoned railway corridors includes planning, acquisition, rehabilitation, and development of corridors for public uses, including bicycle and pedestrian use. This provision permits the development and rehabilitation of privately owned rail corridors open to the public without charge.

Control and Removal of Outdoor Advertising

"Control and removal of outdoor advertising" refers to existing signs, displays, and devices, which is an addition to the requirement to exercise "effective control" of outdoor advertising under Section 131 of Title 23. Only in unusual circumstances should expenditures for removal of nonconforming billboards be considered eligible, since such removal is a function of maintaining "effective control" and is otherwise funded under Section 104 of Title 23.

Expenditures shall be made according to a legal process that bases payment on an equitable appraisal. Priority should be given to the removal of outdoor advertising signs, displays, and devices on scenic roads, areas where local or state laws or ordinances ban new billboards, and cases that occur in conjunction with other transportation enhancement projects.

In using funds under this category for the control of outdoor advertising signs, states may use funds to provide additional resources to ensure that new outdoor advertising is permitted only in areas actually used for commercial and industrial purposes. Included is compilation of an accurate inventory of existing conforming signs.

Archaeological Planning and Research

"Archaeological planning and research" includes but is not limited to research on sites eligible for transportation enhancement funds; experimental projects in archaeological site preservation and interpretation; planning to improve the identification, evaluation, and treatment of archaeological sites; problem-oriented synthesis using data derived from transportation-related archaeological projects, though not limited to such projects; development of national and regional research designs to guide future surveys, data recovery, and synthetic research; and projects having similar purposes carried out in partnership with other federal, state, local, and tribal government agencies and nongovernmental organizations.

Expenditures under this category should be used for research and/or interpretation of sites associated with transportation facilities.

Expenditures are not eligible under this category if required by Section 138 of Title 23 and Section 303 of Title 49 in order to avoid or mitigate the effect of a project on any historic place pursuant to 16 USC 470(f) or its implementing regulations or if they involve the requirements of the Archaeological Resources Protection Act and the Archaeological Conservation Act. Funds may be expended for the inventory of known resources in project areas, reconnaissance surveys where resources are likely to occur, and evaluation of the significance of individual sites for inclusion in the National Register of Historic Places.

Mitigation of Water Pollution Due to Highway Runoff

"Mitigation of water pollution due to highway runoff" is limited to facilities and programs that minimize pollution from stormwater runoff from transportation facilities. Eligible facilities and program must be additions to current requirements and procedures for such mitigation. Projects that demonstrate aesthetic and ecological methods for mitigation and enhance recharge are eligible.

Conclusion

The enhancements provision illustrates the wholly new direction for transportation policy that ISTEA represents. By linking transportation plans, programs, and projects to the goals of preserving community quality and protecting the environment and defining a broader role for citizens in meeting those goals, the successful implementation of enhancements provision will have an impact on the overall success of the new law.

The broad popular support already stimulated by the transportation enhancements provision is advantageous to the whole concept of public involvement and broader planning of transportation for long-term social, environmental, and economic goals. Enhancements are a key to unlocking public enthusiasm not only for individual projects, but also for participation in the entire planning process.

Notes

1. Memorandum from Anthony Kane, Associate Administrator for Program Development to Regional Federal Highway Administrators and Federal Lands Highway Program Administrators on the subject of Transportation Enhancement Activities (April 24, 1992), page 1.
2. 23 USC 101 (a).
3. Memorandum from Anthony Kane, Associate Administrator for Program Development to Regional Federal Highway Administrators and Federal Lands Highway Program Administrators on the subject of Transportation Enhancement Activities (April 24, 1992), page 2.
4. Memorandum form Anthony Kane, Associate Administrator for Program Development to Regional Federal Highway Administrators and Federal Lands Highway Program Administrators on the subject of Transportation Enhancement Activities (April 24, 1992), page 2.
5. Memorandum from Anthony Kane, Associate Administrator for Program Development to Regional Federal Highway Administrators and Federal Lands Highway Program Administrators on the subject of Transportation Enhancement Activities (April 24, 1992), page 3.
6. 23 USC 134 (g)(2)
7. Memorandum from Anthony Kane, Associate Administrator for Program Development to Regional Federal Highway Administrators and Federal Lands Highway Program Administrators on the subject of Transportation Enhancement Activities (April 24, 1992), page 3.
8. Joint Interim Guidance on statewide planning issued May 28, 1992.
9. Memorandum from Anthony Kane, Associate Administrator for Program Development to Regional Federal Highway Administrators and Federal Lands Highway Program Administrators on the subject of Transportation Enhancement Activities (April 24, 1992), page 2.

11

Metropolitan Planning Requirements

The primary planning provisions of ISTEA are found in Sections 134 and 135 of ISTEA, which pertain to metropolitan and state transportation planning, respectively. ISTEA strengthens the previous federal requirement for comprehensiveness in transportation planning by specifying consideration of social, economic, and environmental factors and their use as the basis for selecting projects (See the two lists in the chapter appendix for details on the factors to be considered.) ISTEA also requires financial planning in the development of a transportation improvement program and incorporation of a bicycle and pedestrian plan into both the metropolitan and state transportation plans. Finally, ISTEA mandates consistency with the requirements of the Clean Air Act. The financial and air quality planning requirements of ISTEA are dealt with in the following chapter.

For regional planning, Section 134 of ISTEA lists fifteen factors that metropolitan planning organizations must consider. States must consider twenty-three items during the state planning process, as required by Section 135(c) and amended by the regulations governing ISTEA planning that were issued by the federal government on October 28, 1993. Many of the requirements imposed on MPOs and DOTs are the same, but each has specific requirements as well. The collective effect is to make transportation planning more comprehensive. The requirements reassert the primacy of policy, reinforce the link between planning and policy, and establish broader relationships between transportation planning and other functional planning, such as planning for air quality and land use.

Creating the Conditions for Effective Planning

Strengthening the planning process as called for by ISTEA will require a number of federal, state, regional, and local actions. The following are the four most important.

First, the U.S. DOT must strictly enforce its requirement to certify that transportation planning processes comply with federal law. The federal requirement that transportation planning be comprehensive was first put into law thirty years ago. The Federal-Aid Highway Act of 1962 required that transportation projects in urbanized areas be based on a "continuing, comprehensive transportation planning process carried out cooperatively by states and local communities," the so-called 3C process.[1]

In the early years of federal involvement in transportation planning, compliance with substantive and process requirements was periodically certified by the U.S. DOT. In 1981, the process was changed to allow metropolitan planning organizations to self-certify their compliance with federal regulations.

Despite the fact that the federal requirement has been in force for many years, not all metropolitan transportation planning processes are comprehensive. Although a number of MPOs have been thorough in examining the relationships of transportation to other societal and environmental considerations, others have given such relationships uneven or inadequate attention. Self-certification removed the federal oversight that would assure adequate attention to all the issues.

ISTEA reinstates the requirement for federal certification. Subsection 134(i)(5) instructs the secretary of the U.S. DOT to assure that MPOs in urbanized areas with a population of more than 200,000 carry out their responsibilities under federal law, such as addressing the list of requirements that are included in the planning process. The ISTEA regulations stop short of assigning an aggressive role to the federal government in certifying MPOs.

The Federal Highway Administration and Federal Transit Administration have indicated plans to issue interim guidance to clarify the certification process. The ISTEA regulations call for a "discretionary certification process"[2] to encourage rather than require MPOs to demonstrate rigorous planning or public involvement processes as a means to being re-certified. The FHWA and FTA did include language to specify that MPOs and states must explicitly consider and analyze each of the planning factors set forth in ISTEA.

The FHWA and FTA also decided to allow conditional certifications when MPOs have not yet altered their planning processes to comply with ISTEA. This aggravates the mixed signals that MPOs are receiving about the urgency of committing staff and resources to reforming their planning procedures.

MPOs and DOTs must also invest adequate resources—both funds and staff—to carry out the added work called for by ISTEA. Many MPOs, particularly those in small and medium-sized metropolitan areas, lack sufficient staff and resources to devote to transportation planning. This is a particular problem in locations where transportation decisions traditionally have been made at some other level of government. Although funds have been available for state planning under previous transportation law, statewide transportation planning has never been required, and some state DOTs have considered the only purpose of planning to be the development of a capital improvement program.

ISTEA will help strengthen the role of comprehensive planning through the added funding it authorizes for planning.

These funds can support additional staff and expanded planning activities. But the funds will make a difference only if MPOs and state DOTs use them to hire the necessary staff and undertake the required work.

The planning process itself must also change to address the new planning factors, partnerships, and strengthened public involvement in ISTEA. MPOs and state DOTs must expand the planning process to bring in new participants, address environmental concerns, locate private funds for transportation projects, and provide for freight shipping and public transit services. Public agencies such as those with responsibility for environmental planning and regulation must be involved in the planning process. Private companies that develop or operate parts of the transportation system also need better representation. Public interest groups concerned with clean air, bicycle and pedestrian transportation, and urban development must have input in state and metropolitan plans. Broader inclusion of participants may require reconsideration of MPO board structure and voting powers and revision of the organization of advisory committees at the state and regional levels.

The ISTEA planning regulations clearly define the metropolitan planning organization as "the forum for cooperative transportation decisionmaking for an urbanized area."[3] The ISTEA regulations include new language to emphasize the need for states and metropolitan areas to collaborate in carrying out their planning processes. The role of tribal governments in transportation planning is also strengthened under ISTEA.

The regulations also substantially strengthen and clarify the public involvement process under ISTEA. Among other refinements, the regulations state that the basic approach and philosophy behind public involvement is that the planning process is open to all and should provide anyone who wishes to participate the opportunity to do so. Importantly, as mentioned in the previous chapter, state and metropolitan agencies must "seek out and consider the needs of those traditionally underserved by existing transportation systems, including but not limited to low-income and minority households."[4]

The FHWA and FTA also state in Section 450.212 of the regulation that "it is up to the participating parties [in the planning process] to define a process which provides the opportunity for participation for the interested parties,"[5] including both the private and public sectors.

Finally, regional and state agencies must develop adequate technical methods for carrying out the new requirements. Some of the procedures to be considered are new, and others are stated in new ways. These methods require types of analysis that have not been widely performed in the past.

The planning factors discussed in the following sections are divided into two types: procedural and specific. Procedural factors change the planning process itself, while specific factors require consideration of specific subjects or development of specific methodologies for analyzing decisions and impacts.

Metropolitan Planning—Procedural Factors

The numbers in parentheses in the following discussion are paragraph numbers in Subsection 134(f) of ISTEA.[6]

The most basic of the metropolitan factors requires the process to address the overall social, economic, energy, and environmental effects (13) of transportation decisions. Addressing this factor will require each metropolitan planning organization to adopt explicit policies defining the values that will guide transportation decisions in that metropolitan area. The planning process must then address these policies. In a sense, the other factors are all means to addressing this one.

A second procedural factor requires consideration of the effect of transportation decisions on land use (4) and the consistency between transportation and land-use plans.

Traditionally, transportation planning begins with the present land-use pattern or a postulated future one and identifies the resulting transportation needs and effects. The new requirement calls for analyzing the reverse relationship, i.e., a recognition that land-use patterns are not given but rather are at least partially the result of the accessibility created by the transportation system. Achieving a region's desired land-use pattern therefore requires transportation decisions that support that pattern. Analyzing the land-use effects of transportation is a difficult and complex task; present attempts are general and rely on inexact methods. Improving the ability to address this factor calls for new planning techniques.

One effect of the requirement to consider the consistency of transportation planning with federal, state, and local energy goals (2) will be emphasis on the need for such goals to be defined. But a more important effect will be to make energy consumption a decision criterion, along with cost and the other values that determine the best transportation solution.

Another basic requirement is to preserve existing facilities (1) and meet transportation needs by using those facilities more efficiently. No longer can the solution to a given transportation problem be presumed to require the construction of new facilities. Instead, the planning process must seek to improve the performance of existing facilities. Planning must be more than the development of a capital improvement program. The process must also include transportation system management strategies that increase the usefulness of the existing system and transportation demand management strategies that reduce the number of trips the system must accommodate. Low-cost improvements, ride sharing, pricing, and encouragement of transit use must be integral to the process. Although such strategies have been formally required since 1975 and have been applied in many areas, this requirement strengthens their ability to command serious attention.

The general scope of the planning process is defined by the requirement to consider all projects in the metropolitan area, including those not publicly funded. This will require assessment of all types of transportation system changes, no matter who sponsors them. Typically, the planning process now addresses projects developed with federal and state funds. Those projects that use exclusively local funds—county or city—are not always included. Privately funded projects, including such transportation system elements as freight railroads, freight terminals, intercity bus stations, and parking facilities, are often ignored. Considering those projects in the planning process will assure their incorporation into the overall transportation system.

The factor requiring consideration of six state-developed management systems (9) will change the intergovernmental nature of the planning process. Section 303 of ISTEA requires that states develop management systems for highway pavement of federal-aid highways, bridges on and off federal-aid highways, highway safety, traffic congestion, public transportation facilities and equipment, and intermodal facilities and systems. States are to develop and implement these systems in metropolitan areas in cooperation with MPOs. To assure that the management systems adequately reflect responsibilities for both planning and implementation, new means of state-local cooperation must be established.

Metropolitan Planning—Specific Factors

Specific factors define subjects and methodologies that the planning process must include. Some specific factors will cause major change; others are relatively simple additions. Some are already included in the planning process in many metropolitan areas.

The need to relieve congestion and prevent congestion from occurring where it does not now exist (3) focuses the planning process on system performance rather than facility construction. This factor requires not only planning for the construction of new facilities but also the application of transportation system management and transportation demand management techniques. Addressing this factor requires the same approach as does the procedural factor requiring efficient use of existing facilities.

Related to the focus on efficient use of facilities is the factor calling for the preservation of rights-of-way (10). This factor acknowledges that existing rights-of-way can be less expensive than newly created ones, as well as less disruptive to natural ecosystems and established communities. Addressing this factor will require that all transportation modes be considered and that presently used rights-of-way and those not now used for transportation be considered.

The requirement to consider life-cycle costs (12) is a significant change for some types of projects. This requirement ensures that investment decisions take into account not just the initial capital costs of a facility, but also the operation and maintenance costs during the period the facility will be in use. In some cases, those costs can be substantial and, if properly recognized, could change the identification of the most cost-effective solution to a given problem.

The factor that calls for the programming of Section 133 transportation enhancement projects (5) ensures that these types of projects receive adequate attention in the metropolitan planning process. This requirement is further strengthened by the requirement in Subsection 134(g) that enhancement activities be addressed in each region's long-range plan.

A separate section in ISTEA recognizes the importance of bicycle and pedestrian facilities as a mode of transportation and requires that they be incorporated into regional and state plans. Section 217(g) requires that an overall metropolitan bicycle and pedestrian plan be incorporated by the MPO into the regional long-range plan.

The requirement to consider the efficient movement of freight (11) introduces a new subject for analysis in many areas. Typically, planners assume that if the roadway network functions as it should, it will serve freight movement as well as passenger transportation. This assumption ignores the differences between the two in terms of needs and usage patterns. It also ignores the rail, water, and air modes of freight movement, as well as the importance of intermodal trans-shipment points. Addressing this factor will require many areas to undertake studies on movement of goods.

Two factors relate to the connectivity of the transportation system. One specifies a number of locations to be considered, including ports, recreation areas, and military installations (7). The other requires consideration of the connectivity between roads within and outside the metropolitan area (8). Both of these factors will require that studies of facilities in the vicinity of the identified locations give attention to the issues of access and system continuity. Where particular problems exist, specific studies may need to be undertaken to address this factor.

Methods to expand and enhance transit services and increase their use (14) are already addressed in many metropolitan areas. The significance of this item's inclusion in the list of fifteen factors lies in the increased importance of transit as intrinsic to the planning process in those areas where it is not now adequately considered.

Probably the most detailed of the required factors is that for investments to increase security in transit systems (15). This factor can be addressed through individual studies of security problems in those metropolitan areas where this is a concern.

State Planning—Procedural Factors

The greatest significance in the requirements for state planning is that they exist at all, since this is the first federal mandate for statewide transportation planning. Most of the requirements for the state planning process are similar to those for the metropolitan planning process, with some differences and a few additions reflecting the roles of state DOTs. More of the factors are procedural for the state simply because the state process is new.

Numbers in parentheses in the following discussion are paragraph numbers in Subsection 135(c) of ISTEA.[7]

The requirements that shape the state planning process are the same as those for metropolitan areas: requirements for considering the overall social, economic, energy, and environmental effects of transportation decisions (11); efficient use of existing facilities (10); effects of transportation decisions upon land use (14); and energy goals (2).

Intergovernmental relationships are more broadly expressed from the state perspective than from the metropolitan perspective. States must consider the transportation needs identified through the use of the six management systems (15) that in metropolitan areas must be developed in cooperation with MPOs. But states are also subject to three additional items affecting how they relate to their municipal jurisdictions. One calls for states to consider any plan developed under Section 134 for metropolitan areas (6). The second addresses nonmetropolitan areas and instructs states to consider the transportation needs of those areas through a process that includes consultation with local elected officials with jurisdiction over transportation (5). These requirements will ensure that as states establish their planning processes, they will give particular attention to establishing effective intergovernmental mechanisms, and planning processes will be coordinated with those of local governments.

ISTEA also requires coordination of transportation plans and programs developed for metropolitan planning areas with the statewide transportation plans and programs, and the reconciliation of such plans and programs as necessary to ensure connectivity within transportation systems (21).

The state list includes the requirement to consider methods to reduce traffic congestion (12). Although that requirement is not considered procedural for MPOs, it is for states because the state process is new. Because some states deal with transportation systems solely as facilities, the emphasis upon performance created by this factor is a sweeping change at the state perspective.

An additional factor was added by the ISTEA regulations to strengthen the states' unique role in working with Native Americans. Factor 23 calls for consideration of the concerns of tribal governments that have jurisdiction over lands within the boundaries of the state.

State Planning—Specific Factors

As with the procedural factors, many of the specific factors for states mirror those for metropolitan areas, although in some cases their impact is different because of the larger scale of planning. There are requirements for preservation of rights-of-way (17) and the use of life-cycle costs (20). Freight movement is addressed (19), although the focus is narrower; states are required to consider only commercial motor vehicles. Access to special facilities is addressed (4), as is connectivity (7), although here the connectivity is between metropolitan areas. Expanded transit services must also be considered (13).

Requirements that appear only in the list for states include the need to address long-range needs of the state transportation system (18). This will ensure that state planning is more than the programming of projects for short-term implementation.

Innovative financing of projects must also be considered (16). Since states are a major source of funding for many types of transportation improvements, this requirement should foster creativity that could generate additional funding. A new factor was added by the regulations to require consideration of investment strategies to improve adjoining state and local roads that support rural economic growth, tourism development, federal agency renewable resources management, and multipurpose land management practices, including development of recreation.

Consideration of state plans developed under the federal Water Pollution Control Act (9) will ensure that the water quality effects of transportation projects, such as runoff from roadways and impacts on environmentally sensitive areas, will be adequately addressed.

Incorporation of bikeways and pedestrian facilities in projects throughout the state (3) is identified as a state responsibility, as well as being identified in the general requirements for both MPOs and DOTs and in Section 217(g), which calls for coordination of state bicycle and pedestrian plans with state long-range plans. This responsibility raises the question of the importance of nonmotorized transportation in the range of issues that the states must consider. Like a number of other requirements, it also will necessitate cooperation between various levels of government, since local jurisdictions also have responsibility for such facilities.

Finally, consideration of recreational travel and tourism (8) places responsibility for this subject at the appropriate level of government, since many states now promote tourism and many recreational facilities are in nonmetropolitan areas. Consideration of this factor will require balancing the promotional aspects of attracting tourists with the need to protect the environmental qualities that create the value of many recreational locations.

Summary

MPOs and state DOTs must respond to the requirements of ISTEA by establishing transportation planning and programming processes to address the factors listed above. In some cases, this will require modifying existing practices; in others, it will mean creating entirely new ones. To ensure that each MPO and state DOT fully complies with the act, the regulations should be augmented with guidance on certification criteria that reflect the concerns discussed here. As ISTEA is implemented, citizens and organizations interested in effective transportation planning should continue to participate in the design of certification criteria.

Meanwhile, the changes ISTEA creates are so basic to the planning process that they cannot wait for the regulatory process to be completed. MPOs and state DOTs must begin now to review their existing practices and respond to the opportunity ISTEA creates for more comprehensive planning.

Appendix
Factors for Consideration in Metropolitan Planning

Subsection 134(f) of ISTEA states, "In developing transportation planning plans and programs pursuant to this section, each metropolitan planning organization shall, at a minimum, consider the following":

(1) Preservation of existing transportation facilities and, where practical, ways to meet transportation needs by using existing transportation facilities more efficiently.

(2) The consistency of transportation planning with applicable federal, state, and local energy conservation programs, goals, and objectives.

(3) The need to relieve congestion and prevent congestion from occurring where it does not yet occur.

(4) The likely effect of transportation policy decisions on land use and development and the consistency of transportation plans and programs with the provisions of all applicable short- and long-term land-use and development plans.

(5) The programming of expenditure on transportation enhancement activities as required in Section 133.

(6) The effects of all transportation projects to be undertaken in the metropolitan area, without regard to whether such projects are publicly funded.

(7) International border crossings and access to ports, airports, intermodal transportation facilities, major freight distribution

routes, national parks, recreation areas, monuments and historic sites, and military installations.

(8) The need for connectivity of roads within the metropolitan area with roads outside the metropolitan area.

(9) The transportation needs identified through use of the management systems required by Section 303 of this title.[8]

(10) Preservation of rights-of-way for construction of future transportation projects, including identification of unused rights-of-way which may be needed for future transportation corridors and identification of those corridors for which action is most needed to prevent destruction or loss.

(11) Methods to enhance the efficient movement of freight.

(12) The use of life-cycle costs in the design and engineering of bridges, tunnels, or pavement.

(13) The overall social, economic, energy, and environmental effects of transportation decisions.

(14) Methods to expand and enhance transit services and to increase the use of such services.

(15) Capital investments that would result in increased security in transit systems.

Factors for Consideration in State Planning

Subsection 135(c) as amended by the regulations governing ISTEA, issued October 28, 1993, states: "Each State shall undertake a continuous transportation planning process which shall, at a minimum, consider the following":

(1) The transportation needs (strategies and other results) identified through the management systems required by 23 U.S. Code 303.

(2) Any federal, state, or local energy goals, objectives, programs, or requirements.

(3) Strategies for incorporating bicycle transportation facilities and pedestrian walkways in projects where appropriate throughout the state.

(4) International border crossings and access to ports, airports, intermodal transportation facilities, major freight distribution routes, national parks, recreation and scenic areas, monuments and historic sites, and military installations.

(5) The transportation needs of nonmetropolitan areas through a process that includes consultation with local elected officials with jurisdiction over transportation.

(6) Any metropolitan area plan developed pursuant to Section 134.

(7) Connectivity between metropolitan areas within the state and with any metropolitan areas in other states.

(8) Recreational travel and tourism.

(9) Any state plan developed pursuant to the Federal Water Pollution Control Act.

(10) Transportation system management and investment strategies designed to make the most efficient use of existing transportation facilities.

(11) The overall social, economic, energy, and environmental effects of transportation decisions.

(12) Methods to reduce traffic congestion and to prevent traffic congestion from developing in areas where it does not yet occur, including methods which reduce motor vehicle travel, particularly single occupant motor vehicle travel.

(13) Methods to expand and enhance transit services and increase the use of such services (including commuter rail).

(14) The effect of transportation decisions on land use and land development, including the need for consistency between transportation decision making and the provisions of all applicable short-range and long-range land-use and development plans.

(15) Strategies for identifying and implementing transportation enhancements where appropriate throughout the state.

(16) The use of innovative mechanisms for financing projects, including value capture pricing, tolls, and congestion pricing.

(17) Preservation of rights-of-way for construction of future transportation projects, including identification of unused rights-of-way that may be needed for future transportation corridors, and identification of those corridors for which action is most needed to prevent destruction or loss.

(18) Long-range needs of the state transportation system.

(19) Methods to enhance the efficient movement of commercial motor vehicles.

(20) The use of life-cycle costs in the design and engineering of bridges, tunnels, or pavement.

(21) The coordination of transportation plans and programs developed for metropolitan planning areas with the statewide transportation plans and programs, and the reconciliation of such plans and programs as necessary to ensure connectivity within transportation systems.

(22) Investment strategies to improve adjoining state and local roads that support rural economic growth and tourism development, federal agency renewable resources management, and multipurpose land management practices, including recreation development.

(23) The concerns of Indian tribal governments having jurisdiction over lands within the boundaries of the state.

The consideration of these factors "should be based on the scale and complexity of many issues, including transportation problems, land use, employment, economic development, environmental and housing and community development objectives, the extent of overlap between factors and other circumstances statewide or in subareas within the state," according to Section 450.208 of the ISTEA regulations.

Notes

1. Phil Braum, "New Rules: Developing Transportation Plans and Programs," (Washington, DC: *STPP Resource Guide*, 1992).
2. 23 Code of Federal Regulations, General Preamble (Washington, DC: *Federal Register*, Volume 58, Number 207, October 28, 1993). Page 58043.
3. 23 CFR, Chapter I, Part 450.104 (Washington, DC: *Federal Register*, Volume 58, Number 207, October 28, 1993). Page 58064.
4. 23 CFR, Chapter I, Part 450.212, (Washington, DC: *Federal Register*, Volume 58, Number 207, October 28, 1993). Page 58067.
5. Ibid.
6. These are codified and expanded upon in 23 CFR Chapter I, Parts 450.208 and 450.316 (Washington, DC: *Federal Register*, Volume 58, Number 207, October 28, 1993). Pages 58067 and 58072.
7. Codified and expanded upon in 23 CFR Chapter I, Part 450, Section 208 (Washington, DC: *Federal Register*, Volume 58, Number 207, October 28, 1993). Page 58067.
8. The six management systems identified in Section 303 are as follows: pavement, bridge, safety, congestion, public transportation, and intermodal transportation.

12
Planning, Project Selection, and Financing

This chapter considers how ISTEA's planning requirements are supported by its project selection and financial constraint requirements. In turn, all of these provisions support the implementation of the Clean Air Amendments of 1990, since the financially constrained project selection process helps assure that low-cost, management-oriented projects receive strengthened consideration over new road construction for ISTEA funds.

Project selection under ISTEA is the result of two sequential processes: development of a twenty-year long-range plan and development of a three-year transportation improvement program. The principal thrust of ISTEA's new planning requirements is to open up the transportation planning and programming process in states and metropolitan areas. Under the old federal aid transportation programs, state transportation agencies made many of the important decisions on what metropolitan projects would be selected for federal funding. Since most of the federal transit funding coming into metropolitan areas was allocated to designated transit recipients, transit projects were generally selected by the operators without much consultation between them and the state DOTs. The fragmentation of these programming arrangements was further exacerbated by the U.S. DOT planning regulations, which did not require the transportation improvement programs of metropolitan planning organizations to be constrained by the available federal and local funds. Thus, the plans and TIPs grew into "wish lists." Project sponsors, in the main, selected projects from the lists on the basis of subjective rather than negotiated objective priorities for the region.

Under ISTEA, the opportunity now exists to develop a collaborative process whereby state and local governments and transportation providers are partners in the planning and programming process. Interest groups and community leaders can also participate in the development and implementation of transportation investments. To achieve successful negotiations among the new partners, two factors are paramount: enough must be at stake for the participants to want involvement, and each participant must have enough bargaining power to ensure basic equivalency in the negotiation process. The money provided by ISTEA is enough to address the first factor, and the vested right of local government and transit representatives to help select the federally assisted projects provides sought-after bargaining clout.

ISTEA refers in its planning provisions to the selection of projects (Sections 134 and 135, codified in 23 CFR Chapter I, Parts 450.208 and 450.316). The process and standards for making these decisions are not specifically defined. But a complete reading of the planning and programming sections of ISTEA establishes a firm basis for an operational definition.

The term *project selection* refers to that part of the planning and programming process in which specific projects in the long-range plan of the metropolitan planning organization are identified and included in the transportation improvement program, based on priority merit and certainty of financing.

Under Section 134(g) of ISTEA, MPOs in urbanized areas (areas of 50,000 or more population) must develop a twenty-year plan that considers the fifteen new factors described in Section 134(f).

Based on the long-range plan, the metropolitan planning organization develops a transportation improvement program, in cooperation with the state and affected transit operators, that includes a priority list of projects for a three-year period and a financial plan for how the TIP can be implemented. To be eligible for federal funds, projects must be incorporated into the TIP, which must in turn be consistent with the long-range plan.

ISTEA creates a more equal partnership among state DOTs, local governments, and transit operators in the selection process, particularly in metropolitan areas. Section 450.216 of the regulations issued in October 1993 by the FHWA and FTA states:

> Each state shall develop a statewide transportation improvement program for all areas of the state . . . The portion of the STIP in a metropolitan planning area shall be developed in cooperation with the MPO . . . Metropolitan planning area TIPs shall be included without modification in the STIP, directly or by reference, once approved by the MPO and the Governor after needed conformity findings are made.[1]

Transportation Management Areas

ISTEA refers to the largest regions (with populations of more than 200,000) as "transportation management areas." In these large areas, new project selection rights are vested in the local governments functioning through the metropolitan planning organizations. This new selection requirement can be the basis for putting all parties on a substantially equal footing.

All highway projects within the boundaries of the transportation management areas (except National Highway System projects and bridge and interstate maintenance) and transit projects under the Federal Transit Act "shall be selected by the metropolitan planning organization designated for such area in consultation with the state, and in accordance with the priorities in the approved metropolitan TIP."[2] This represents a radical change for most MPOs.

The basis for creating a new programming arrangement is found in the provisions for a long-range plan which must cover the twenty-year forecast period. The plan should identify the transportation facilities that will function as an integrated metropolitan system, giving emphasis to those that serve important national and regional transportation functions. Among other things, the plan must include a financial component showing how the long-range plan can be implemented. The plan can include revenues "reasonably expected" to be available. Thus, in the planning phase, new revenue sources can be identified if reasonable evidence suggests that they will materialize.

Further, in nonattainment areas, the long-range plan must be coordinated with the development of transportation control measures in the state implementation plan, as required by the Clean Air Act Amendments of 1990. (See the list of required measures in the chapter appendix.)

Clean Air Act Amendments of 1990

The Clean Air Act Amendments of 1990 (CAAA) require states to integrate their air quality and transportation planning processes by establishing better coordination between those planning processes and setting a firm schedule for states to attain air quality standards. ISTEA strengthens these reforms by requiring that local and state transportation plans be consistent with state air plans, introducing incentives to control transportation demand, and removing traditional federal inducements to build new roads.

Perhaps the most important and far-reaching provision of the CAAA is the requirement that metropolitan transportation plans conform to state air plans. Although a similar provision has been in the Clean Air Act since 1977, it was never formally interpreted to mean that transportation plans as a whole must conform to air plans, only that transportation plans had to list the transportation control measures included in the air plans. The CAAA broadens the interpretation by prohibiting the expenditure of any funds on projects in a transportation plan or program unless that plan and program conforms on the whole to the state air plan. The projects must meet the state plan's purpose of eliminating and reducing air quality violations.

The CAAA also requires greatly increased attention to mobile source emissions as part of the new requirements for ozone control. Mobile sources (cars, buses, and trucks) account for 88 percent of carbon monoxide and 50 percent of oxides of nitrogen and volatile organic compounds, which are the major contributors to ground-level ozone, smog, global warming, and health problems associated with those environmental problems. (In California, volatile organic compounds are known as reactive organic gases.) Traffic congestion and mobile source pollution compromise the environment, damage human health, and take a heavy financial toll through fuel consumption, car maintenance costs, and lost productivity.

Nonattainment areas are required to develop air quality plans and take steps on a specific timetable to demonstrate reductions in ground-level ozone and carbon monoxide. States containing areas with serious, severe, or extreme air quality nonattainment must submit air plans demonstrating emission reductions averaging three percent per year for each consecutive three-year period after 1996. States that contain areas with moderate ozone air quality must submit air plans that demonstrate a 15 percent reduction in emissions of volatile organic compounds by 1996. Penalties for noncompliance include the freezing of federal transportation funds and/or the imposition of a federal implementation plan to help attain air quality standards.

The freezing of federal transportation funds does not apply to funds that are spent on safety programs or projects that will improve air quality.³ A partial list of eligible projects includes capital expenditures for public transit, construction of bus or HOV lanes, traffic flow improvements that achieve a net reduction of emissions, park-and-ride lots at transit stops, and programs to limit vehicle use in high-traffic areas through tolls, parking surcharges, or other congestion pricing measures to control the social and environmental costs of driving.

The EPA gives states with nonattainment areas eighteen months to revise deficient air plans after the EPA's initial review. If that deadline is missed, the nonattainment areas may either have their federal funding withheld or be required to reduce emissions from industry and businesses at a rate that could negatively affect their ability to expand or add new industrial facilities. If an area is still in nonattainment after twenty-four months, both sanctions kick in. The EPA may also apply the sanctions statewide at that time.

Section 134(g)(3) of ISTEA requires MPOs for nonattainment areas to coordinate the development of their long-range plans with the development of the state implementation plans required by the Clean Air Act. A substantial challenge for some metropolitan areas is the requirement that their boundaries must at least include the boundaries of the nonattainment area.⁴

ISTEA also requires the planning process to attempt to solve transportation needs by using existing facilities more efficiently before building new capacity. No longer can the solution to a given transportation problem be assumed to require the construction of new facilities. The metropolitan plan must include transportation system management strategies that increase the usefulness of the existing system and transportation demand management strategies that reduce the travel volumes the system must accommodate. This provision reinforces the funding preference given by the CAAA to transportation control measures over new construction.

As mentioned in the previous chapter, Section 303 of ISTEA requires states to develop management systems for highway pavement of federal-aid highways, bridges on and off federal-aid highways, highway safety, traffic congestion, public transportation facilities and equipment, and intermodal transportation facilities and systems. States are to develop and implement these systems in metropolitan areas in cooperation with MPOs. To ensure that the management systems adequately reflect responsibilities for both planning and implementation, new means of state-local cooperation will need to be established. The establishment of these management systems also requires the states to think through the management and operation of existing facilities and to place decisions about construction of new facilities in a broad management context.

The CAAA legislation provides that the state implementation plan and the MPO's plan and program must be mutually supportive. In this regard, the CAAA relates not only to ISTEA funding for special congestion mitigation, but to all projects in the transportation improvement program and their effect on air quality. To ensure the conformity of both, the CAAA requires that the MPO's long-range plan be detailed enough so the probable emissions from proposed transportation projects can be estimated. This will cause significant changes in the nature of the long-range plans of most MPOs. Plans must specify projects or project alternatives to meet the defined transportation needs of the region and can no longer be conceptual and general. Projects that meet the identified needs and can be implemented in the near term should be listed in the plan so priorities for implementing them can be developed.

This requirement identifies the other critical amendment to the planning process that creates the context for the project selection process: financial constraint. Section 134(h)(2) of ISTEA requires a financial plan demonstrating the resources that are reasonably expected to be available to carry out the TIP. This financial feasibility test is reinforced in Section 134(h)(5) of the law and in the ISTEA regulations, which mandate that the TIP shall include "only projects for which construction and operating funds can reasonably be expected to be available."[5]

Financial Constraint

Under ISTEA, metropolitan planning organizations and state departments of transportation must demonstrate that projects included in transportation improvement programs are likely to be funded. In addition, MPOs must demonstrate adequate financial commitments for transportation projects and activities in their long-range plans.

At the metropolitan level, the new law requires that long-range plans include a financial plan that demonstrates methods of implementation, indicates resources from public and private sources that are reasonably expected to be made available to carry out the plan, and recommends any innovative financing techniques for needed projects and programs, including such techniques as value capture, tolls, and congestion pricing.[6] The new law imposes the same requirements on transportation improvement programs.[7]

Although states are not required to establish funding sources for their long-range plans, the new law requires states to include projects in their transportation improvement programs only under the same full funding condition required of TIPs in general.

These provisions originated in the Senate bill and were subsequently included in the House bill and conference report. Of particular relevance, therefore, is the language in the Senate report describing the rationale for these provisions. According to the Senate report,

> Historically, TIPs have included projects for which funding could not be reasonably anticipated. Before passing of the Clean Air Act Amendments of 1990, inclusion of such projects in a TIP had no adverse effect on project priorities and spending. However, the amended conformity provisions of the Clean Air Act have made it imperative that TIPs contain only projects for which funding is reasonably anticipated. The likelihood that funding will be available for future projects will be a factor in evaluating the conformity of long-range plans.
>
> The conformity provisions of the Clean Air Act, as amended, require an MPO to evaluate a TIP for conformity with the emission reduction schedules and other provisions of the applicable implementation plan based on the assumption that each of the projects and programs in the TIP will be implemented in accordance with the timetable in the TIP. If projects and programs for which there is no reasonably anticipated source of funding are included in the TIP, the air quality benefit or detriment of such projects and programs could skew the expected air quality impact of the TIP. As a result the TIP may only contain projects for which there is a reasonably anticipated source of funding. However, many transit projects rely on the Federal appropriations process for funding and such funding may change from year to year. It is not the intention of the Committee to exclude such projects from a TIP because such funding depends on Federal appropriations.
>
> Nor must each project to [sic] have earmarked federal, state, and local funds identified in the TIP. Historical funding levels, existing bonding authority, existing state and local tax revenues, allocation of Federal funds under the Surface Transportation Program and other relevant factors may be used in determining whether funding can be reasonably anticipated.[8]

The legislative language and accompanying Senate report make clear that an MPO must exclude any project or program from its long-range plan and transportation improvement program if funding is not reasonably available. Therefore, a financial plan must demonstrate reasonably available funding for all projects listed in the transportation improvement program and long-range plan.

The Federal Highway Administration and the Federal Transit Administration, in their ISTEA regulations, took a broad view of what constitutes "reasonably available funding." For areas in attainment of National Ambient Air Quality Standards, the definition indicates that funding need not be currently available or committed. With regard to federal funds, this means either authorized or appropriated. Proposed state or local legislation identifying potential funds are acceptable as long as the TIP identifies how the legislation will be achieved.

Air quality nonattainment areas and areas that recently reached attainment (maintenance areas) must base the first two years of their TIP on available or committed funding, not proposed or potential funding. The third year, however, can be based on "reasonably available" funds.

In addition, Congress determined that funding for completing the project must be shown to be available "within the time period contemplated for completion of the project." Therefore, any financial plan must be tied to the priorities and timetables set forth in the TIP. A "reasonably anticipated funding" determination is not possible if no time frame is established for a program or project. In order to comply with ISTEA, a financial plan must not only identify funding sources and revenues, but also indicate whether such resources will be available within the time frame established by the transportation improvement program and the long-range plan.

Finally, each state must also demonstrate in its TIP that each project has "reasonably available" funding in the same manner as the metropolitan TIP. State TIPs must also include a timetable of construction and completion in order to allow an evaluation of the financial plan.

The following requirements, then, must be satisfied by local and state agencies and enforced by federal transportation agencies:

Metropolitan Requirements

Each MPO must prepare a financial plan to accompany its long-range plan and transportation improvement program. Each MPO must exclude from its TIP any project for which funding is not reasonably available.

State Requirements

Each state must prepare a financial plan to accompany its TIP. Each state must exclude from its TIP any project for which funding is not reasonably available.

General Requirements

MPOs and states must rely on existing sources of revenue rather than speculative or prospective revenues. In addition, revenues must be linked to project timing: no project may be included in an MPO or state TIP unless funding is demonstrated to be "reasonably available" within the time contemplated for completion of the project.

Summary

The time is ripe for nationwide changes in transportation policy. To move forward, however, transportation and air quality officials must coordinate their planning efforts and create a climate more responsive to public activism and involvement. In turn, members of the public must educate themselves regarding transportation needs to improve understanding of the role of transportation in neighborhood vitality and quality of life. They must move from a focus on projects to a focus on process.

Long-range plans, on which project decisions will be based, must be more inclusive and definitive than ever before. In addition to addressing the broad range of considerations called for under ISTEA, long-range plans should contain detailed information on the specific transportation facilities to meet their goals. The proposed facilities should be compatible with the strategy to attain and sustain federal air quality standards and must be financially constrained. No wish lists can survive.

This approach establishes the foundation and dynamics for the ideal of collaborative negotiation. The states, local governments, and transit operators will have a blueprint for negotiation around the regional table. The project selection process can provide each player with nearly comparable bargaining chips. Another leveling influence will be the public participation requirements. Citizens, public interest groups, and business groups will be given the opportunity to argue for their interests and preferences when the TIP is being formulated.

A new arrival on the scene is the governor. He or she will have to concur with the TIPs once they are adopted. It is to be hoped that the governor will encourage the public and state agencies responsible for the environment, parks, or land use to be part of transportation decisions.

The state is still in the best position to select projects. But new and equalizing forces can be engaged if they are orchestrated as suggested above. One of the most important accomplishments of ISTEA is the fact that the priority and financial plan requirements cited above establish a framework of action for the state DOT, which in turn strengthens the ability of MPOs and local governments to negotiate.

The challenge in this approach is that it requires local governments to reach agreement and form a coherent strategy for the use of project funds. Otherwise, they will lose the opportunity to influence project selection, and the state DOT will then have to make the important decisions on behalf of all parties. It is equally critical for citizens, transit operators, labor, business representatives, and public interest groups to have input into the planning process and determine the services really needed in their neighborhoods, cities, and towns, as well as the best ways to provide those services so that they contribute to the attainment of healthier air and a better quality of life.

Appendix
Transportation Control Measures

Section 108 of the Clean Air Act Amendments of 1990 suggests sixteen *transportation control measures*, and Section 176(d) mandates that they be given priority consideration in transportation planning and funding. These measures are listed below.

- Improved public transit;
- Limitations and restrictions of certain roads or lanes to transit and HOVs;
- Employer-based transportation management;
- Trip reduction ordinances;
- Traffic flow improvements to achieve emissions reductions;
- Park and ride/fringe parking;
- Programs to limit auto travel during peak periods (including congestion pricing);
- Ride-sharing programs;
- Pedestrian and bicycle facilities;
- Bicycle storage facilities;

- Programs to reduce extended vehicle idling;

- Programs to reduce extreme cold starts;

- Flexible work schedules;

- Programs to promote nonautomobile travel to special events and major activity centers such as shopping centers;

- Programs for new construction and major reconstruction of paths, tracks, or areas solely for the use of pedestrian or other nonmotorized means of transportation; and

- Voluntary removal of pre-1980 vehicles ("Cash for Clunkers").

Notes

1. 23 Code of Federal Regulations, Section 450.216(a) (Washington, DC: *Federal Register*, Volume 58, Number 207, October 28, 1993). Page 58068.
2. 23 CFR, Section 450.332(b) (Washington, DC: *Federal Register*, Volume 58, Number 207, October 28, 1993). Page 58078.
3. Clean Air Act Amendments of 1990, Section 176(a).
4. 23 CFR, Chapter I, Part 450, Section 308 (Washington, DC: *Federal Register*, Volume 58, Number 207, October 28, 1993). Page 58071.
5. 23 CFR, Section 450.324(e) (Washington, DC: *Federal Register*, Volume 58, Number 207, October 28, 1993). Page 58076.
6. 23 CFR, Chapter I, Part 450.322(b)(11) (Washington, DC: *Federal Register*, Volume 58, Number 207, October 28, 1993). Page 58075.
7. 23 CFR, Chapter I, Part 450.324(e) (Washington, DC: *Federal Register*, Volume 58, Number 207, October 28, 1993). Page 58076.
8. Senate Report 102-71, p. 30.

Afterword

How ISTEA Will Help Us Serve Communities

Interstate 90 connects Boston to Seattle, but it also connects the practices of the past to the efforts of the present. On the East Coast, the older city struggles to repair and restore the damage done to communities, historic areas, and open space by several decades of road-focused policy. The result of this struggle is the CAT project, funded through ISTEA Interstate Completion funds. Thus, one of the final acts of the Interstate program will be to tunnel underground and bury its own. On the West Coast, community activists have been working to protect and enhance the area along the final segment of I-90 before it is transformed into Anywhere, U.S.A. by intense growth pressure and strip development. The relatively small transportation enhancements program in ISTEA has given the Mountains-to-Sound Greenway movement a tangible incentive for realizing their vision.

The Boston-Seattle Interstate represents the fundamental change afoot in transportation policy. Forty years ago, the primary focus of our federal decision-making was connecting economic centers in the straightest line possible, for the quickest and most efficient trips. Today, citizens in both the Boston and Seattle "markets" have opened the eyes of transportation officials to see these regions as places in their own right, where the protection of unique scenic and historic values and local economies are as important as maintaining a connection to other places.

All the cases examined in this book, both before and after ISTEA passed, featured committed citizens who gained the attention and cooperation of transportation agencies. In some cases, as in both Connecticut cases, in the regulations phase of the Maine Sensible Transportation Act, and in the new regional planning processes in Albany, Pittsburgh, and northern California, transportation agencies responded early enough to citizen pressures to create an effective forum for their involvement. In other cases, such as the Maryland 301 Task Force case, the Freedom Parkway, and Boston CAT, projects were so well advanced that citizens had to escalate their efforts to the level of political or legal action before their concerns were heeded. In many cases, including the Maryland 301 Task Force, the James River ferry project, and the Freedom Parkway case, a change in political or institutional leadership led to the crucial shift in decision-making.

Transportation trend-watchers expect to see still more changes in political and institutional leadership over the next decade. Since the 1980s, a new kind of state transportation director has been coming to the fore, one who is more politically attuned and often is trained in planning or public service rather than in a technical field such as civil engineering. This new breed of director is exerting increased influence over the ranks of thirty-year veterans with engineering expertise. For example, just prior to ISTEA's passage, the Texas Legislature consolidated several agencies into a new Texas DOT. In October 1993, the new DOT underwent massive staff changes, in which almost 15 percent of the staff retired, including most of the agency's senior management.

At the helm of the Delaware Department of Transportation, Anne Canby, a professional planner and one of the few women in a senior transportation position in the U.S., is shifting the focus of the agency toward a more multi-modal approach to policy. Canby is a strong supporter of the National Transportation System required by ISTEA, which includes rail, major transit systems, major roads, major ports and airports, and connecting or adjacent bicycle and walking routes. Delaware was one of only two states to recognize and test the eligibility of railroad corridors for designation as part of the National Highway System (New Jersey was the other state).

Many of these changes began long before the passage of ISTEA and would have occurred with or without it. In a very real sense, ISTEA was crafted as the result of the existing groundswell of public opinion and efforts, and it codifies a new technical and administrative approach to policy, lending credibility to what many members of the public have been saying for decades: that transportation policy should be decided in a broader context, that the public is entitled to a system of checks and balances to ensure this context is heeded, and that the focus of transportation service should be communities. ISTEA has undoubtedly accelerated the pace of change since 1991. To reach the "accessibility paradigm" described at the beginning of the book, the service of community must be seen in terms of making each community more self-sustaining and coherent, rather than simply connecting places to one another like so many dots on the map.

Post-ISTEA: Creating a Context with Checks and Balances

During the debate over ISTEA, several citizen groups who had helped pass the Clean Air Act Amendments the previous year called for ISTEA's public participation requirements to enable citizens to sue public entities for noncompliance, similar to the provision in the Clean Air Act. Instead, ISTEA built in a series of provisions to assure that local and state transportation decisions take place in the context of the built and natural environment and that a set of checks and balances is in place to ensure regional-state collaboration, financial constraints on planning, and meaningful public involvement in the planning and project selection process. The overarching aim of these new measures is transportation that serves the broader aims of communities, including citizens' concerns about equal access to opportunities, transportation options, recreation, community design, and the health of local economies.

The planning requirements in ISTEA call for regions and states to assemble the broad context in which their decisions must take place. By considering the implications of their policies for land use, energy conservation, scenic and historic quality, public transportation, bicycling and walking, public officials are beginning to place mobility in a more balanced setting, among a host of other important goals which are not all best-served by moving vehicles and people around at the highest possible volume and speed.

Recognizing that it is not enough simply to require public review of complex technical processes, ISTEA includes practical measures to assure that the goals set by officials in their plans are reflected in the actions recommended in their programs. For example, ISTEA requires both plan and program to describe likely funding sources for each activity or project described. This requirement for financial constraint was a crucial inclusion, because it gives low-cost and cost-effective projects an advantage over high-profile, costly construction projects. It also marks the difference between "pie-in-the-sky" planning that results in project wish-lists, and meaningful goal-setting tied to available funds. The Jump-Start program, as described in Chapter 9, illustrates the effectiveness of using financial constraint not only to keep the planning process in the realm of the possible, but to focus participation and provide real incentives for creative competition among a variety of project sponsors.

ISTEA also strengthened the certification process whereby metropolitan planning organizations are certified by the U.S. DOT. Many planning agencies have been reluctant to change their processes at all, for fear that new federal procedures for planning and certification will render any efforts obsolete. The Capital District Transportation Committees, Southwest Regional Planning Commission, and Georgia Department of Transportation provide examples of agencies willing to alter their existing practices in ways that allow them to make adjustments as the federal framework for their decisions becomes clearer.

To consider the planning factors set forth in ISTEA, planning agencies will be called on to develop new technical procedures, particularly for measuring the impacts of transportation options across a broad range of considerations. The MTC in San Francisco, the CDTC in Albany, and the SWRPC in Pittsburgh are examples of regional agencies which have adapted their technical practices to the task of ISTEA planning. However, dramatic overhaul has yet to occur. It will take some time before most state and regional agencies absorb new practices, for very different reasons. Most state transportation agencies must change their administrative practices and agency goals before they can focus on new technical methods. The Minnesota Department of Transportation Strategic Management Process illustrates that altering management practices is a challenge as daunting in the long run as changing technical procedures. At most metropolitan planning organizations, the reform of technical practices must wait until the staff and resources are in place to back up technical assumptions, a state of affairs still out of reach at many MPOs. As illustrated by the SWRPC example in Pittsburgh, even when technical assumptions can be tested by agency staff and presented to the public, there may not be immediate consensus on how to act on the results.

Because ISTEA calls on states and Metropolitan Planning Organizations to work more closely together in their project selection, one solution to the problem of reforming technical practices may lie in the creative tension between the levels of government. State DOTs are well-funded and have the staff to conduct detailed technical analyses. MPOs have the political understanding and contact with the public which could allow them to more clearly define the goals of technical research and evaluation. States and MPOs could pool their resources, staff expertise, political acumen, and connection to the public in order to create new models for technical evaluation which reflect and answer to the concerns of the public. Placing technical evaluation requirements hand in hand with public information needs is a valuable action for helping clarify the goals of the former and the results of the latter.

Defining Access in Terms of Community

If the new contextual planning and system of checks and balances called for by ISTEA are meant to serve communities, how is that new goal related to the accessibility paradigm? Simply, accessibility places the overall needs of community residents at the pinnacle of the hierarchy of values under consideration. While the needs of the individual are still given great emphasis, those needs are placed in the context of the community, just as the private vehicle is placed in the broader context of its environment. As opposed to the mobility paradigm, which enshrines individual mobility at the expense of other goals, the access paradigm re-enacts the social contract on which democracies are based, in that each individual shares in the benefits of his or her community rather than some individuals enjoying complete autonomy while others are left to fend for themselves.

What this implies, of course, is that the ability to go anywhere, anytime, at any speed is not a fundamental right, nor even an ideal for individuals to aspire to. Instead, the ability to locate and have access to equal opportunities is a protected right, against which each individual must negotiate his or her own personal choices of residence, job, and lifestyle. It is neither possible nor desirable to place all goods, services, and jobs farther and farther out, while placing greater and greater power to travel in the hands of those who can afford it. Instead, opportunities must be placed where people already are, so that they can tap into the power that resides within their cities, towns, neighborhoods, and ultimately within themselves.

Suggested Reading

Several books, articles, and reports are mentioned in this book or have informed the authors and others on the debate over transportation and land use. Some of these are suggested in the following list for further exploration by the interested reader.

Burrington, Stephen, *Road Kill: How Solo Driving Runs Down the Economy,* Boston: Conservation Law Foundation, 1994. (617) 350-0990.

> *This report distills information from a larger study conducted by Apogee Research, Inc. that looks at the costs of transportation in the Boston, Massachusetts, and Portland, Maine, metropolitan areas. It examines existing conditions, hidden subsidies/ real costs, inexpensive alternatives, and options for more sustainable future transportation systems.*

Calthorpe, Peter, *The Next American Metropolis: Ecology, Community, and the American Dream,* New York: Princeton Architectural Press, 1993.

> *This book discusses how to build a transit-oriented development, eliminate sprawl, support the pedestrian, and move toward a sustainable future. It is a perfect counterpoint to Edge City (see Garreau entry below). Mr. Calthorpe does not thrill to the entrepreneurial exploits of shopping mall developers but rather seeks to order life in a less car-dependent way.*

Chasan, Dan, *Mountains to Sound: The Creation of a Greenway across the Cascades,* Seattle: Sasquatch Books, 1993.

> *This book tells the history and the possible future of the I-90 highway corridor. It is a sophisticated example of legitimizing an idea—in this case the concept of a park, open space, heritage, and economic development corridor—by presenting it in a beautifully illustrated, well-written book.*

Citizens Against Route 20 (CART), *Traffic Calming: The Solution to Route 20 and a New Vision for Brisbane*, Ashgrove, Queensland, Australia, 1989. Available from STOP, Portland, Oregon, (503) 624 6083.

This citizen's guide to reducing auto impacts on neighborhoods is easily accessible and rich with examples from northern Europe. If you want to learn about Woonerfs and speed tables as a way to calm traffic in your community, this is the source for you.

Downs, Anthony, *Stuck in Traffic: Coping with Peak-Hour Traffic Congestion*, Washington, D.C.: The Brookings Institution, 1992.

This book is an excellent compendium of transportation demand management alternatives, with descriptions, examples, and evaluations. It covers the broad array of alternatives with a presentation of land use and job concentration options that is perhaps too pessimistic.

Garreau, Joel, *Edge City: Life on the New Frontier*, New York: Doubleday, 1991.

Mr. Garreau is convinced that he has found the new urban future in the form of new, dense, employment and residential centers located in metropolitan areas outside of the traditional central city. These edge cities, he contends, are our new cities in the making. The book is thoughtful, synthetic, and irreverent, and it challenges many assumptions about transportation and our culture. A great read.

Kunstler, James Howard, *The Geography of Nowhere: The Rise and Decline of America's Man-Made Landscape*, New York: Simon & Schuster, 1993.

Mr. Kunstler gives a vivid description of the drawbacks of the auto-oriented development in the United States. This book paints a very complete (and often gloomy) picture of development that challenges us to do things differently.

1000 Friends of Oregon, *Making the Land Use, Transportation, Air Quality Connection: A National Growth Management Research Project (LUTRAQ)*, Portland, Oregon, 1993. (503) 223-4396.

LUTRAQ serves as the current state-of-the-art work in analyzing and projecting the interrelationship between land uses and transportation now and in the future. The project, written by nationally recognized experts, enjoyed the support of private foundations, the regional government, and the Oregon Department of Transportation.

Untermann, Richard, *Linking Land Use and Transportation: Design Strategies to Serve HOV's and Pedestrians*, Seattle: Washington Department of Transportation, 1991.

Is it possible to take pre-interstate highways bordered by strip development and reconfigure them into pedestrian-friendly suburban centers? This concise study looks at specific ways to retrofit a typical sprawling strip mess.

Yaro, Robert, Randall Arendt, and Harry Dodson, *Dealing with Change in the Connecticut River Valley: A Design Manual for Conservation and Development*, Cambridge, Massachusetts: Lincoln Institute of Land Policy, 1989. (617) 661-3016.

If you wonder whether there is really any way to save our vistas, farmland, and community character while accommodating growth, this is the guide for you. Using growth management principles the authors explain and, most importantly, show in simple drawings how alternate futures can be created by placing roads in the right places and by developing in concert with the land. This work has inspired many community visioning processes and countless public reports.

Index

AASHTO, 34, 38
accessibility
   as transportation paradigm, 9, 16, 79, 156
   urban, 56
accidents, automobile, 11, 15
accountability mechanisms, 56. *See also* litigation
advertising, outdoor, 17, 72, 132
advisory committees, 56, 96–98, 103, 107
aesthetics, 32–33, 38, 131
agencies, changing role of, 17–18, 105–111
agricultural lands
   and I-90 corridor, 73
   impact of transportation modes, 4
   loss of, 7, 11, 29
   transportation planning and, 31, 64
air quality, 3, 15, 31. *See also* Clean Air Act Amendments of 1990
   cost of inhaling gasoline fumes, 15
   under ISTEA, 18
   in land use accounting, 4
   LUTRAQ, 14, 64–69, 80
   nonattainment of NAAQS, 15, 18, 38, 66, 147–148
   smog, 6, 15
Albany, New York, 101–103
all-terrain vehicles, 97
American Association of State Highway and Transportation Officials (AASHTO), 34, 38
American Lung Association, 15
Americans with Disabilities Act of 1990, 100, 129
Anne Arundel County Government, 31
Anton Nelleson Associates, 11
archaeological planning, 17, 31, 72, 132–133
Association for the Preservation of Virginia Antiquities, 24
Association of Bay Area Governments, 100
Atlanta, 46, 47, 50
   case study, 4, 44–50
   Great Park, possible scenario, 4
Atlanta Journal-Constitution, 46
Audubon Society, 31
automobile accidents, 11, 15
automobile industry, 5, 6
automobiles
   auto-oriented urban design, 10, 80
   car/road construction equilibrium, 8
   cost and ownership statistics, 5, 14–16
   early history of, 5, 6–7
   freedom limited by, 5, 7
   funding for. *See* ISTEA
   as primary means of travel, 5

balanced transportation, 39
Baltimore, 96, 97–98
Baltimore Bicycling Club, 96
Baltimore Metropolitan Council, 97
Bay Area Clean Air Plan, 98
Bechtel, 50
behavior modification, incentives for commuters, 8–9, 62
Bellevue, Washington, 76
Bethel, Maine, 123
Beverly Hills Freeway, proposed, 22
bicycle facilities, 7, 9
   bike lanes, 9, 46, 48, 63, 72, 139
   funding for, 17, 91, 130. *See also* ISTEA
   percent of work trips, 9
   transportation system management for, 8, 62–64
Big Dig. *See* Central Artery/Tunnel (CAT)
Blue Grass Land and Nature Trust, 43
Bluegrass Tomorrow, 42, 43
B&O Railroad Museum, 96, 97
Boston, 4, 50
   case study, 4, 50–59, 63–64
   cost of parking in, 15
   Southwest Freeway, 121
Boston Building and Construction Trades Council, 21
Boston Greenspace Alliance, 54, 56
Boston Harbor, 52
Boston Preservation Alliance, 21

Boston Societies of Architects, Civil Engineers and Landscape Architects, 21
Bourbon Fiscal Court, 43
Bowie, Maryland, 31
brainstorming, 42, 57, 94, 97
Bridge Design and Review Committee, 57
bridges
   congestion pricing on, 62
   historic, 131–132
   Lake Washington, Washington, 73
   Merritt Parkway, Connecticut, 36–37
   options in planning, 57
   Quinnipiac River, Connecticut, 39, 107–109
   vs. ferries, 22–26
Bronx River Parkway, 33
Bullitt Foundation, 77
Burrington, Steve, 16
buses and busing
   funding for, 17, 91
   proposed in Portland area, 68
   transportation system management for, 8, 62–64
businesses
   in compact community development, 80
   mall as threats to local, 13
   Portland area forecasts, 69
   relocation from urban areas, 6

California, transportation planning, 98–101
Calthorpe, Peter, 11
Calthorpe Associates, 67
Cambridge, Massachusetts, 4, 56
Cambridge City Council, 56, 57
Cambridge Systematics, Inc., 67
Camden Yards, 96
canals, historic, 131–132
Canby, Anne, 154
Candler Park, Georgia, 44, 46
capacity, as transportation paradigm, 8, 14, 52, 79
Capital District Transportation Committee, 101, 155
carbon monoxide, 6, 15
carpools
 Commute Trip Reduction Act of 1991, 62
 in mobility paradigm, 8
 percent of work trips, 9
Carroll Park Restoration Foundation, 96
cars. See automobiles
Carter, James Earl, Jr., 44, 46
Carter Library and Presidential Center, 45, 47, 48, 50
case studies, 4–5. See also Central Artery/Tunnel (CAT); Freedom Parkway; I-90 Corridor; Lower James River Crossing; Merritt Parkway; Washington Bypass; Western Bypass
CAT project. See Central Artery/Tunnel (CAT)
CAUTION citizens group, 46–48
Central Artery Environmental Oversight Committee, 56

Central Artery/Tunnel (CAT)
 case study, 4, 50–59
 TDM strategies for the, 63–64
Central Park, New York, 11
Century Freeway, 63
charettes, 122
Charles County government, 31
Charles River, Massachusetts, 4, 52
Charles River Crossing Design Review Committee, 56–58
Charlestown, Massachusetts, 56
Chase, Tyler, 32
Chattahoochee-Flint Heritage Highway, 95–96
Chattahoochee-Flint Regional Development Center, 95, 112–113
Chattahoochee Trace Bike Path, 96
checks and balances, of planning, 154–156
Chesapeake Bay Commission, 30, 31
Chesapeake Bay Foundation, 12, 24, 29, 31
Chinatown Neighborhood Association, 21
Citizens Against Unnecessary Thoroughfares in Older Neighborhoods (CAUTION), 46–48
Citizens for a Better Environment, 98
citizens groups. See *individual group names*; public involvement
Citizens Planning and Housing Association, 96
City Beautiful movement, 33
City Council of Williamsburg, 23
Clean Air Act Amendments of 1990, 19, 145
 and ISTEA, 135, 147–149

transportation control measures of, 151–152
Coalition for Quality Growth, Inc., 25
coalitions, 21–26. See also decision-making processes; *individual coalition names*
 as consensus-builders, 43, 47
 establishing, 57–58, 83, 103–105, 118–119
 as implementation vs. opposition groups, 48
 lists of post-ISTEA members, 112–115
 Mountains-to-Sound Greenway, 77
 Virginia, 92–93
 Washington Regional Network, 93–95
Colonial Williamsburg Foundation, 24
Colorado Department of Transportation, 106–107
Commission on the Condemnation of Public Property, 47
committees
 establishing, 120–121
 integration of, 57–58
Commonwealth of Massachusetts. See Massachusetts
Commonwealth of Virginia. See Virginia
Commonwealth Transportation Board, 25
communication, during planning, 118–123
communities
 definition, 3–4
 design of. See urban design

how ISTEA will serve, 153–156
 physical cohesion of, 7
 quality of life, 3, 9, 15. See also transportation enhancements; urban design
 social aspects, 7, 9, 80, 81
Commute Trip Reduction Act of 1991, 62
commuting
 highway corridors opening new areas for, 73–76
 pick-up areas, 62
 to suburbia office parks, 6
competitions, 123
computers, telecommuting with, 9, 13, 81, 99
conferences, 29, 34, 92, 105–106, 121–122
conflict resolution. See coalitions; litigation; mediation
congestion. See traffic congestion
Congestion Mitigation and Air Quality Improvement Program, 18, 92, 111
congestion pricing, 15–16, 17, 62
Connecticut, case study, 32–39
Connecticut Department of Transportation, 32, 34, 35, 36
 institutional changes, 107–109
Connecticut State Historic Preservation Office, 35
Connecticut Trust for Historic Preservation, 35, 39
Conservation Law Foundation, 16, 54, 55, 57, 64
conservation of resources, 9, 16
consortiums, 99
consultants, for technical support, 123

contacts
    Atlanta Bureau of Planning, 50
    Capital District Planning
        Committee, 103
    CAUTION, 50
    Central Artery/Tunnel Project, 59
    Chattahoochee-Flint Regional
        Development Commission, 98
    Chesapeake Bay Foundation, 32, 95
    Colorado Department of
        Transportation, 107
    Connecticut Department of
        Transportation, 38
    Connecticut Fund for the
        Environment, 109
    Connecticut Trust for Historic
        Preservation, 39
    Conservation Law Foundation, 59
    Georgia Transportation Alliance,
        106
    Lower James River Association,
        26
    Maine Department of
        Transportation, 91
    Maryland Department of
        Transportation, 32
    mediators, 59
    Metropolitan Transportation
        Commission, 101
    Minnesota Department of
        Transportation, 111
    Mountains-to-Sound Greenway
        Trust, 78
    Natural Resources Council of
        Maine, 91
    1000 Friends of Oregon, 69
    Portland Area Comprehensive
        Transportation Committee, 92
    Sensible Transportation Options
        for People (STOP), 69
    Southwestern Pennsylvania
        Regional Planning Commission,
        104–105
    Trust for Public Land, 98
    Virginia Surface Transportation
        Coalition, 93
contests, 123
corridor management, 82–84
    and commuting, 73–76
    funding for, 84
    and historical preservation, 76–78
    for I-5, 64
    for I-90, 12–13, 72–78
    natural area preservation, 76–78,
        131
    Route 301, 28–32, 84
    Southwest Corridor, 57, 64–65
cost/benefit analyses, 102
cost effectiveness, 155
    life-cycle analyses, 139, 140
    of transportation systems, 62–63
Cougar Mountain County Park, 78
3C Process, 136
cul de sacs, 11
cultural uses, 4. *See also* transportation enhancements

Dahms, Larry, 99
Daily Press, 25
deadlines, and decision-making, 48, 50
Deakin, Elizabeth, 8–9
debates, 121–122
decision-making processes, 30,
        42–43, 84
    and deadlines, 48, 50
    screening processes, 100, 102,
        109, 145–151
    Western Bypass, 67–68

DeKalb County, 44
DeKalb Superior Court, 47
Delaware Department of
    Transportation, 154
delivery services, 81
Depression, The, 5, 6
DeVillars, John, 56–57
Dietrich, Bill, 78
disabled persons, 100, 129
drainage basins, 78
drive-in services, 7
Druid Hills, Georgia, 44
Druid Hills Historic District, 46
Duany, Andres, 11
Dukakis administration, 53, 56
Dunaway Gardens, 96

easements, 17, 72, 83
    funding for, 130–131
Ebenezer Baptist Church, 44
ecosystem management, 76–78, 83
    funding for, 17, 131
Edge City, 6
education
    of the public, 29, 34, 66, 77, 93
    of transportation professionals,
        85
elderly, Americans with Disabilities
    Act of 1990, 100, 129
electronic communications, 9, 13,
    81, 99
Ellis, Jim, 76, 77
Emory University, 45
energy crises, 8
enhancements. *See* transportation enhancements
environment
    impact of transportation modes
        on, 4

scenic/historic easements, 17, 72,
    83, 130
transportation enhancements, 1,
    71–72, 92
Environmental Impact Statements
    Central Artery/Tunnel (CAT), 53,
        56, 58
    Lower James River Crossing, 23,
        24
    Quinnipiac River freeway bridge,
        39, 107–109
    Scheme Z, 56–57
Eplan, Leon, 48
errands, 6, 13
Europe, and pedestrianization, 11

facilitators, 122
Fairfield County Planning
    Association, 33
farmlands. *See* agricultural lands
fatalities, 15
fax machines, 9
Federal-Aid Highway Act of 1962,
    136
Federal Highway Administration
    (FHWA), 31, 48, 124
    and enhancements, 127, 129
    resistance to transportation
        growth management, 54, 63
Federal Highway Aid Act of
    1956, 6
Federal Transit Act, 146–147
Federal Transit Administration, 17
ferries, 22, 23, 24, 25, 53
Final Forest, The, 78
financial planning, ISTEA, 135,
    149–150
flextime, 9, 62
focus groups, 123

forums, 121–122
Frankel, Emil, 35, 38
Franklintown Road Improvement Association, 96
Freedom Parkway
  case study, 4, 44–50
  maps, 45, 49
freeways. *See* highways
Friends of Oregon, 14
full-cost pricing, 9, 14–16
Fulton County, Georgia, 44
funding
  automobiles. *See* ISTEA
  and corridor/greenway management, 84, 97
  financial constraints under ISTEA, 149–150
  innovative, 140
  by ISTEA, 71–72, 99–101
  jeopardized by litigation, 42, 46
  LUTRAQ, 66
  mass transit, 17, 91
  nonmotorized transportation, 17, 91, 100
  transition from private to government, 83
  of transportation enhancements, 89–90, 92, 130–133

Garreau, John, 6
gasoline, cost of inhaling fumes, 15
Geography of Nowhere, The, 6
Georgia
  case study, 44–50
  public involvement, 90
  transportation enhancements, 95–96
Georgia Department of Transportation, 42, 44–48

institutional changes, 105–106, 155
Georgia 400 freeway, 47
Georgia Transportation Alliance (GTA), 106
Gifford, K. Dun, 58
Girls United to Save the Environment (GUTSE), 97
Golden Gate Bridge, California, 62
Goldsboro Park, Georgia, 46
Governor's Land, Virginia, 24
Grasso, Ella, 35
Gray, Elmon, 23
Great Depression, The, 5, 6
Greater Boston Real Estate Board, 21
Great Park, Georgia, 44–45
Great Park Authority, 45, 46
Greenber, Blayney Dyett, 67
Greenway Concept Plan, 77
greenways, 22, 76–78, 96–98
grid system of arterials, 63
Gross National Product, 6
growth management, 9, 11–13, 75
  conflicting goals for, 29
  regional, 61–70, 77, 91
Growth Management Act, 75
Gwynns Falls Greenway, 96–98, 113–114

habitats, 52, 131. *See also* natural areas
Hague Consulting Group, 67
health costs, 4
High Occupancy Vehicle (HOV) lanes, 8, 17, 53–54, 109
  transportation system management for, 62–64
Highway Act of 1962, 18

highways. *See also* roads
  automated, 8, 81–82, 99
  construction of, 8, 15, 29, 45, 104
  creation of infrastructure, 8
  design and aesthetics, 32–33, 38, 131
  enhancing the existing system, 71–78, 138, 148
  focus on high speed, 4
  interstate system, 6, 17
  managing corridors, 82–84
  runoff from, 17, 72, 133
  subsidized development of, 6
  support through ISTEA. *See* ISTEA
historical background, 5–7
  of land use and transportation planning, 80
historical preservation, 17. *See also* transportation enhancements
  archaeological planning, 17, 31, 72, 132–133
  bridges, 36–37
  funding, 130–132
  Georgia, 4, 44–50, 95–96
  in highway corridors, 76–78
  impact of land use changes on, 4, 31
  Maryland, 96–98
  and safety considerations, 34, 38
  scenic roadways. *See* Freedom Parkway; Merritt Parkway; Paris Pike
  transportation buildings, 131–132
Historic American Engineering Record Study, 38
Hogansville Amphitheatre, 96

holistic transportation, 79, 82–84, 85
home ownership, subsidizing of, 6
horses, 5
housing, Portland area forecasts, 69
HOV lanes, 8, 17, 53–54, 62–64, 109

I-5 Corridor, 64
I-90 Corridor, 153
  aerial views, 74–75
  case study, 12–13, 72–78
immigration, increasing town size, 5
implementation of plans, 48, 56
incentives. *See also* congestion pricing
  for commuters, 8–9
  for low car-ownership, 14–15
inclusiveness of public involvement, 118–119
industrial growth, 5
information gathering, 119–120
Inman Park, Georgia, 44, 46
Inner Harbor, Maryland, 96
Institute for Local Self-Reliance, 16
Intelligent Transportation System (ITS), 8, 81–82
Intelligent Vehicle Highway System (IVHS). *See* Intelligent Transportation System (ITS)
Intermodal Concept Development Committee, 108, 114–115
Intermodal Surface Transportation Efficiency Act of 1991. *See* ISTEA
interstate highways. *See* highways
Interstate Highway System, 6, 17
interviews, 123
Issaquah, Washington, 75

Issaquah Alps Trail Club, 76
ISTEA, 3, 9
    Central Artery/Tunnel, 53
    certification of MPOs, 136, 155
    financial planning, 135, 149–150
    first steps toward compliance, 89–112
    committee members lists, 112–115
    funding, 17, 136–137
    how communities will be served, 153–156
    metropolitan planning, 135, 137–139, 141–142
    Metropolitan Transportation System, 99
    and National Environmental Policy Act, 72
    project selection, 145–151
    provisions of, 16–17
    public involvement requirements, 118, 123–124
    reauthorization in 1997, 112
    and role of regional agencies, 17–18, 83
    Scenic Byways Program, 130
    state planning, 135, 139–141, 142–143
    and transportation demand management, 62, 71
    transportation enhancements, 95–98, 127–133
    transportation management areas, 146–147
    used in Albany, New York, 101–103
    used in Pittsburgh, 103–105, 155
    used in San Francisco Bay Area, 98–101
ITS (Intelligent Transportation System), 8, 81–82
IVHS. *See* Intelligent Transportation System (ITS)

Jackson, Maynard, 47
James City County, Virginia, 23
James River Crossing, 4, 22–26
James River Crossing Coalition, 24–25
Jamestown, Virginia, case study, 4, 22–26
Jamestown National Historical Park, 22
Jersey Barrier, 38
jogging paths, 46, 72
Joint Urban Mobility Program, 99
JUMP Start, 99, 155
Justice Center of Atlanta, 47

Kentucky Transportation Cabinet, 43
King, Martin Luther, Jr., 44
King County, Washington, 76, 77
Kustler, James Howard, 6

Lake Claire, 44
land, pavement as percentage of, 6
landscaping, 17, 32, 34, 72
    funding for, 131
land use. *See also* growth management; ISTEA
    forecasting, 13–14, 100–101
    historical relations of, 80–81
    impact of the Interstate Highway System, 6
    and transportation planning, 9, 12, 13–14, 31, 100, 104
Land Use, Transportation, Air Quality Connection (LUTRAQ), 14, 64–69, 80
lead emissions, 6, 15
leadership
    within departments of transportation, 39, 154
    impacts of personnel changes on policy, 47–48, 50
least-cost planning, 9, 16
legal action. *See* litigation
Lewis, John, 47
Lexington-Fayette Urban County Government, 43
life-cycle analyses, 139, 140
Lighthizer, O. James, 98
litigation, 42, 154
    Central Artery/Tunnel, Massachusetts, 54, 64
    and Paris Pike, Kentucky, 43
    and Presidential Parkway, Georgia, 44, 46, 50
    Scheme Z, Massachusetts, 53, 54, 56–59
    Western Bypass, Oregon, 65–66
Logan International Airport, 52
Long Beach Freeway, 22
Long Island Motor Parkway, 33
Lower James River Association, 24–25
Lower James River Crossing
    case study, 4, 22–26
    map, 23
LUTRAQ (Land Use, Transportation, Air Quality Connection), 14, 64–69, 80

MacKaye, Benton, 33
magnetic levitation transportation, 17
mailing lists, 122

Maine, 90–92
Maine Department of Transportation, 90–91
malls
    mimicry of community life, 7
    redesign of, 11
    as threat to local businesses, 13
Martin Luther King Center, 48, 50
Maryland
    case studies, 27–32, 84
    public involvement, 90, 96–98
    transportation enhancements, 96–98
Maryland Department of Transportation, 28, 30, 31, 32
Maryland Historical Trust, 98
Maryland National Capital Park and Planning Commission, 31
Mashpee Commons, 7, 11
Massachusetts
    case study, 4, 50–59, 63–64
    Mashpee Commons, 7, 11
Massachusetts Department of Transportation, 52
Massachusetts Mediation Service, 54
Massachusetts Transportation Agenda, 53
mass transit
    Boston area, 54
    funding for, 17, 91
    magnetic levitation transportation, 17
    in metopolitan planning, 139
    in mobility paradigm, 8, 63
    percent of work trips, 9
    subsidies of passes, 8, 15
    transit-oriented development, 68–69, 80–81
Mass Transit Administration, 31

MAX light rail system, 64
mediation, 42, 84, 122
    Central Artery/Tunnel, 56–59
    Freedom Parkway, 47–48
meetings, 121–122
Merritt, Schuyler, 33
Merritt Parkway
    case study, 4, 32–39
    historical background, 34–35
    map, 33
Merritt Parkway Citizens Advisory Committee, 35
Merritt Parkway Working Group, 38
Metropolitan Boston Transit Authority, 63
Metropolitan Development Commission, 54
metropolitan planning organizations (MPOs), 17, 18, 101–103, 106–107
    certification of, 136, 155
    ISTEA, 135, 137–139, 141–142
    partnership with state agencies, 155–156
    and public involvement, 117
metropolitan sprawl, 11–12, 31, 35
    automobile domination of, 80
    drive-in services, 7
    I-90 Corridor, 73
    malls, 7
    in old *vs.* new cities, 61
    parking lots, 7
    strip development, 7, 80, 153
Metropolitan Transportation Commission, 98
miles traveled, 6, 68
military installations, 139
Milliken, John, 25

Minnesota Department of Transportation, institutional changes, 109–111, 155
mitigation, 54
    Central Artery/Tunnel, 64
    I-90 Corridor, 73
mobility, as transportation paradigm, 8, 16, 79
modeling, 13–14. *See also* LUTRAQ
modems, in telecommunication, 9, 13, 81, 99
Moreland Old Mill, 96
Morris, David, 16
Mountains-to-Sound Greenway, 76–78. *See also* I-90 Corridor
    charette, 122
Mountains-to-Sound Greenway Trust, 5, 22, 76–77, 78, 83
Mount Baker-Snoqualmie National Forest, 73
Mount Hood Freeway, proposed, 64
Mount Si, Washington, 78
Move Massachusetts 2000, 21
MSTA (Maine's Sensible Transportation Act), 90–92
multi-modal transportation systems, 8, 39, 62–64
Mumford, Lewis, 33

National Ambient Air Quality Standards (NAAQS), 15, 18, 38, 66, 147–148
National Association of Railroad Passengers, 56
National Highway System (NHS), 6, 17
National Park Service, 23, 38, 48, 83

National Register of Historic Places, 35
National Trust for Historic Preservation, 46
natural areas, 6, 7
    funding, 131
    from highway corridors, 76–78
    impact of transportation modes on, 4, 31
Natural Resources Defense Council, 32
negotiation processes, 90, 122
neighborhoods
    decentralization with modern technology, 81
    redevelopable and infill sites for, 68
    retrofitting, 68
New Haven Harbor, 107
New Haven Harbor Crossing Intermodal Concept Development Committee, 114–115
newsletters, 66, 77, 98
New York City, horses in, 5
New York State Department of Transportation, 101
Nike, 64
NIMBY (not in my backyard), 68
Nintendo of America, 75
nitrogen dioxide, 6, 15
nitrous oxide, 6, 15
noise, 4, 6, 31
nonattainment areas. *See* air quality, nonattainment of NAAQS
nonmotorized transportation. *See also* bicycle facilities; walking facilities
    funding for, 17, 91, 100

integrated with existing facilities, 99, 138
    percent of work trips, 9
    subsidizing automobile transportation, 14
    system integration of, 8, 62–64
North Bend, Washington, 73
Northwest Greenwich Association, 35

office parks, origins of, 6
oil, energy crises, 8
Olmsted, Frederick Law, 11, 33, 46, 47, 96
Olympics of 1996, 47, 48, 50
1000 Friends of Massachusetts, 53, 54
1000 Friends of Oregon, 61, 65
open space, 29
    from Artery/Tunnel project, 54, 56, 57
    and urban compact form, 80
Oregon
    case study, 5, 64–69
    LUTRAQ, 14, 64–69, 80
    regional growth management, 12, 14, 61
Oregon Department of Transportation, 65, 66, 67, 68
Oregon Land Conservation and Development Commission, 66
Oriole Park at Camden Yards, 96
outdoor advertising, 17, 72, 132
oversight committees, 56

Palo Alto, California, 9
Paris, Kentucky, 42, 43
Paris Pike, Kentucky, 42–44
Paris Pike Review Committee, 43

Paris Pike Study Committee, 43
parking, 7, 15, 54
   in Boston, 63
   cost of, 15
   disincentives, 8–9, 14, 62
   preferential incentives, 8, 63
   zoning laws, 62
parks. *See also* open space
   from the Central Artery/Tunnel, 54
   to cover freeway scars, 73
   Department of Transportation control of, 46
   in urban areas, 56
parkways, 33, 76–78
   implementing agreements for, 48, 77–78
Parsons Brinckerhoff, 50
Partnership for Regional Excellence, 93
Patapsco River Greenway, 96, 97
pavement
   to increase road capacity, 8, 14
   as percentage of arable land, 6
   surface area of, 5–6
peak travel, 8, 15–16, 17, 62
pedestrian facilities. *See* walking facilities
pedestrian-oriented communities, 7, 10–11, 72, 80
pedestrian pocket development concept, 11, 62
Pennsylvania, case study, 103–105, 155
Pine Mountain Trail, 96
Pittsburgh, public involvement, 103–105
Pittsburgh Planning Department, 104
Pittsburgh Port Authority, 103

Pittsburgh Regional Transportation Partnership, 103
Plater-Zyberk, Elizabeth, 11
political activism, 22, 46, 66. *See also* coalitions; public involvement
political power
   and coalitions, 25–26, 30
   impacts of personnel changes on, 47–48, 50
polls, 123
Poncey Highlands, Georgia, 46
population growth, forecasting, 13–14, 69, 100–101
Portland, Oregon, case study. *See* LUTRAQ; Western Bypass
Portland Area Comprehensive Transportation Committee (PACTC), 91
Portman, John, 45
ports, 139
Preservation Alliance of Virginia, 24
Presidential Parkway, 45–46
Preston, Washington, 73
Prince George's Civic Federation, 32
Prince George's County government, 32
project selection, 100, 102, 109, 145–151
proximity, of transportation enhancements, 128
public education
   access to information, 119–120
   campaigns, 122–123
   conferences, 29, 34, 92, 121–122
   printed matter, 66, 77, 98
public hearings, 118
public involvement, 98–105, 117–125, 155

   access to information, 119–120
   Albany, New York, 101–103
   citizen advisory committees, 56, 96–98, 103
   early involvement in the process, 119, 154
   education, 29, 34, 66, 77
   Georgia, 105
   inclusiveness, 118–119
   in metropolitan planning, 124–125
   Pittsburgh, 103–105
   project selection, 146
   San Francisco Bay Area, 98–101
   shift to long-term planning, 90, 92, 99
   in state planning, 124
public meetings, 121–122
public opinion surveys, 123
public participation. *See* public involvement
public relations, 47, 77–78
Puget Sound, case study. *See* I-90 Corridor
Puget Sound Council of Governments, 12
Puget Sound Regional Council, 14

quality of life, 3, 4, 9, 15
Quinnipiac River bridge, Connecticut, 39, 107–109

Radburn, New Jersey, 11
rail corridors, rehabilitation of, 17, 72, 132
rail services, 39, 80
   Boston area, 53–54, 56
   in Central Artery/Tunnel, 63
   electric, 5

   funding for, 17, 83
   light rail lines, 14, 68, 83
   Portland area, 64, 68
   transportation system management for, 8, 62–64
Rails-to-Trails program, 17
Rattlesnake Ridge, Washington, 78
reading, suggested, 157–158
real estate development
   early railway rights-of-way, 5
   for greenways, 77–78
   and new highway construction, 29
   Portland area forecasts, 69
   strip development, 7, 153
Recreational Equipment Inc. (REI), 76
Region 2040, 67
Regional Alliance For Transit (RAFT), 100–101
Regional Plan Association (RPA), 33
regional planning, 17–18, 33, 61–70, 77
   establishing committees, 91, 93, 99, 103–105, 106–107
   of highway corridors, 83
   ISTEA, 135
Regional Transportation Advisory Committees (RTACs), 91
regulatory negotiations (Reg-Negs), 90–92, 122
resolution techniques. *See* coalitions; litigation; mediation
retail. *See* businesses
retrofitting neighborhoods, 68
Rives, Hal, 48
Roadbusters, 47
roads
   car/road construction equilibrium, 8

roads (continued)
    cost of construction and maintenance of, 15
    creation of infrastructure, 8
    funding for, 17, 91
    mileage statistics, 5
    surface area of pavement, 5–6
    transportation system management for, 8, 62–64
Robert Moses Parkway, 33
RPA (Regional Plan Association), 33
runoff, from highways, 17, 72, 133
rural communities, telecommuting in, 9, 13, 81
rush hour, 8, 15–16, 17, 62

safety, 102
    automobile accidents, 11, 15
    and historical preservation, 34, 38
Salvucci, Fred, 53, 56
Sammammish Plateau, 73
San Fernando Valley, California, 8–9
San Francisco Bay Area, public involvement, 98–101
San Francisco Bay Area Metropolitan Transportation Commission (MTC), 14, 155
San Francisco-Oakland Bay Bridge, 62
satellite offices, 13
Save the Merritt Committee, 35
Scenic Byways Program, 130
Scheme Z, 53, 54, 56–59
Schmoke, Kurt, 97
screening processes, 100, 102, 109, 145–151
Seattle
    case study, 12–13, 53, 72–78
    vehicle miles traveled, 6

Security Pacific Bank, 76
Seeliger, Clarence, 47
Sensible Transportation Options for People, 61, 64, 65, 66
Sensible Transportation Policy Act of 1991 (MSTA), 90
S.H. Putnam Associates, 67
Shackelford, Wayne, 48
Shadyside Park, Georgia, 46, 48
Shopping. See businesses; malls
Sierra Club, 32, 56, 67, 98
single occupancy vehicles (SOVs), 8–9, 54
    Commute Trip Reduction Act of 1991, 62
    current increase in, 9
    reduction with urban compact form, 81
smog, 6, 15
Snoqualmie, Washington, 73, 74
Southern California Edison, 16
South Pasadena, California, 22
Southwest Corridor, 57
Southwest Corridor Transportation Study, 64–65
Southwestern Pennsylvania Regional Planning Commission, 103, 155
Southwest Freeway, Massachusetts, 121
Spectacle Island, Massachusetts, 52, 54
speed limits, 34, 48, 63
Squak Mountain State Park, Washington, 78
state agencies
    institutional changes, 105–112
    partnership with MPOs, 155–156
state planning, and ISTEA, 135, 139–141, 142–143

Stein, Clarence, 11, 33
Stone Mountain Tollway Study Commission, 44
stop lights, 8, 63
STP (Surface Transportation Program), 17, 71–72
Strategic Plan for Action, Maryland transportation enhancement plan, 96
streams. See natural areas; water quality
strip development, 7, 153
subsidies, of "free" parking, 15
Suburban Maryland Builders Association, 32
suburbia
    origin of, 5
    pollution from, 27
    uncontrolled development, 29
    World War II promotion of, 6
suggested reading, 157–158
sulfur dioxide, 6, 15
Surface Transportation Assistance Act, 29
Surface Transportation Program (STP), 17, 71–72
Surrey County Board of Supervisors, 23, 25
surveys, 123
symposia. See conferences

Tallahassee, Florida, 123
task forces, 30–32, 82–83, 97, 98–99
    establishing, 120
tax incentives
    for local businesses, 13
    for parking, 15
TDM (transportation demand management), 8–9, 62, 63–64

technical support, 123
telecommuting, 9, 13, 81
    funding, 99
telephone systems, 9
Texas Department of Transportation, 154
301 Corridor, Maryland, 28–32, 84
Tidewater, Virginia, 25
Tiger Mountain State Forest, 78
time, wasted in traffic congestion, 6
TIP. See transportation improvement programs (TIPs)
TMA (transportation management areas), 18, 146–147
toll roads, 16, 17, 62
tourism, 76, 141
Traditional Neighborhood Development, 11
traffic congestion, 5, 6
    economic impacts, 6-7
    Intelligent Transportation System (ITS), 8, 81–82
    ISTEA initiative for, 92
    during peak-hour travel, 8, 16, 62
    in suburbs of Portland, 67, 68
traffic control technology, 8
traffic signals, 8, 63
transit-oriented development, 68–69, 80
Transportation Act of 1966, 43
transportation control measures, 151–152
transportation demand management (TDM), 8–9, 62, 63–64
transportation enhancements, 17, 71–72, 92
    definitions of, 127–133
    funding of, 89–90, 92, 130–133
    Georgia, 95–96

transportation enhancements (*continued*)
  Maryland, 96–98
  role in planning, 129–130
transportation improvement programs (TIPs), 17–18, 98, 101–102, 110–111
  financial constraint, 149–150
  and public involvement, 117
transportation management areas (TMAs), 18, 146–147
transportation paradigms
  accessibility as, 9, 16, 79, 156
  capacity as, 8, 14, 79
  holistic, 79, 82–84, 153–156
  mobility as, 8–9, 16, 79
transportation planning
  Albany, New York, 101–103
  checks and balances, 154–156
  and coalitions, 21–26, 92
  compared to electric utility sector, 16
  establishing committees, 120–121
  evaluation of impacts, 31
  holistic approach. See ISTEA
  and land use, 9, 12, 13–14, 80, 100. See also growth management; ISTEA
  long-term goals, 30–31
    Maine, 90–91
    San Francisco Bay Area, 98–101
    Washington, D.C., 94–95
  options, 31
  Pittsburgh, 103–105, 155
  public involvement in, 117–125
  questions to apply to choices, 79–80
  role of enhancements, 129–130

screening process for projects, 100, 102, 109, 145–151
task forces, 30–32, 38, 82–83, 97, 120
Virginia, 92–93
Transportation Planning Board of the Metropolitan Washington Council of Governments, 93–95
transportation planning regions (TPRs), 106
Transportation Planning Rule of 1991, 66–67
transportation policies
  full-cost pricing, 14–16
  integrating metropolitan with state, 56–58
  paradigms of, 8–17, 82–84, 153–156
transportation system management (TSM), 8, 62–64. See also transportation demand management (TDM)
trends, 154
Tri-County Council, 32
trip substitution, 81–82
trolleys, horse-drawn, 5
trucks, 81. See also ISTEA
Trust for Public Land, The, 76, 96
TSM (transportation system management), 8, 62–64
tunnels, 131–132. See also Central Artery/Tunnel (CAT)

University of California, Davis, 15
urban compact form
  loss of, 6
  in new paradigms, 14, 80–81, 104
  redevelopable and infill sites, 68
  reinforced by access, 56
  in the 1800s, 5

urban growth boundaries, 64, 68
urban design
  and accessibility, 9, 16, 79, 156
  auto-oriented, 10
  community-oriented, 9–11
  pedestrian-oriented, 7, 10–11, 72, 80
urban growth boundaries, 64, 68
Urban Mass Transit Administration. See Federal Transit Administration
urban sprawl. See metropolitan sprawl
urban village development, 62, 68, 80–81
U.S. Army Corps of Engineers, 32
U.S. Department of Transportation, 136, 145–146
  telecommuting study, 13
U.S. Environmental Protection Agency, 31
U.S. Fish and Wildlife Service, 32
U.S. Forest Service, 83
U.S. Government Accounting Office, 7

Vanderbilt, William, Jr., 33
Vanderbilt Cup race course, 33
vanpools, 8, 62
Virginia
  case study, 4, 22–26
  public involvement, 90, 92–93
Virginia Department of Transportation, 23, 92
Virginia Gazette, 25
Virginia Surface Transportation Coalition, 92, 112
visual impacts, 32–33, 38

impact of land use changes, 4, 57

walking facilities
  coalitions for trails, 96
  danger of, 7
  funding for, 17, 91, 100, 130, 139. See also ISTEA
  and limitation of town size, 5
  paths, 46, 72
  pedestrian-scaled communities, 7, 10–11
  percent of work trips, 9
  transportation system management, 8, 62–64
Washington, D.C., 28
  case study, 4, 12, 27–32
  public involvement, 90, 93–95
Washington Board of Trade, 32
Washington Bypass, 12
  case study, 4, 27–32
  map, 28
Washington Council of Governments, 32
Washington Department of Natural Resources, 77
Washington Department of Transportation, 12, 77
Washington Regional Network for Livable Communities (WRN), 93–95
Washington State, case study, 12–13, 72–78, 153
Washington State Commissioner of Public Lands, 76
Water Pollution Control Act, 140–141
water quality, 6, 27
  mitigation by ISTEA, 17, 72, 133, 141

watershed management, and highway corridor planning, 83
Weld, William, 57
Western Bypass
  case study, 5, 64–69
  map, 65
Westport Improvement Association, 96
wetlands, 4, 7, 29, 31
Weyerhaeuser Company, 76, 77
Wilder, Douglas, 25
wildlife habitats, 131. *See also* natural areas
  artificial habitat design, 52
Wofford, John, 57
Wolf's Den Loop, 96
women, in the workforce, 6
woods. *See* natural areas
working at home, 9, 13, 81
Working Group on Community Development, 104
workshops. *See* conferences
World War II, 5, 6

Yale University, 96
Young, Andrew, 45–46, 47

zoning laws, 62, 67

ABOUT THE AUTHORS

DANIEL CARLSON is a research consultant in the Institute for Public Policy and Management at the University of Washington in Seattle. His areas of interest are community development, preservation, and empowerment. He is a graduate of Oberlin College and the University of California, Berkeley, where he received a master's degree in city and regional planning. He is also the author of *Reusing America's Schools,* a guide for converting closed schools into centers of community and economic activity.

LISA WORMSER was a founding staff member of the Surface Transportation Policy Project in 1991. As communications manager, she oversaw all aspects of STPP's public information programs. She is a graduate of Southern Methodist University and is now the owner of Two Heads, a communications consulting firm.

CY ULBERG is a research associate professor in the Graduate School of Public Affairs at the University of Washington. He is also associated with the Washington State Transportation Center, a consortium of the University of Washington, the Washington State University, and the Washington State Department of Transportation. He holds a bachelor's degree in physics from Stanford University and a doctorate in social psychology from the Univeristy of Michigan. His interests are in community development, transportation policy, and land use.

ISLAND PRESS BOARD OF DIRECTORS

CHAIR **SUSAN E. SECHLER**
Executive Director, Pew Global Stewardship Initiative

VICE-CHAIR **HENRY REATH**
President, Collector's Reprints, Inc.

SECRETARY **DRUMMOND PIKE**
President, The Tides Foundation

TREASURER **ROBERT E. BAENSCH**
Consulting Partner, Scovill, Paterson Inc.

PETER R. BORRELLI
Executive Vice President, Open Space Institute

CATHERINE M. CONOVER

LINDY HESS
Director, Radcliffe Publishing Program

GENE E. LIKENS
Director, The Institute of Ecosystem Studies

JEAN RICHARDSON
Director, Environmental Programs in Communities (EPIC), University of Vermont

CHARLES C. SAVITT
President, Center for Resource Economics/Island Press

PETER R. STEIN
Managing Partner, Lyme Timber Company

RICHARD TRUDELL
Executive Director, American Indian Resources Institute